Innovative Strategies Against Blood Parasites

Innovative Strategies Against Blood Parasites

Advancing Control Through Natural Products and Next-Generation Technologies

Edited by

MOHAMED DKHIL
Department of Zoology and Entomology, Faculty of Science,
Capital University, Cairo, Egypt

ACADEMIC PRESS
An imprint of Elsevier

Academic Press is an imprint of Elsevier
125 London Wall, London EC2Y 5AS, United Kingdom
50 Hampshire Street, 5th Floor, Cambridge, MA 02139, United States

ISBN: 978-0-443-48509-1

For Information on all Academic Press publications
visit our website at https://www.elsevier.com/books-and-journals

Publisher: Andre Wolff
Acquisitions Editor: Kirti Sharma
Editorial Project Manager: Ashavari Bhattacharya
Production Project Manager: Rajeswari R.
Cover Designer: Raman Kumar

Typeset by MPS Limited, Chennai, India

Dedication

This volume is dedicated to the scientists, clinicians, and public health professionals around the world who devote their knowledge, time, and perseverance to understanding and combating blood parasitic diseases. Their unwavering commitment continues to improve the lives of millions, often in the most challenging settings.

It is also dedicated to the patients and communities affected by these infections, whose resilience inspires the pursuit of better therapies, innovative technologies, and sustainable solutions.

Finally, this work is dedicated to my mentors, colleagues, and students, whose collaboration, curiosity, and passion for discovery make progress possible and meaningful.

Contents

List of contributors

Rewaida Abdel-Gaber
Zoology Department, Faculty of Science, Cairo University, Cairo, Egypt

Abdulsalam Alkhudhayri
Department of Biology, College of Science, University of Hafr Albatin, Saudi Arabia

Malek Al-Najjar
Faculty of Medicine, Jordan University of Science and Technology, Irbid, Jordan

Mohammad A A Al-Najjar
Department of Pharmaceutical Sciences and Pharmaceutics, Applied Science Private University, Amman, Jordan

Huda A. Alqahtani
Department of Zoology, College of Science, King Saud University, Riyadh, Saudi Arabia

Raja'a Al-Qudah
Department of Clinical Pharmacy and Therapeutics, Applied Science Private University, Amman, Jordan

Khalid Awad Elkareem Ahmed
Tropical Medicine Research Institute, National Centre for Research, Ministry of Science & Technology, Khartoum, Sudan

Muna Barakat
Department of Clinical Pharmacy and Therapeutics, Applied Science Private University, Amman, Jordan

Mohamed Dkhil
Department of Zoology and Entomology, Faculty of Science, Capital University, Cairo, Egypt

Rania Ali El-Hadi Mohamed
Department of Biology, Faculty of Science, Princess Nourah bint Abdulrahman University, Riyadh, Saudi Arabia

Youssef A. El-Sayed
Genetic Engineering and Biotechnology Program, Faculty of Science, Helwan National University, Helwan, Egypt

Ahana Ghosh
Cell and Developmental Biology Special, Department of Zoology, University of Kalyani, Kalyani, West Bengal, India

Omnia Hamed
Department of Zoology and Entomology, Faculty of Science, Capital University, Cairo, Egypt.

Shaimaa M. Kasem
Zoology Department, Faculty of Science, Kafrelsheikh University, Kafr Elsheikh, Egypt

Debdiya Majumdar
Cell and Developmental Biology Special, Department of Zoology, University of Kalyani, Kalyani, West Bengal, India

Andreas Meryk
Department of Pediatrics, Medical University of Innsbruck, Innsbruck, Austria

Diptangshu Modak
Cell and Developmental Biology Special, Department of Zoology, University of Kalyani, Kalyani, West Bengal, India

Sisir Nandi
Global Institute of Pharmaceutical Education and Research, Kashipur, Uttarakhand, India

Amin Omar
Department of Pharmaceutical Sciences and Pharmaceutics, Applied Science Private University, Amman, Jordan

Shubhradip Singha Roy
Cell and Developmental Biology Special, Department of Zoology, University of Kalyani, Kalyani, West Bengal, India

Riddha Saha
Cell and Developmental Biology Special, Department of Zoology, University of Kalyani, Kalyani, West Bengal, India

Asmita Samadder
Cell and Developmental Biology Special, Department of Zoology, University of Kalyani, Kalyani, West Bengal, India; Cytogenetics and Molecular Biology Lab., Department of Zoology, University of Kalyani, Kalyani, West Bengal, India

Simeon Santourlidis
Epigenetics Laboratory for Human Health and Longevity, Institute of Transplantation Diagnostics and Cell Therapeutics, Medical Faculty, Heinrich Heine University Duesseldorf, Duesseldorf, Germany

Soni Shaw
Cell and Developmental Biology Special, Department of Zoology, University of Kalyani, Kalyani, West Bengal, India

Mahek Sultana
Cell and Developmental Biology Special, Department of Zoology, University of Kalyani, Kalyani, West Bengal, India

Felwa A. Thagfan
Department of Biology, College of Science, Princess Nourah Bint Abdulrahman University, Riyadh, Saudi Arabia

Preface

Blood parasitic diseases remain a major challenge at the interface of human and veterinary health, continuing to affect millions of people and animals worldwide. Despite decades of progress in chemotherapy, vector control, and diagnostics, the persistence of infections caused by *Plasmodium*, *Trypanosoma*, *Leishmania*, and *Babesia* underscores the complexity of host–parasite interactions and the adaptive capacity of these organisms. The rapid emergence of drug resistance, environmental changes influencing transmission, and the limitations of existing therapies collectively highlight the urgent need for innovative and integrative approaches.

Innovative Strategies Against Blood Parasites: Advancing Control Through Natural Products and Next-Generation Technologies was conceived to provide a comprehensive and forward-looking perspective on the evolving landscape of antiparasitic research. The central aim is to bridge traditional knowledge with cutting-edge scientific advances, illustrating how multidisciplinary collaboration can accelerate the discovery and implementation of more effective and sustainable interventions.

This book begins with a foundational overview of blood parasitic diseases, outlining their biology, epidemiology, and global burden, followed by a critical discussion of current therapeutic strategies and the growing challenge of resistance. These chapters set the stage for exploring alternative solutions rooted in natural products, highlighting the remarkable diversity of plant, marine, and microbial compounds with antiparasitic potential. The mechanistic insights presented emphasize how these agents interfere with parasite survival, replication, and host invasion, providing a scientific basis for their continued development.

A major focus of this work is the integration of next-generation technologies into parasitology research. Advances in nanotechnology have opened new avenues for targeted drug delivery and improved bioavailability, while omics platforms have transformed our ability to identify molecular targets and understand parasite biology at an unprecedented resolution. In parallel, artificial intelligence and in silico tools are reshaping drug discovery pipelines, enabling the faster and more precise identification of promising therapeutic candidates. The concluding chapters address the translational pathway, discussing clinical evaluation, safety considerations, and regulatory aspects that determine whether promising discoveries can ultimately benefit patients.

As editor, I had the privilege of working with an exceptional group of contributors whose expertise spans parasitology, pharmacology, biotechnology, and computational science. Their collective insights reflect not only the current state of knowledge but also the future directions of the field. I am deeply grateful for their dedication, collaboration, and commitment to excellence throughout the preparation of this volume.

It is my hope that this book will serve as a valuable resource for researchers, clinicians, graduate students, and policymakers, fostering new ideas and encouraging interdisciplinary partnerships. By combining the wisdom of natural product research with the power of modern technologies, we move closer to achieving more effective control strategies and, ultimately, reducing the global burden of blood parasitic diseases.

Prof. Mohamed Dkhil
Department of Zoology and Entomology, Faculty of Science,
Capital University, Cairo, Egypt

CHAPTER 1

Overview of blood parasitic diseases

Shaimaa M. Kasem[1], Omnia Hamed[2], and Mohamed Dkhil[2]
[1]Zoology Department, Faculty of Science, Kafrelsheikh University, Kafr Elsheikh, Egypt,
[2]Department of Zoology and Entomology, Faculty of Science, Capital University, Cairo, Egypt

1.1 Introduction

Parasitic illnesses significantly impact the health of both animals and humans globally. Various parasites, including detrimental protozoa, helminths, and ectoparasites such as ticks and mosquitoes, affect humans, pets, and cattle regarding the severity of sickness and the number of individuals or animals impacted (Kaminsky and Mäser, 2025). Blood parasites are infections induced by certain protozoa residing in the host's bloodstream. Trypanosomes are a category of parasites, namely unicellular organisms that induce a disease known as trypanosomiasis in animals such as camels, horses, cattle, sheep, and goats. This disease is mostly transmitted by the tsetse fly, however other hematophagous insects may potentially facilitate its spread (Malik et al., 2025). For instance, malaria, a prominent disease transmitted by insects. The parasites responsible for malaria are several kinds of Plasmodium, which are transmitted by Anopheles mosquitoes (St. Laurent, 2025). In general, diseases passed on by ectoparasites such as ticks and mosquitoes, including parasitic ones, make up more than 17% of all human infectious diseases worldwide (Kaminsky and Mäser, 2025). Visceral leishmaniasis, or kala-azar, is a zoonotic illness caused by *Leishmania donovani* and *L. infantum*, which reside in canines and are transmitted by sandflies (Scarpini et al., 2022). Because diseases that spread from animals to humans and chronic animal illnesses have a big effect on people, it is really important to control parasites to protect both animal and human health (Rahman et al., 2020). Therefore, the aim of this chapter was to provide a comprehensive and integrated overview of blood parasitic diseases affecting humans and animals, with particular emphasis on their biological, epidemiological, and public health significance.

1.2 Major blood parasites and transmission

Blood parasites are a varied assemblage of pathogenic entities that invade and multiply within the circulatory system of people and animals, resulting in considerable clinical and socioeconomic repercussions globally. This encompasses protozoa, helminths, and many opportunistic parasites, many of which are disseminated by blood-feeding vectors. Their epidemiological success is augmented by their capacity to endure within blood cells or plasma while circumventing host immune responses (World Health

Innovative Strategies Against Blood Parasites
DOI: https://doi.org/10.1016/B978-0-443-48509-1.00005-7

Organization, 2023). *Plasmodium* spp., the etiological agents of malaria, are among the most significant blood parasites. Transmission transpires via the bite of infected female Anopheles mosquitoes (Ménard, 2001). Upon entering the host, *Plasmodium* parasites invade hepatic cells and subsequently erythrocytes, resulting in cyclical febrile sickness, hemolytic anemia, hepatosplenomegaly, and severe complications, including cerebral edema and multi-organ failure (White et al., 2014). Another genus within the Apicomplexa is *Babesia* spp., primarily transmitted by Ixodes ticks, which induce babesiosis. Clinical signs mimic malaria, frequently characterized by fever, hemolytic anemia, and significant consequences in elderly or immunocompromised patients (Vannier and Krause, 2012). *Toxoplasma gondii*, likewise classified among the Apicomplexa, is spread congenitally, through the ingestion of oocysts, or via undercooked meat. Although frequently asymptomatic, it can induce severe systemic disease in immunocompromised individuals (Nayeri et al., 2024).

Blood flagellates are significant infections delivered by vectors. *Trypanosoma brucei*, conveyed by tsetse flies, induces African trypanosomiasis (sleeping sickness), whereas *Trypanosoma cruzi*, communicated by triatomine bugs, results in Chagas disease. These parasites invade the bloodstream and deep tissues, leading to hepatosplenomegaly, leukopenia, bone marrow suppression, and persistent cardiac and neurological consequences (Manful et al., 2024). *L. donovani*, another significant blood flagellate, is transmitted by sandflies and causes visceral leishmaniasis (Kala-Azar). The parasite multiplies within macrophages and is marked by prolonged fever, significant splenomegaly, and pronounced leukopenia, constituting a potentially lethal illness if left untreated (Pasha et al., 2022).

Helminths significantly contribute to blood-borne parasite illnesses. Traditional vector-borne species, including *Wuchereria bancrofti* and *Onchocerca volvulus*, are responsible for lymphatic filariasis and onchocerciasis, respectively (Hassen et al., 2023). Nevertheless, several developing or overlooked helminths have attracted interest. The organisms comprise *Gnathostoma spinigerum*, the causative agent of larva migrans profundus; *Angiostrongylus cantonensis* (rat lungworm); *Baylisascaris procyonis* (raccoon roundworm); and *Anisakis simplex* (herring worm), all of which can induce severe or migrating tissue infections in humans (Hotez et al., 2009). Certain blood parasites may also be transmitted through non-vector routes, such as congenital transmission, blood transfusions, organ transplantation, and infected needles, hence amplifying their public health implications (Singh and Sehgal, 2010).

1.3 Pathogenicity and host–parasite interactions

A fundamental characteristic of pathogenic blood parasites is their capacity to circumvent host immune responses through mechanisms such as antigenic variation and intracellular persistence. Antigenic variation is notably elucidated in Trypanosoma infections, characterized by fluctuating waves of parasitemia as the quantity of bloodstream trypomastigotes increases and decreases over time. Blood-stage trypomastigotes are enveloped in densely arranged variant-specific glycoproteins (VSGs), creating a surface layer of 12–15 nm in thickness (Choi et al., 2024). These VSGs exhibit significant immunogenicity and function as the primary antigens identified by the mammalian host immune system. Nonetheless, *Trypanosoma* species harbor thousands of VSG genes, facilitating the frequent alteration of the produced surface glycoprotein (Fig. 1.1). Consequently, when the host generates an antibody response against a certain VSG type, the majority of parasites expressing the targeted variant are eradicated; however a minority that have transitioned to an alternative VSG evade annihilation and perpetuate the infection (Beaver et al., 2024). This mechanism recurs cyclically, producing the distinctive parasitemia waves and facilitating prolonged life in the bloodstream. Comparable techniques are evident in other blood parasites. Relapsing forms of *Plasmodium* and *Babesia* can exhibit antigenically diverse variants over consecutive infection cycles, allowing them to endure despite the host's immune response (Baral, 2010). By incessantly modifying or concealing their principal surface antigens, these parasites evade neutralization, extend infection duration, and enhance the probability of transfer to new hosts. Consequently, antigenic diversity is a highly effective evolutionary adaptation that supports the persistence and harmful capacity of numerous vector-borne blood parasites (Li et al., 2025).

Numerous parasites circumvent host immunity by inhabiting immunologically favorable places, such as within host cells or in hollow organs, which lack host immunological elements. *Leishmania* promastigotes are consumed by macrophages and convert into amastigotes, rendering them inaccessible to antibodies and complement proteins. The *Leishmania* amastigotes endure and proliferate within these phagocytes by

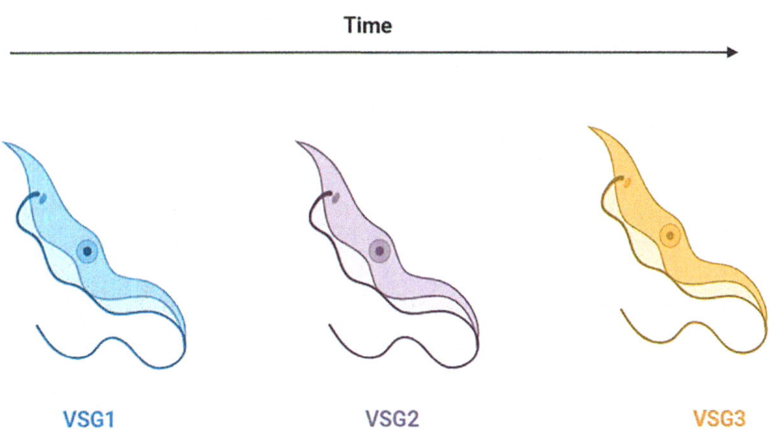

Figure 1.1 Schematic representation for *Trypanosoma brucei* infection. As infection with *T. brucei* progresses, the dominant expressed VSG transitions sequentially from VSG1 to VSG2 and then to VSG3, allowing the parasite to persist despite ongoing immune responses.

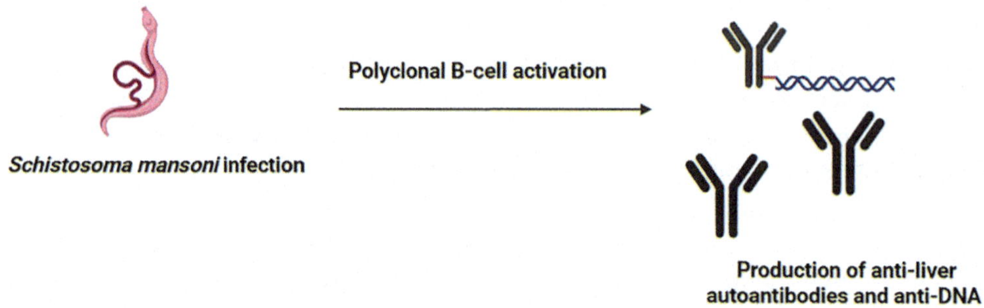

Figure 1.2 Host immune response during *Schistosoma mansoni* infection. Polyclonal B-cell activation leads to the production of anti-liver autoantibodies, anti-DNA antibodies, and circulating immune complexes, all of which play key roles in disease progression.

counteracting several intracellular microbicidal factors of the host, thereby establishing a chronic infection (Elmahallawy et al., 2021). *Plasmodium* sporozoites utilize perforin-like protein (PLP1) to evade disintegration by host cell lysosomes during cellular traversal. Within invaded hepatocytes, *Plasmodium* sporozoites inhabit parasitophorous vacuoles (PVs), where they produce merozoites (Loubens et al., 2021).

The eggs produced by female *Schistosoma* worms elicit an immune-mediated granulomatous response, resulting in both local and systemic pathological effects. Polyclonal B-cell activation, noted in *Schistosoma mansoni* infection, may result in the generation of anti-liver autoantibodies and anti-DNA, as well as the development of circulating immune complexes (Fig. 1.2 Lundy and Lukacs, 2013). In patients with *L. donovani*, polyclonal lymphocyte activation correlates with autoantibodies to ribonucleoproteins, which impair the host immune system's functionality (Argov et al., 1989). *T. brucei* synthesizes a protein known as TbKHC1 that impedes nitric oxide (NO) production, thereby exacerbating liver pathogenicity at the advanced phase of infection (De Muylder et al., 2013) Fig. 1.2.

1.4 Epidemiology and global burden

Vector-borne parasitic infectious diseases (vb-pIDP) are globally prevalent, found in diverse habitats from tropical rainforests to arid deserts. Notwithstanding their extensive existence, their geographical distribution is markedly varied and influenced by ecological, climatic, socioeconomic, and vector-related factors (Zhu et al., 2024). In 2021, the age-standardized prevalence and disability-adjusted life year (DALY) rates for most vb-pIDP were elevated in low Socio-Demographic Index (SDI) locations, indicating disparities in living conditions, healthcare systems, and illness management capabilities. Chagas disease represented a significant deviation from this trend (Zhu et al., 2024). With the rise in national SDI levels, both prevalence and DALY rates exhibited a notable decrease, illustrating the robust correlation between socioeconomic advancement and enhanced outcomes in parasite diseases (Zhao et al., 2025). Numerous vb-pIDP exhibit distinct demographic trends regarding risk and illness burden. Malaria is especially lethal for young children, resulting in almost half a million fatalities per year, predominantly among those under five years old in sub-Saharan Africa. The prevalence and DALY rates of malaria are highest in children under five and decrease progressively with age (Zhu et al., 2024). Worldwide, childhood underweight (0.14%) and stunting (0.08%) significantly contribute to malaria-related DALYs, underscoring the impact of dietary inadequacies on illness severity (Ijaiya et al., 2024). Lymphatic filariasis exhibits the greatest incidence and DALY burden in young adults, particularly peaking within the 20–24-year age cohort. Chagas disease exhibits a distinct demographic pattern, with DALY rates significantly elevated in males compared to females throughout various age groups, including 35–39, 40–44, 45–49, 50–54, 55–59, and 60–64 years (Wang et al., 2025).

1.5 Socioeconomic impact

Neglected tropical diseases (NTDs) have significant socioeconomic impacts on individuals, communities, and nations, perpetuating a cycle of poverty and illness. The most immediate consequence is the financial strain on healthcare systems. In numerous developing nations, the expenses associated with diagnosis, treatment, and prolonged care for NTD infections impose a significant financial burden on both individuals and healthcare systems. The lack of social protection systems results in impacted communities incurring catastrophic health expenses, which intensifies poverty (Hudu et al., 2024). In addition to direct medical expenses, NTDs considerably diminish production and educational achievements. Infected adults often suffer economic loss due to illness, exacerbated by the absence of sickness or disability insurance in many endemic areas (Turner et al., 2016). Children are disproportionately impacted; NTD infections, especially soil-transmitted helminths (STH), have been demonstrated to hinder school attendance, concentration, and academic achievement. These educational failures may lead to a decline in human capital, resulting in sustained decreases in economic productivity (Donkoh et al., 2022). The ramifications for community and national development in the long term are as grave. Chronic infections can adversely affect nutritional status, growth, and cognitive development in children, resulting in diminished educational achievement and decreased earning potential in adulthood. As a result, people afflicted by NTDs have ongoing socioeconomic disadvantages, perpetuating intergenerational cycles of poverty. Addressing these health disparities is essential not only for enhancing individual health outcomes but also for fostering more equitable chances for personal improvement and national progress (Hudu et al., 2024). The social stigma and diminished quality of life exacerbate the socioeconomic consequences of NTDs. Numerous neglected tropical diseases exhibit apparent physical symptoms that lead to social exclusion, discrimination, and reduced psychosocial well-being. Efficient control and management of NTDs can mitigate these burdens, thereby inhancing the capacity of affected individuals to engage fully in social, educational, and economic activities (Koschorke et al., 2022).

1.6 Diagnostic approaches

A significant number of the conventional diagnostic instruments employed in contemporary microbiology laboratories continue to depend on technologies that are millennia outdated and necessitate considerable human labor. Microscopy, for instance, continues to serve as the cornerstone for identifying many parasite illnesses and has seen minimal alteration since its inception in the 15th century. For decades, it functioned as the sole technique for identifying parasites in blood smears, tissue specimens, fecal matter, lymph node aspirates, bone marrow, and cerebrospinal fluid. However, the preparation of these materials is arduous and time-intensive, and precise interpretation relies significantly on proficient laboratory professionals. The diagnosis of all significant intestinal helminth infections now depends only on microscopic investigation (Momčilović et al., 2019). When tissue or other biological specimens cannot be obtained, serology has emerged as the diagnostic gold standard. Serological methods are classified into two primary categories: antigen-detection and antibody-detection assays. They include various techniques, such as enzyme-linked immunosorbent assay (ELISA), hemagglutination tests, indirect and direct immunofluorescent antibody tests, complement fixation tests, immunoblotting, and rapid diagnostic tests. In comparison to microscopy, these assays often provide enhanced sensitivity and specificity (Haselbeck et al., 2022).

Since the advent of polymerase chain reaction (PCR), there have been few significant advancements in clinical diagnostic testing. Since the introduction of PCR, parasitologists have adopted molecular-based methodologies to enhance current diagnostic techniques. Molecular techniques, including real-time PCR (RT-PCR) and loop-mediated isothermal amplification (LAMP), demonstrate significant potential for parasite identification, exhibiting enhanced specificity and sensitivity (Bretagne, 2003). The National Reference Centre for Parasitology (NRCP) use RT-PCR for diagnosing Leishmaniasis and Chagas disease. DNA-based techniques have demonstrated exceptional sensitivity and specificity. Additional molecular-based methodologies encompass Luminex and proteomic technologies that utilize mass spectrometry platforms (Ndao, 2009).

Diagnostic efforts in endemic, resource-limited settings face substantial challenges that hinder accurate detection and proper patient management. Conventional and immunodiagnostic methods often fall short because of issues such as difficulties in obtaining reliable slide readings, the inability to distinguish among different stages of infection, and susceptibility to cross-reactivity in regions with multiple co-circulating parasites. Although molecular approaches such as PCR offer greater sensitivity, especially for low-density infections, their integration into routine practice remains limited. Together, these constraints highlight the urgent need for more accessible, accurate, and stage-specific diagnostic tools to improve outcomes in affected populations (Oyeyemi et al., 2024).

1.7 Treatment and control strategies

Antiparasitic medications have been effectively utilized for several years to manage parasitic infections in animals because of their safety, affordability, and efficacy against a wide range of parasites. A major drawback of this achievement appears to be the emergence of drug resistance in many target parasites. Moreover, apprehensions regarding residues in the food chain and environment have emerged, jeopardizing their further utilization. Control strategies that include vaccines as a core component present appealing choice. Although attenuated parasite vaccinations have proven effective, subunit vaccines remain uncommon (Tenorio, 2025). Capela et al. (2019) indicated that resistance to artemisinin-based therapy in *P. falciparum* has been documented in Southeast Asia, presenting a significant challenge to malaria control initiatives. Resistance to antimonial medicines has similarly been demonstrated in *Leishmania* species, complicating the treatment of leishmaniasis. The absence of new pharmaceuticals with innovative modes of action intensifies this problem, as cross-resistance may render several treatments ineffective (Capela et al., 2019). Numerous current medications are linked to toxicity and detrimental side effects, constraining their applicability (Kaushik et al., 2025).

Prior to the 19th century, medicinal herbs were employed for several ailments based on empirical experience, devoid of any mechanistic understanding of their application. Rational drug research commenced in the 19th century with the extraction of the analgesic morphine (Atanasov et al., 2015). Plants produce a diverse range of chemicals that fulfill specialized functions in metabolism. Natural chemicals derived from plant extracts exhibit significant chemical diversity relative to manufactured molecules and frequently result in distinct biological functions (Newman et al., 2008). Concerning parasitism, medicinal plants have been utilized for centuries to address these ailments and continue to be employed for this purpose in many regions globally (Newman and Cragg, 2007). Nanotechnologies are employed to create advanced instruments for managing the vectors of parasitic diseases, notably malaria. Studies indicate that metallic nanoparticles derived from plants and plant extracts are efficacious against mosquito eggs, larvae, pupae, and adults, specifically targeting Anopheles mosquitoes (Onen et al., 2023). These bio-derived nanoparticles are low-toxicity agents, and they may offer numerous advantages over conventional insecticides, such as ease of formulation, low toxicity, and the absence of known resistance to date (Auysawasdi et al., 2016).

1.8 Challenges and emerging concerns

Environmental, societal, and microbiological factors are progressively influencing the global prevalence of blood parasites and vector-borne illnesses. Increasing temperatures and altered precipitation patterns have expanded the habitats of vectors, including mosquitoes, facilitating the dissemination and recurrence of diseases such as malaria (Semenza and Paz, 2021). Simultaneously, accelerated urban expansion and increased human mobility facilitate the dissemination of diseases across regions, resulting in both localized epidemics and global health emergencies (Zumla and Hui, 2019). In numerous tropical and subtropical regions, inadequate sanitation and socioeconomic adversity exacerbate transmission by fostering environments conducive to vector proliferation (Qian and Zhou, 2016). NTDs, encompassing protozoan blood parasites such as *Trypanosoma* spp., *Plasmodium* spp., and *Trypanosoma cruzi*, persist as underreported and extremely frequent in Africa, Asia, and Latin America. Inadequate access to clean water, sanitation, and healthcare sustains the cycle of infection and hinders effective surveillance and control measures (Zumla and Hui, 2019).

1.9 Future perspectives

Future progress in the control of blood-borne parasites will be strongly shaped by breakthroughs in molecular parasitology and host-pathogen immunology. High-throughput sequencing, single-cell genomics, and CRISPR-based functional studies are poised to deepen our understanding of parasite biology, virulence factors, and immune evasion mechanisms. These insights will support the development of next-generation diagnostics capable of detecting low-density and mixed infections, as well as innovative therapeutics and vaccines tailored to specific parasite stages. Improved immunoprofiling strategies may also enable more accurate differentiation among acute, chronic, and past infections, thereby addressing one of the major limitations in current diagnostic approaches.

The integration of artificial intelligence (AI), machine learning, and big data analytics is transforming global disease surveillance. AI-driven models can predict vector distribution changes under shifting climate patterns, detect outbreak hotspots in real time, and analyze vast diagnostic datasets to identify early warning signals. Coupled with mobile health platforms and digital reporting tools, AI-enabled systems have the potential to strengthen early detection, guide resource allocation, and support rapid response efforts in both endemic and emerging transmission zones.

Nanotechnology and biotechnology offer promising avenues for improving the diagnosis, treatment, and prevention of blood-borne parasitic diseases. Nanoparticle-based biosensors may enable ultrasensitive point-of-care diagnostics, while nanoformulated drugs could enhance therapeutic efficacy and reduce toxicity. Concurrently, natural products remain an invaluable source of novel antiparasitic compounds, especially when paired with modern bioengineering approaches such as synthetic biology and metabolomics. These innovations have the potential to overcome drug resistance and expand the arsenal of safe and effective interventions.

Sustainable control of blood-borne parasites will require harmonized, multidisciplinary approaches. Integrated strategies may combine vector control, enhanced sanitation, community education, climate-informed risk mapping, and improved access to diagnostics and treatment. Strengthening health systems, particularly in resource-limited regions, is essential for implementing these measures. Cross-sector collaboration involving public health agencies, environmental scientists, social scientists, and policymakers will be central to reducing transmission and mitigating the socioeconomic drivers of disease.

Although eradication remains a complex challenge, sustained progress is achievable through long-term commitment and innovation. Future efforts will likely focus on developing highly sensitive surveillance systems capable of identifying residual hotspots, improving vaccine availability, and implementing adaptive management plans that incorporate environmental and social change. An emphasis on sustainability through community engagement, continued research investment, and global partnerships will be crucial for maintaining gains and preventing re-emergence. Moving forward, the integration of emerging technologies with traditional public health practices offers a promising path toward the eventual elimination of major blood-borne parasitic diseases.

References

Argov S, Jaffe CL, Krupp M, Slor H, Shoen feld Y. Autoantibody production by patients infected with leishmania. Clinical and Experimental Immunology 1989;76(2):190–7.

Atanasov AG, Waltenberger B, Pferschy-Wenzig EM, Linder T, Wawrosch C, Uhrin P, et al. Discovery and resupply of pharmacologically active plant-derived natural products: a review. Biotechnology Advances 2015;33(8):1582–614. Available from https://doi.org/10.1016/j.biotechadv.2015.08.001.

Auysawasdi N, Chuntranuluck S, Phasomkusolsil S, Keeratinijakal V. Improving the effectiveness of three essential oils against Aedes aegypti (Linn.) and Anopheles dirus (Peyton and Harrison). Parasitology Research 2016;115(1):99–106. Available from https://doi.org/10.1007/s00436-015-4725-3.

Baral TN. Immunobiology of African trypanosomes: need of alternative interventions. Journal of Biomedicine and Biotechnology 2010;2010. Available from https://doi.org/10.1155/2010/389153.

Beaver AK, Keneskhanova Z, Cosentino RO, Weiss BL, Awuoche EO, Smallenberger GM, et al. Tissue spaces are reservoirs of antigenic diversity for *Trypanosoma brucei*. Nature 2024;636(8042):430–7. Available from https://doi.org/10.1038/s41586-024-08151-z.

Bretagne S. Molecular diagnostics in clinical parasitology and mycology: limits of the current polymerase chain reaction (PCR) assays and interest of the real-time PCR assays. Clinical Microbiology and Infection 2003;9(6):505–11. Available from https://doi.org/10.1046/j.1469-0691.2003.00677.x.

Capela R, Moreira R, Lopes F. An overview of drug resistance in protozoal diseases. International Journal of Molecular Sciences 2019;20(22):5748. Available from https://doi.org/10.3390/ijms20225748.

Choi B, Vu HT, Vu HT, Radwanska M, Magez S. Advances in the Immunology of the host–parasite interactions in african trypanosomosis, including single-cell transcriptomics. Pathogens 2024;13(3). Available from https://doi.org/10.3390/pathogens13030188.

De Muylder G, Daulouède S, Lecordier L, Uzureau P, Morias Y, Van Den Abbeele J, et al. A *Trypanosoma brucei* kinesin heavy chain promotes parasite growth by triggering host arginase activity. PLoS Pathogens 2013;9(10):e1003731. Available from https://doi.org/10.1371/journal.ppat.1003731.

Donkoh ET, Berkoh D, Boadu IWO, Raji AS, Asamoah S, Fosu-Gyasi S, et al. Evidence of reduced academic performance among school children with helminth infection independent of nutritional status. Research Square 2022. Available from https://doi.org/10.21203/rs.3.rs-1153467/v1.

Elmahallawy EK, Alkhaldi AAM, Saleh AA. Host immune response against leishmaniasis and parasite persistence strategies: a review and assessment of recent research. Biomedicine and Pharmacotherapy 2021;139. Available from https://doi.org/10.1016/j.biopha.2021.111671.

Haselbeck AH, Im J, Prifti K, Marks F, Holm M, Zellweger RM. Serology as a tool to assess infectious disease landscapes and guide public health policy. Pathogens 2022;11(7). Available from https://doi.org/10.3390/pathogens11070732.

Hassen M, Mohammed A, Endeshaw T, Seid T, Samuel F, Asmare T, et al. Integrated prevalence assessment of wuchereria bancrofti and onchocerca volvulus in three co-endemic districts of Gambella Region, Ethiopia. American Journal of Tropical Medicine and Hygiene 2023;109(4):844–9. Available from https://doi.org/10.4269/ajtmh.22-0392.

Hotez PJ, Fenwick A, Savioli L, Molyneux DH. Rescuing the bottom billion through control of neglected tropical diseases. The Lancet 2009;373(9674):1570–5. Available from https://doi.org/10.1016/s0140-6736(09)60233-6.

Hudu SA, Jimoh AO, Adeshina KA, Otalike EG, Tahir A, Hegazy AA. An insight into the success, challenges, and future perspectives of eliminating neglected tropical disease. Scientific African 2024;24. Available from https://doi.org/10.1016/j.sciaf.2024.e02165.

Ijaiya MA, Anjorin S, Uthman OA. Quantifying the increased risk of illness in malnourished children: a global meta-analysis and propensity score matching approach. Global Health Research and Policy 2024;9(1). Available from https://doi.org/10.1186/s41256-024-00371-0.

Kaminsky R, Mäser P. Global impact of parasitic infections and the importance of parasite control. Frontiers in Parasitology 2025;4. Available from https://doi.org/10.3389/fpara.2025.1546195.

Kaushik A, Makarani N, Bharadava K, Gehlot J, Naik BV, Singh A, et al. Antiprotozoal agents – integration of drug discovery, medicinal chemistry, and advanced computational approaches: an in-depth review. The Microbe 2025;7:100395. Available from https://doi.org/10.1016/j.microb.2025.100395.

Koschorke M, Al-Haboubi YH, Tseng PC, Semrau M, Eaton J. Mental health, stigma, and neglected tropical diseases: a review and systematic mapping of the evidence. Frontiers in Tropical Diseases 2022;3. Available from https://doi.org/10.3389/fitd.2022.808955.

Li J, Xiao C, Li C, He J. Tissue-resident immune cells: from defining characteristics to roles in diseases. Signal Transduction and Targeted Therapy 2025;10(1). Available from https://doi.org/10.1038/s41392-024-02050-5.

Loubens M, Vincensini L, Fernandes P, Briquet S, Marinach C, Silvie O. Plasmodium sporozoites on the move: switching from cell traversal to productive invasion of hepatocytes. Molecular Microbiology 2021;115(5):870–81. Available from https://doi.org/10.1111/mmi.14645.

Lundy SK, Lukacs NW. Chronic schistosome infection leads to modulation of granuloma formation and systemic immune suppression. Frontiers in Immunology 2013;4. Available from https://doi.org/10.3389/fimmu.2013.00039.

Malik S, Shahzad MI, Shah ZA, Qadeer I, Parveen S, Maqbool U, et al. Zoonotic diseases: trypanosomiasis - an overview. Bahawalpur, Pakistan: The Government Sadiq College Women University; 2025. p. 257–62.

Manful EE, Dofuor AK, Gwira TM. The role of tryptophan derivatives as anti-kinetoplastid agents. Heliyon 2024;10(1). Available from https://doi.org/10.1016/j.heliyon.2023.e23895.

Ménard R. Gliding motility and cell invasion by Apicomplexa: insights from the Plasmodium sporozoite. Cellular Microbiology 2001;3(2):63–73. Available from https://doi.org/10.1046/j.1462-5822.2001.00097.x.

Momčilović S, Cantacessi C, Arsić-Arsenijević V, Otranto D, Tasić-Otašević S. Rapid diagnosis of parasitic diseases: current scenario and future needs. Clinical Microbiology and Infection 2019;25(3):290–309. Available from https://doi.org/10.1016/j.cmi.2018.04.028.

Nayeri T, Sarvi S, Daryani A. Effective factors in the pathogenesis of Toxoplasma gondii. Heliyon 2024;10(10):e31558. Available from https://doi.org/10.1016/j.heliyon.2024.e31558.

Ndao M. Diagnosis of parasitic diseases: old and new approaches. Interdisciplinary Perspectives on Infectious Diseases 2009;2009:1–15. Available from https://doi.org/10.1155/2009/278246.

Newman DJ, Cragg GM. Natural products as sources of new drugs over the last 25 years. Journal of Natural Products 2007;70(3):461–77. Available from https://doi.org/10.1021/np068054v.

Newman DJ, Cragg GM, I. Kingston DG. Chapter 8 - Natural products as pharmaceuticals and sources for lead structures. In: Wermuth CG, editor. The Practice of Medicinal Chemistry. third ed.Academic Press; 2008. p. 159–86. Available from https://doi.org/10.1016/B978-0-12-374194-3.00008-1.

Onen H, Luzala MM, Kigozi S, Sikumbili RM, Muanga CJK, Zola EN, et al. Mosquito-borne diseases and their control strategies: an overview focused on green synthesized plant-based metallic nanoparticles. Insects 2023;14(3). Available from https://doi.org/10.3390/insects14030221.

Oyeyemi OT, Ogundahunsi O, Schunk M, Fatem RG, Shollenberger LM. Neglected tropical disease (NTD) diagnostics: current development and operations to advance control. Pathogens and Global Health 2024;118(1):1–24. Available from https://doi.org/10.1080/20477724.2023.2272095.

Pasha F, Saleem S, Nazir T, Tariq J, Qureshi K. Visceral leishmaniasis (Kala-Azar): a triumph against a trickster disease. Cureus 2022;14(6):e25698. Available from https://doi.org/10.7759/cureus.25698.

Qian MB, Zhou XN. Global burden on neglected tropical diseases. The Lancet Infectious Diseases 2016;16(10):1113–4. Available from https://doi.org/10.1016/S1473-3099(16)30328-0.

Rahman MT, Sobur MA, Islam MS, Ievy S, Hossain MJ, Zowalaty MEE, et al. Zoonotic diseases: etiology, impact, and control. Microorganisms 2020;8(9):1–34. Available from https://doi.org/10.3390/microorganisms8091405.

Scarpini S, Dondi A, Totaro C, Biagi C, Melchionda F, Zama D, et al. Visceral leishmaniasis: epidemiology, diagnosis, and treatment regimens in different geographical areas with a focus on pediatrics. Microorganisms 2022;10(10):1887. Available from https://doi.org/10.3390/microorganisms10101887.

Semenza JC, Paz S. Climate change and infectious disease in Europe: impact, projection and adaptation. The Lancet Regional Health - Europe 2021;9:100230. Available from https://doi.org/10.1016/j.lanepe.2021.100230.

Singh G, Sehgal R. Transfusion-transmitted parasitic infections. Asian Journal of Transfusion Science 2010;4(2):73. Available from https://doi.org/10.4103/0973-6247.67018.

St. Laurent B. Mosquito vector diversity and malaria transmission. Frontiers in Malaria 2025;3. Available from https://doi.org/10.3389/fmala.2025.1600850.

Tenorio JCB. Drug resistance in parasites: a review of mechanisms, drivers, and mitigation strategies. Microbes and Infectious Diseases 2025;6(3):6152–60. Available from https://doi.org/10.21608/MID.2024.317774.2189.

Turner HC, Bettis AA, Chu BK, McFarland DA, Hooper PJ, Ottesen EA, et al. The health and economic benefits of the global programme to eliminate lymphatic filariasis (2000-2014). Infectious Diseases of Poverty 2016;5(1). Available from https://doi.org/10.1186/s40249-016-0147-4.

Vannier E, Krause PJ. Human babesiosis. New England Journal of Medicine 2012;366(25):2397–407. Available from https://doi.org/10.1056/NEJMra1202018.

Wang C-C, Zhang W-X, He Y, Liu J-H, Ju C-S, Wu Q-L, et al. Global Epidemiology of vector-borne parasitic diseases: burden, trends, disparities, and forecasts (1990–2036). Pathogens 2025;14(9):844. Available from https://doi.org/10.3390/pathogens14090844.

White NJ, Pukrittayakamee S, Hien TT, Faiz MA, Mokuolu OA, Dondorp AM. Malaria. The Lancet 2014;383(9918):723–35. Available from https://doi.org/10.1016/S0140-6736(13)60024-0.

World Health Organization. Vector-borne and parasitic diseases global report. WHO Press; 2023.

Zhao H, Xu T, Shen H, Ionica AM. Global, regional, and national disability-adjusted life years and prevalence of lymphatic filariasis from 1990 to 2021: a trend and health inequality analysis based on the global burden of disease study 2021. PLoS Neglected Tropical Diseases 2025;19(4):e0013017. Available from https://doi.org/10.1371/journal.pntd.0013017.

Zhu Y-S, Sun Z-S, Zheng J-X, Zhang S-X, Yin J-X, Zhao H-Q, et al. Prevalence and attributable health burdens of vector-borne parasitic infectious diseases of poverty, 1990–2021: findings from the global burden of disease study 2021. Infectious Diseases of Poverty 2024;13(1). Available from https://doi.org/10.1186/s40249-024-01260-x.

Zumla A, Hui DSC. Emerging and reemerging infectious diseases: global overview. Infectious Disease Clinics of North America 2019;33(4):xiii. Available from https://doi.org/10.1016/j.idc.2019.09.001.

CHAPTER 2

Drug resistance and the urgent need for novel therapies

Raja'a Al-Qudah[1], Malek Al-Najjar[2], Mohammad A A Al-Najjar[3], Amin Omar[3], and Muna Barakat[1]
[1]Department of Clinical Pharmacy and Therapeutics, Applied Science Private University, Amman, Jordan,
[2]Faculty of Medicine, Jordan University of Science and Technology, Irbid, Jordan,
[3]Department of Pharmaceutical Sciences and Pharmaceutics, Applied Science Private University, Amman, Jordan

The second section critically evaluates the limitations of current antiparasitic therapies, addressing both clinical and operational gaps. These include drug toxicity, narrow therapeutic windows, prolonged treatment regimens, poor patient adherence, limited efficacy against resistant strains, and challenges in treating co-infections and vulnerable populations. Operational constraints, such as high costs, limited drug availability, inadequate diagnostic tools, and weak health system infrastructure in endemic regions, further contribute to treatment failure and resistance spread. By integrating mechanistic insights with clinical and programmatic challenges, this chapter highlights the pressing need for innovative therapeutic approaches, including new drug targets, combination therapies, host-directed treatments, and advanced drug delivery systems. Addressing these gaps is essential to curb resistance, improve treatment outcomes, and ensure sustainable control of blood-borne protozoan diseases.

2.1 Mechanisms of drug resistance in blood-borne Protozoa

The massive health, social, and economic effects of protozoal infections contribute considerably to the global burden of infectious diseases. Malaria (*Plasmodium spp.*), cutaneous and visceral leishmaniasis (*Leishmania spp.*), African sleeping sickness (*Trypanosoma brucei*), Chagas disease (*Trypanosoma cruzi*), amoebic dysentery (*Entamoeba spp.*), and toxoplasmosis (*Toxoplasma spp.*) are some of the life-threatening diseases caused by protozoa that afflict nearly a sixth of the world's population (Breman, 2001; Fletcher et al., 2012). Nevertheless, control programs depend, for the most part, on a limited number of antiparasitic drugs. As these drugs are applied on a broad scale, parasite populations continue to acquire reduced susceptibility, leading to treatment failure and endangering extermination initiatives. Drug resistance among blood-borne protozoa contributes to our failure of combating these infections (Capela et al., 2019; De Koning, 2017). This chapter explores the major biological mechanisms by which blood-borne protozoa acquire drug resistance, Fig. 2.1.

Innovative Strategies Against Blood Parasites
DOI: https://doi.org/10.1016/B978-0-443-48509-1.00010-0

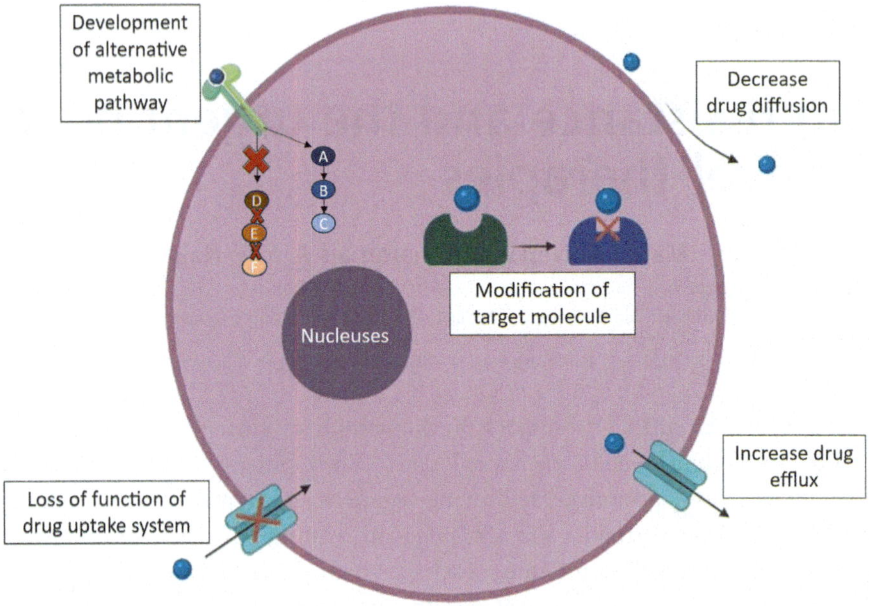

Figure 2.1 The major biological mechanisms by which blood-borne protozoa acquire drug resistance.

2.2 Drug resistance in malaria

Malaria is a serious medical problem in tropical and subtropical countries, affecting roughly 200 million people annually and killing more than two million (Nnamonu et al., 2020; Sankineni et al., 2023). Malaria is treated mainly by chemotherapy, but the parasite has developed resistance to commonly used treatments and prevention methods. The most serious form of malaria, *Plasmodium falciparum*, is the one transmitted by mosquitoes and is responsible for almost all human malaria mortality (Daskum et al., 2021). For the control of *P. falciparum*, antimalarial drugs such as quinine, chloroquine, mefloquine, and halofantrine are widely used, along with the antifolate antagonists sulfadoxine and pyrimethamine (Yadav et al., 2024). The widespread resistance of *P. falciparum* to medicines necessitates the development of new antimalarial medications as well as a better understanding of the parasite's resistance mechanisms.

2.3 The history of drug resistance in malaria and the shift to new-generation agents

In malaria control, antimalarial medications are the only choice for managing malaria and preserving at-risk people; safe and effective therapies save malaria patients from having serious infections and from dying. For more than four decades, chloroquine (CQ) was the first-line therapy for malaria, and molecular markers for its resistance were discovered in 2001 (Djimdé et al., 2001). Artemisinin (ART)-based combination treatments (ACTs) were launched following widespread resistance to CQ (Valecha et al., 2009). The World Health Organization (WHO) (WHO, 2023) promoted ACTs as a first-line therapy between 2001 and 2004, and ACTs were introduced in 20 African nations based on WHO recommendations. Six ACTs are now used to treat malaria globally. ACT currently is used throughout the world and has demonstrated significant malaria decline (Rasmussen et al., 2022). In spite of stringent malaria treatment guidelines and surveillance by WHO, the emergence and spread of ART-resistant (Artemisinin resistance) *P. falciparum*, with initial cases in the Greater Mekong Subregion and now in East Africa, constitute a major threat to worldwide malaria elimination efforts (Kamau et al., 2015; Ngwa et al., 2022). Moreover, eleven years later, in February 2018, Southeast Asia showed ART-resistance, specifically to the dihydroartemisinin/piperaquine combination treatment (Win et al., 2022). Resistance to the partner drugs in ACTs has continued to pose a problem in malaria treatment. However parasites with reduced susceptibility to ACTs have lost susceptibility to ART and the resistance of combined antimalarial drugs containing ART (Kamau et al., 2015).

New antimalarials, in view of the failure of previous monotherapies and the emerging gaps in ACT effectiveness, are designed to avoid current resistance mechanisms and allow longer cure periods. The leading next-generation therapy with a completely novel mechanism and once-daily dose is ganaplacide-lumefantrine. It has shown ~97–99% Phase III success rates in Africa, including against resistant strains, with no field resistance documented yet (Manaranche et al., 2024). Cipargamin (KAE609) is a fast-acting *PfATP4* Na^+-pump inhibitor that clears parasites and transmission stages (Schmitt et al., 2022). However *PfATP4* resistance mutations have already been seen (Qiu et al., 2022). MMV390048 (MMV048) acts on several life-cycle phases as an inhibitor of *PfPI4K* and does not have cross-resistance with drugs previously used. No common clinical resistance has been confirmed (Moolman et al., 2020).

2.4 Resistance mechanisms for classical and next-generation antimalarials

Drug resistance has been recognized as a major challenge to malaria control efforts. Chemoprophylaxis/chemotherapy is the main way to control malaria, since many mosquito vectors are resistant to pesticides and an effective vaccine is currently unavailable. Since the advent of synthetic antimalarials 60–70 years ago, only a few molecules from three major families have proven clinically effective (Grimberg and Mehlotra, 2011). The parasite's capacity to develop resistance to antimalarial medicines has significantly degraded the limited arsenal available. Resistance to a single medication varies significantly depending on geography. Southeast Asia has varying levels of *P. falciparum* medication resistance (Wernsdorfer et al., 1994), some areas developing total resistance to many treatments, while in other areas the disease remains sensitive to a wide range of drugs (White, 1997).

Antimalarial medication resistance involves two processes: (1) the rate of resistance mutations arising from medication usage inside an individual, and (2) the transmission of resistant alleles to others (Le Bras and Durand, 2003; White, 2004). High rates of mutations at the cellular level enable the parasite to escape the host's immune system and, within a host, select for resistance. Variation in transmission and host susceptibility also affect selection at the population level (Klein, 2013).

Genetic crosslinking and mapping of parasites allowed the discovery of medication resistance genes. Crosslinking between CQ-sensitive and resistant strains identified a 36 kb stretch on chromosome 7 of *P. falciparum* (Wellems et al., 1991). Molecular analysis linked mutations in the *P. falciparum* CQ-resistance transporter (*Pfcrt*) gene to both susceptibility and drug-resistant strains in laboratory and field studies (Baro et al., 2013; Durand et al., 2001; Fidock, 2000). Mutations in the *Pfcrt* gene impact CQ resistance and phenotype significantly. Also, the K76T mutation is considered the major determinant for CQ resistance and susceptibility. This mutation in the first transmembrane domain of the PfCRT protein, replacing a positively charged lysine at position 76 with a neutrally charged threonine, might enhance the active transport of diprotonated CQ from the gastric vacuole (Fidock et al., 2000). Other mutations (C72S, M74I, N75E, A220S, Q271E, N326S, I356T, and R371I) contribute to resistance in association with the K76T mutation (Tun et al., 2015).

Sulfadoxine/pyrimethamine, an antifolate medication, inhibits *P. falciparum* dihydropteroate synthetase (PfDHPS) and *P. falciparum* bifunctional dihydrofolate reductase-thymidylate synthase (PfDHFR), enzymes involved in the folate production pathway. In biochemical and genetic cross-linkage studies, *P. falciparum* mutations in the genes *Pfdhps* and *Pfdhfr* confer reduced drug susceptibility of sulfadoxine/pyrimethamine (Cowman, Morry et al., 1988; Peterson et al., 1988; Triglia and Cowman, 1999). Whole-genome sequencing of ART-resistant parasites identified a mutation in the Kelch 13 propeller protein that has been associated with resistance in clinical and field isolates (Ariey et al., 2014; Ashley et al., 2014; Tun et al., 2015). Table 2.1 summarizes the major antimalarial drug classes, representative drugs, and the key mechanisms by which *P. falciparum* develops resistance.

2.5 Drug resistance in leishmaniasis

Leishmania are protozoan parasites caused by *leishmania spp.* (Protozoa, Kinetoplastida, Trypanosomatidae), and travel between sandflies and mammals. It can result in skin sores, serious deformity, and even death because of systemic infection (Handman, 1999). According to the WHO, the disease infects 2 million people annually, threatens 350 million people in 88 countries, and currently infectes 12 million people throughout the world (Alvar et al., 2012). Leishmaniasis treatment options are limited including the

Table 2.1 Classes of antimalarial drugs and their mechanisms of resistance.

Class of antimalarial drug	Drug	Mechanism of resistance	References
Folate antagonists	Sulfa drugs, dihydrofolate reductase inhibitors	Point mutations in the treatment target has been found to contribute to treatment resistance	Plowe (2001)
Quinoline-containing antimalarials	Quinine, mefloquine, 4-amino-quinoline, chloroquine	• Reduced drug accumulation because of reduced vacuolar proton pump activity. • Amplification and overexpression of the *pfmdr1* gene.	Egan (2001), Ginsburg and Krugliak (1992)
Artemisinin-based combination treatments (ACTs)	Artemether–lumefantrine, artesunate–amodiaquine, dihydroartemisinin–piperaquine, artesunate–mefloquine, artesunate–sulfadoxine–pyrimethamine, pyronaridine–artesunate	• Reduce drug susceptibility via *pfcrt* K76 and *pfmdr-1* N86 and *pfmrp1* polymorphisms point mutations in the *pfcrt* and *pfmdr1* genes • A triple mutation in pfdhfr (51I, 59 R, 108 N) and a double mutant in pfdhps (437 G and 540E) were shown to enhance the probability of treatment failure in vivo	Breman (2012), Ward et al. (2022)
Ganaplacide/lumefantrine combination	Ganaplacide/lumefantrine (KAF156 + lumefantrine)	-	Manaranche et al. (2024)
Cipargamin	Cipargamin (KAE609)	*PfATP4* resistance mutations	Goldgof et al. (2016)
PI4K inhibitor MMV390048	MMV390048 (MMV048)	-	Demarta-Gatsi, et al. (2022), Mathews and Odom John (2018)

use of antimonial salts (sodium stibogluconate (Sb^{V}) and meglumine antimonate (Sb^{III})), miltefosine, amphotericin B, pentamidine, azoles (ketoconazole, itraconazole, and fluconazole), allopurinol, sitamaquine, antiretroviral drugs, and combination therapy (Braga, 2019; Dietze et al., 2001; Koutinas et al., 2001).

In general, pentavalent antimonials have long been the first-line antileishmanial therapy and continue to play an important role in treatment, but resistance to this class of medication is so strong in some regions in the world, notably in Bihar (India), that it is soon becoming obsolete (Fidock, 2000; Sundar et al., 2000). Amphotericin B and pentamidine represent second-line therapies but their toxicity and high cost limit their usefulness. Fluconazole, administered orally, was likewise effective in the treatment of cutaneous leishmaniasis. Further drugs with demonstrated efficacy or in clinical trials may help improve the limited options available to treat leishmania infections (Berman, 2003; Croft and Coombs, 2003). For that, combination therapy has emerged as a viable option for treating leishmaniasis, while monotherapeutic regimens have become less effective. Combining antileishmanial medicines may lessen harmful side effects and avoid resistance. Research suggests that some medications might enhance their antileishmanial effects when used together (Bryceson, 2001).

2.6 The history of drug resistance in *Leishmania* and the shift to combination therapy

Antimonials (Sb^{V}, Sb^{III}) represent the principle of drugs used in the treatment of leishmaniasis. They have been in use since the 1920s. These toxic chemicals have a narrow therapeutic window, and their use has been largely replaced in the Indian subcontinent, where resistance has developed in 2005. They are, however still being used in several parts of the world, including Latin America and East Africa (Elammari and Sariti, 2021; Mitropoulos et al., 2010).

Miltefosine is an alternative drug invented in the middle of the 1980s, and has replaced antimonials in the kala-azar eradication program in the Indian subcontinent but lost its effectiveness within ten years (Rijal et al., 2013; Sundar et al., 2012). In the initial period, the loss of effectiveness of miltefosine could not be attributed to resistance among the parasites (Rijal et al., 2013). However a few resistant clinical isolates have been reported, first in France in an HIV-coinfected patient and then in two Indian patients (Cojean et al., 2012; Mondelaers et al., 2016; Srivastava et al., 2017).

Then the free deoxycholate form of amphotericin B was used to treat leishmaniasis. It is very effective but moderately hazardous. Toxicity risk is lowered by liposomal administration, although such administration is enormously expensive and limits its use. Moreover, the resistance of amphotericin B has been reported.

After that, paromomycin was used. It targets only a narrow spectrum of leishmania species, and field resistance is currently unknown. However laboratory-derived resistant isolates have been generated (García-Hernández et al., 2012; Hendrickx et al., 2016; Jhingran et al., 2009).

2.7 Resistance mechanisms for classical and combination antileishmanial therapy

There are several suggested processes for antimonial resistance. Resistance to antimony has been linked to a lower biological conversion of Sb^{V} to Sb^{III}, reduced drug internalization, the overexpression of the ABC transporters, elevated levels of MRPA (multidrug resistance protein A), overexpression of tryparedoxin peroxidase, and higher levels of trypanothione, which increases thiol redox susceptibility (Ponte-Sucre et al., 2017). Downregulation of AQP1 has also been found as a cause of resistance in *L. donovani* isolates from the Indian subcontinent (Ponte-Sucre et al., 2017).

The failure of miltefosine therapy was initially assumed to be a result of host variables such as immunological factors, drug exposure, or parasite pathogenicity. Miltefosine is transported across the parasite cell membrane by the *L. donovani* miltefosine transporter and the protein LdRos3 (Rai et al., 2013). Recently, two laboratories reported miltefosine-resistant visceral leishmaniasis isolates in the Indian subcontinent. The principal mechanism of resistance identified was a significant reduction in drug internalization or increased efflux. Genomic studies showed single-nucleotide polymorphisms in the parasite LdMT gene (Rai et al., 2013). The increased miltefosine resistance in leishmania has also been associated with overexpression of ABC transporters ABCB4 (MDR1), ABCG4, and ABCG6 that enhance the efflux of the drug. One study from Nepal also showed that higher parasite infectivity was correlated with miltefosine relapse (Pandey et al., 2009).

Resistance to amphotericin B therapy is rare, even among immunocompromised individuals. However there have been recent reports of therapy failures involving both competent and immunosuppressed patients because of the detection of resistant organisms in one study (Morizot et al., 2016; Purkait et al., 2012; Srivastava et al., 2011). Resistance has been associated with the depletion of ergosterol, alterations in sterol 14α-demethylase genes, and drug-induced oxidative stress. Given this situation, early diagnosis and monitoring of the effectiveness of the regimen in order to minimize the spread of amphotericin B resistance are important in the Indian subcontinent, where single dosing is prevalent (Ponte-Sucre et al., 2017).

Resistance to paromomycin in visceral leishmaniasis is unknown because it has not been widely used. In addition, in a study of 60-day cutaneous leishmaniasis therapy in two cases of *L. aethiopica*, isolates from relapsed patients were 3–5 times less sensitive to the drug following treatment compared with isolates taken before treatment in an amastigote-macrophage test. There are only a few reports that indicate that resistance is linked to reduced drug uptake, diminished mitochondrial and cytoplasmic protein synthesis, and reduced drug accumulation along with a significant decrease in the initial binding to the cell surface (Chakravarty, 2010; Jhingran et al., 2009; Croft et al., 2006).

Fluconazole, itraconazole, and ketoconazole have been used for cutaneous leishmaniasis in a number of studies (Alrajhi et al., 2002). These drugs are active against the ergosterol production of leishmania parasites. In a small study of cutaneous leishmaniasis patients in India, itraconazole was superior to placebo, but the findings were not replicated in a study conducted in Iran. In a Saudi Arabian study, fluconazole cured 79% of patients with cutaneous leishmaniasis caused by *L. major*, compared to 34% with placebo (Alrajhi et al., 2002; Dogra and Saxena, 1996; Momeni et al., 1997; Nassiri-Kashani et al., 2005).

2.8 Drug resistance in African sleeping sickness

African sleeping sickness is a very serious disease that follows two phases of development: early and late. After the bite from a tsetse fly, trypanosomes multiply in the circulation and undergo antigenic variation to evade the host's immune system (Vickerman, 1985). The early phase of the disease presents symptoms that are rather nonspecific and can be confused with other conditions such as influenza or malaria: nausea, fever, and lethargy. In the late stage, trypanosomes cross the blood-brain barrier and are found in neural tissue and cerebrospinal fluid. After neuronal damage and the host response, the disease's characteristic symptoms commence: disruption of biological cycles, inappropriate and irregular sleep patterns, and loss of concentration and coordination. Unless the disease is treated, death will occur. The disease progresses from acute, where death results in 6 to 12 months, to chronic, where death results in 5 to 20 years. Very few drugs are available to treat African sleeping sickness, and little progress has been made in developing new treatments in the past 50 years (Croft et al., 1997; Pepin and Milord, 1994).

2.9 The history of drug resistance in African sleeping sickness

Only a few drugs have an efficacy against African sleeping sickness, and few new treatments have been developed in the last 50 years. Pentamidine and suramin, discovered before the 1920s, are still the drugs of choice for early-stage sleeping sickness. Melarsoprol, developed in 1949, is the most effective treatment for late-stage sleeping sickness (Laohasinnarong, 2020). Melarsoprol leads to reactive encephalopathy in 10% of patients, which is fatal in half of those affected. Subsequently, eflornithine (alpha-difluoromethylornithine), also known as DFMO, an ornithine metabolism inhibitor, has been used to treat late-phase sleeping sickness, but it is only effective for the West African form of the disease caused by *Trypanosoma brucei gambiense* and is ineffective for the East African form caused by *T. b. rhodesiense*. Furthermore, DFMO is no longer commercially available (Pepin and Milord, 1994).

2.10 Resistance mechanisms for African sleeping sickness therapy

Although the African trypanosomes were originally reported over a century ago, only a few effective medications have been licensed for therapy. Toxicity, complicated administration, and trypanosome resistance are some of the issues presented by these medications. In certain situations, administering the medications is very expensive and labor-consuming, a disadvantage considering that African trypanosomes are prevalent in rural and resource-limited areas. At the moment, there is no comprehensive therapy medicine or approach for African trypanosomes (Babokhov et al., 2013; Brun et al., 2010; Lopes et al., 2010).

The licensed medications for treating African trypanosomiasis have different mechanisms of action. Pentamidine isethionate (pentamidine) and suramin are used to treat the hemolymphatic stage of chronic and acute African trypanosomiasis, respectively. Melarsoprol (Mel B or Arsobal®) and DFMO are used to treat the meningoencaphalitic stage. DFMO is utilized in situations of meningoencephalitic chronic African trypanosomiasis, while melarsoprol is used in cases of chronic and acute African trypanosomiasis (Babokhov et al., 2013; Lopes et al., 2010). To accelerate the treatment of meningoencephalitic chronic African trypanosomiasis, DFMO is administered in combination with nifurtimox (Lampit®) in what is called nifurtimox-eflornithine combinatorial therapy (NECT). Nifurtimox is a standalone drug that has never received approval for treating African trypanosomiasis but is instead used to treat Chagas disease, a condition caused by *Trypanosoma cruzi*, an American trypanosome (Bisser et al., 2007; Kansiime et al., 2018; Munoz-Calderon et al., 2019; Patterson and Wyllie, 2014).

The mechanisms of melarsoprol resistance are the best studied of any antitrypanosomal drug. Carter and Fairlamb demonstrated, in 1993 (Carter and Fairlamb, 1993) that an adenosine transporter called P2 was probably able to take up melarsoprol, and that loss of this transporter was correlated with drug resistance in the RU15 line, selected *in vivo* for restistance to sodium melarsen. Melarsoprol is rapidly converted *in vivo* to melarsen oxide. The lower polarity of melarsoprol allows for passive diffusion across membranes, while the more polar active metabolite is dependent on carrier-mediated absorption. An early hypothesis speculated that the loss of the P2 transporter alone conferred melarsoprol/melarsen oxide resistance. Support came from the cloning of TbAT1, which encodes the P2 transporter, and was demonstrated to have point mutations in resistant lines that inactivated it or in other instances were deleted from other resistant lines. Gene knockout studies demonstrated that loss of the TbAT1 gene indeed caused functional loss of P2 transporter activity (Maser et al., 1999). However these knockout cells were only moderately less sensitive to melarsen oxide. Loss of P2 was necessary but not sufficient to account for high resistance levels. In an *in vitro* lysis assay, pentamidine delayed the lysis of P2 transporter-deficient cells, indicating that the high affinity pentamidine transporter, HAPT1, could be an alternate route for melamine-based arsenical uptake (Bridges et al., 2007; Matovu et al., 2003). A trypanosome line derived *in vitro* from the TbAT1 knockout precursor was resistant to the drugs pentamidine and melaminophenyl arsenicals, demonstrating functional loss of the HAPT1 transporter. The findings suggest that high levels of melaminophenyl arsenical resistance need the loss of both the P2 transporter and HAPT1. Identifying the HAPT1 carrier's gene and assessing the impact of TbAT1 will help determine other variables that lead to resistance and HAPT1 double-gene knockout (de Koning, 2008).

The resistance to diamidines, especially pentamidine, was reviewed. Carter et al., demonstrated that the P2 transporter can absorb pentamidine, and resistance to the medication is because of the lack of uptake (de Koning, 2008). However the RU15 line chosen for melarsen resistance showed only a minor improvement in resistance to pentamidine. PR32.6, a pentamidine-resistant line, showed minimal reduction in sensitivity to melaminopheny-larsenicals. The situation with diamidine-arsenical cross-resistance seemed convoluted. The finding that pentamidine is transported by more than one transporter, in addition to P2 transporter, helped to simplify the process. HAPT1 is named for the apparent Km for pentamidine was in the mid-nanomolar range, with a modest affinity (Bridges et al., 2007). Through kinetic analysis, a low-affinity carrier, LAPT1 in the tens of μM range was identified. To understand more about the resistance of these other transporters, a line, named B48, was selected, starting using the TbAT1-deficient line for higher levels of resistance to pentamidine. As stated previously, these cells lost their HAPT1 transporter and showed decreased susceptibility to melamine-based arsenicals. It turned out that pentamidine and the melaminophenyl arsenicals enter via both P2 and HAPT1 transporters, and that high levels of resistance need a combination of both (Bernhard et al., 2007).

Bacchi et al., (Bacchi et al., 1993) examined *T. b. rhodesiense* isolates which were naturally resistant to eflornithine. Several results were garnered which could have pointed to the reduced sensitivity of such lines. Two of the isolates accumulated significantly less drug than the sensitive bacteria. One clone strain which had been subjected to eflornithine pressure showed enhanced putrescine uptake. S-adenosyl methionine metabolism in sensitive and resistant lines differed. Sensitive cells treated with eflornithine expressed significantly higher levels of S-adenosylmethionine and its decarboxylated product, which acts as the aminopropyl group donor in polyamine biosynthesis. Refractory cells indeed showed increased levels following therapy, but to a lesser extent. Recent research (Xiao et al., 2009) found that inhibiting ornithine decarboxylase with eflornithine and RNA interference resulted in higher decarboxy-lated S-adenosylmethionine, but not of its precursor. T. *b. rhodesiense* may be resistant to eflornithine because of a shorter half-life of its ornithine decarboxylase enzyme compared to *T. b. gambiense*. This could allow *T. b. rhodesiense* to generate new enzymes to replace activity lost because of the inhibitor-bound enzyme inactivation. Obtaining consistent data on eflornithine-related metabolic processes has been challenging (Iten et al., 1995).

2.11 Limitations of current antiparasitic therapies: clinical and operational gaps

Despite decades of therapeutic interventions, current antiparasitic treatment options exhibit serious clinical and implementation shortcomings. These include the emergence of drug-resistant parasite strains, significant toxicity and adverse effects, suboptimal pharmacokinetics, and limited efficacy against latent or tissue-dwelling parasite stages. From an operational perspective, the effectiveness of existing treatments is further compromised by challenges such as poor accessibility in endemic areas, delayed diagnosis, fragmented follow-up, and an underfunded drug development pipeline. Together, these deficiencies not only reduce treatment success rates but also contribute to the growing threat of resistance, highlighting the urgent need for innovative therapeutic strategies, including advanced drug-delivery platforms such as nanotechnology, to enhance efficacy, safety, and accessibility.

2.12 Clinical gaps in current therapies

2.12.1 Emergence of drug resistance

The growing spread of drug resistance in parasitic diseases poses a significant threat to global control and elimination efforts (Balahbib A et al., 2025; Zhang et al., 2025). Protozoan pathogens have continually evolved mechanisms to evade treatment, especially in cases where monotherapies or suboptimal regimens are widely used (Balahbib A et al., 2025; Zhang et al., 2025). As reported by Capela et al., species such as *Plasmodium falciparum*, *Leishmania* spp., and *Trypanosoma cruzi* frequently acquire genetic mutations, alter metabolic pathways, and upregulate efflux pumps in response to selective drug pressure (Capela et al., 2019). Their resistance is driven by multiple mechanisms, including target modification, enhanced efflux, and metabolic bypass, and is intensified by widespread drug use, poor adherence, and weak surveillance systems (Raya, 2024). Consequently, treatment failures increase not only at the individual level but also across entire populations (Raya, 2024).

Malaria provides a particularly good example of this adaptive capacity. In this disease, resistance has progressed from early monotherapies to current frontline combination regimens. Although chloroquine and sulfadoxine-pyrimethamine have historically been effective, the recent emergence of partial resistance to artemisinin-based combination therapies (ACTs) raises serious concerns. Mutations in the K13 β-propeller domain, a structural region that enables essential protein interactions, serve as validated markers of delayed parasite clearance (Azmi et al., 2023). However artemisinin resistance is often stage specific, especially through increased ring-stage survival, and involves several interconnected pathways, including altered oxidative stress responses, proteasome activity, and metabolic adaptation (Rosenthal et al., 2024; Yu et al., 2023). The complexity and ongoing evolution of these resistance phenotypes demand robust molecular surveillance, new therapeutic combinations, supportive public health strategies, and responsible stewardship of currently effective antimalarials (Rosenthal et al., 2024, Yu et al., 2023).

2.12.2 Narrow therapeutic window and adverse effects

The clinical utility of many antiparasitic agents is severely constrained by their narrow therapeutic index, whereby the margin between effective and toxic dosing is minimal (Dziduch et al., 2022). This risk-benefit imbalance is particularly critical for drugs such as amphotericin B, used in visceral leishmaniasis, which can induce significant nephrotoxicity and electrolyte disturbances. To combat this, intensive monitoring infrastructure is required that is rarely accessible in endemic, low-resource regions (Kennedy, 2013). Similarly, melarsoprol, administered for late-stage *Trypanosoma brucei* infection, carries a high incidence of reactive encephalopathy, occurring in up to 10% of treated individuals and associated with substantial mortality, rendering clinical decision-making ethically and logistically challenging in endemic contexts (Kennedy, 2013). These toxicity-driven constraints not only compromise patient safety but also limit treatment adherence, delay therapeutic initiation, and significantly limit the ability to expand treatment programs in settings with inadequate clinical supervision (Dziduch et al., 2022).

2.12.3 Pharmacokinetic and pharmacodynamic limitations

The pharmacological performance of antiparasitic compounds is often hindered by physicochemical barriers that limit their capacity to reach and sustain therapeutic concentrations at infection sites (Croft et al., 2005). Drugs such as albendazole and nifurtimox exhibit variable oral absorption and require metabolic activation, contributing to inconsistent systemic exposure and treatment outcomes (Croft et al., 2005). Even when active agents are generated, factors such as rapid clearance, limited tissue penetration, and inadequate traversal of the blood-brain barrier restrict their efficacy against tissue-dwelling or neuroinvasive parasites, including *T. brucei* and *T. cruzi*, which can remain sequestered in anatomical niches poorly accessible to current therapies (Sanderson et al., 2008). These pharmacokinetic and pharmacodynamic constraints create conditions where subtherapeutic concentrations persist, fostering not only incomplete parasite elimination but also the selection of drug-resistant subpopulations (Al Jalali and Zeitlinger, 2020).

2.12.4 Limited efficacy against dormant stages

A fundamental biological challenge in parasite control is the fact that some life-cycle stages can enter dormant or metabolically inactive states, presenting natural tolerance to current drug treatments (White, 2011). For instance, in malaria, *Plasmodium vivax* hypnozoites residing in hepatocytes represent a clinically silent reservoir capable of reactivating weeks to months postinfection; their eradication requires primaquine, yet its hemolytic toxicity in individuals with G6PD deficiency restricts widespread use (White, 2011). The tissue-resident stages of helminths and kinetoplastids exhibit similar drug-refractory phenotypes, frequently necessitating prolonged treatment regimens that remain only partially effective (Van den Kerkhof et al., 2020). As a result, relapse, recurrence, and sustained community-level transmission persist, limiting public health interventions aimed at the long-term elimination of parasitic diseases.

2.12.5 Lack of pediatric formulations and coverage for vulnerable populations

Despite the disproportionate burden of parasitic diseases among children, pregnant women, and immunocompromised individuals, drug-development and formulation strategies remain inadequately tailored to these vulnerable groups. The scarcity of age-appropriate or pregnancy-compatible formulations complicates dose selection and administration, often requiring tablet fractionation or off-label regimens that compromise both safety and therapeutic reliability. Moreover, pharmacokinetic profiles can differ markedly in pediatric or immunologically vulnerable populations, heightening risks of toxicity or inadequate exposure (Al Jalali and Zeitlinger, 2020; Bansal et al., 2023). These barriers to accessing effective treatment exacerbate existing health inequalities and impede progress toward global disease control goals.

2.13 Operational and implementation gaps

2.13.1 Access, availability, and affordability

In places where parasitic diseases remain common, people still face barriers to accessing the medicines that could protect their health (Greco et al., 2024). These persistent obstacles reveal broader weaknesses in the global systems meant to support them (Ozawa et al., 2019). Critical medicines such as artemisinin-based combination therapies (ACTs), pentavalent antimonials, and benznidazole are frequently constrained by supply-chain instability, procurement delays, and pricing structures that remain prohibitive for low-income populations (Ozawa et al., 2019). Because access to treatment often depends on international donors and narrowly structured programs, even minor disruptions in funding or coordination can leave clinics without medicines and patients without care (Ozawa et al., 2019). These market and policy vulnerabilities expose national programs to treatment interruptions that risk worsening disease outcomes and accelerating resistance selection (Ozawa et al., 2019).

2.13.2 Weak diagnostic infrastructure

Weak diagnostic systems mean that large numbers of people are forced to wait far too long for the proper treatment. Microscopy remains the primary tool in many endemic settings, yet it often misses infections with low parasite levels and requires trained personnel who are not always available (Wongsrichanalai et al., 2007). Rapid diagnostic tests have helped extend services to remote clinics, but their value is often compromised (Fitri et al., 2022). Without reliable quality checks, backup testing, or steady supplies, patients will continue to face uncertain results and delays in care. Moreover, diagnostic delays not only increase the probability of disease progression but also contribute to inappropriate therapy and unnecessary drug exposure, forces that drive parasites to become drug resistant more quickly, while also limiting how effectively scarce medicines can be used when they are needed most (Fitri et al., 2022).

2.13.3 Poor adherence and follow-up

The complex treatment regimens and prolonged dosing schedules characteristic of many antiparasitic therapies can challenge patient adherence, particularly in settings where socioeconomic insecurity and limited health care literacy are widespread. Diseases such as Chagas disease and leishmaniasis often require extended courses associated with frequent adverse effects, leading to high treatment discontinuation rates. Inadequate follow-up systems and weak pharmacovigilance limit monitoring for toxicity and constrain the detection of relapse or reinfection (Barrett and Croft, 2012; Silva et al., 2019). Together, poor adherence, limited patient support, and inconsistent clinical oversight reduce treatment success and contribute to persistent infection, relapse, and continued transmission.

2.13.4 Inadequate drug development pipeline

The limited number of antiparasitic drug options available today underscores a history of inadequate investment in diseases that overwhelmingly impact populations with the fewest resources (Dziduch et al., 2022). As Pedrique et al., 2013 demonstrated, only a small fraction of global research and development output targets neglected parasitic diseases, resulting in a limited pipeline and slow rates of therapeutic innovation (Pedrique et al., 2013). High attrition rates during the preclinical and early clinical phases, alongside regulatory and financial barriers, further delay innovation (Dziduch et al., 2022). Consequently, clinical reliance on antiquated agents such as suramin, introduced in 1920 and still used against African trypanosomiasis, highlights the lack of meaningful advancement in treatment despite continuing high rates of illness and death (Delespaux and Dekoning, 2007; Wiedemar et al., 2020).

2.14 Implications for novel therapies and nanotechnology

The persistence of therapeutic, biological, and operational limitations across parasitic diseases highlights the need for transformative innovation in drug design and delivery

(Martin, 2022; Rao et al., 2023). Traditional small-molecule drugs are no longer sufficient to tackle parasites that adapt quickly, hide within human tissues, and move through complex stages of disease, leaving patients vulnerable to treatment failure (Martin, 2022; Rao et al., 2023). For patients in resource-constrained settings, the push toward therapies that act specifically on the parasite and last longer in the body, as well as causing fewer adverse effects, is essential, particularly when routine safety monitoring is difficult (Martin, 2022; Rao et al., 2023). Nanotechnology-based formulations directly address these unmet needs by improving the solubility of hydrophobic agents, sustaining therapeutic exposure, and facilitating selective accumulation at infection sites, thereby reducing off-target effects and preserving therapeutic efficacy (Gujjari et al., 2022; Rabie et al., 2025).

Notable successes already validate this paradigm shift. For instance, liposomal amphotericin B represents a clinically established nanocarrier system that significantly reduces nephrotoxicity while maintaining high antileishmanial potency (Date et al., 2007). Similarly, polymeric and lipid-based nanoparticles for antimalarial compounds have demonstrated increased bioavailability, improved intracellular uptake into infected erythrocytes or hepatic reservoirs, and the potential to overcome resistance-linked transport barriers (Pandian et al., 2021). Beyond delivery enhancement, nanostructured systems can be engineered for multi-functional applications, including co-encapsulation of synergistic agents, triggered release in parasite-specific microenvironments, and diagnostic-therapeutic integration, positioning them as key tools in next-generation antiparasitic strategies (Pandian et al., 2021). Continued translational research, regulatory adaptation, and investment in scalable manufacturing will determine whether these promising technologies can transition from experimental success to frontline global health impacts (Eltom et al., 2025).

2.15 Summary and key messages

Significant pharmacological limitations and systemic implementation barriers constrain current antiparasitic therapies. These multidimensional shortcomings impair the effectiveness of treatment, hinder the global response to parasitic diseases, and contribute to sustained transmission and morbidity. Overcoming these challenges requires an integrated approach that combines improvements in healthcare infrastructure with innovation in therapeutic development. Addressing both clinical and operational deficits is imperative for achieving durable and scalable parasite control and elimination.

References

Al Jalali V, Zeitlinger M. Systemic and Target-Site Pharmacokinetics of Antiparasitic Agents. Clinical Pharmacokinetics 2020;59(7):827–47. Available from https://doi.org/10.1007/s40262-020-00871-5.

Alrajhi AA, Ibrahim EA, De Vol EB, Khairat M, Faris RM, Maguire JH. Fluconazole for the treatment of cutaneous leishmaniasis caused by Leishmania major. The New England Journal of Medicine 2002;346(12):891–5.

Alvar J, Vélez ID, Bern C, Herrero M, Desjeux P, Cano J, et al. Leishmaniasis worldwide and global estimates of its incidence. PLoS One 2012;7(5):e35671.

Ariey F, Witkowski B, Amaratunga C, Beghain J, Langlois A-C, Khim N, et al. A molecular marker of artemisinin-resistant *Plasmodium falciparum* malaria. Nature 2014;505(7481):50–5. Available from https://doi.org/10.1038/nature12876.

Ashley EA, Dhorda M, Fairhurst RM, Amaratunga C, Lim P, Suon S, et al. Spread of artemisinin resistance in Plasmodium falciparum malaria. Randomized Controlled Trial 2014;371(5):411–23.

Azmi WA, Rizki AFM, Djuardi Y, Artika IM, Siregar JE. Molecular insights into artemisinin resistance in Plasmodium falciparum: An updated review. Infection, Genetics and Evolution 2023;112:105460.

Babokhov P, Sanyaolu AO, Oyibo WA, Fagbenro-Beyioku AF, Iriemenam and g. health NCJP. A current analysis of chemotherapy strategies for the treatment of human African trypanosomiasis. Pathog Glob Health 2013;107(5):242–52.

Bacchi CJ, Garofalo J, Ciminelli M, Rattendi D, Goldberg B, McCann PP, et al. Resistance to dl-α-difluoromethylornithine by clinical isolates of Trypanosoma brucei rhodesiense: role of S-adenosylmethionine. Biochemical Pharmacology 1993;46(3):471–81.

Balahbib A, El Omari N, Lghazi H, Hatoufi K, El Atki Y, Bouyahya A, et al. Therapeutic of schistosomiasis: mechanisms of action and current limitations. Journal of Parasitic Diseases 2025;49:498–512. Available from https://doi.org/10.1007/s12639-025-01785-4.

Bansal N, Momin S, Bansal R, Venkata SKRG, Ruser L, Yusuf K. Pharmacokinetics of drugs: newborn perspective. Pediatric Medicine 2023;7:19. Available from https://doi.org/10.21037/pm-22-11.

Baro NK, Callaghan PS, Roepe PDJB. Function of resistance conferring Plasmodium falciparum chloroquine resistance transporter isoforms. Biochemistry 2013;52(24):4242–9.

Barrett MP, Croft SL. Management of trypanosomiasis and leishmaniasis. British Medical Bulletin 2012;104(1):175–96. Available from https://doi.org/10.1093/bmb/lds031.

Berman J. Current treatment approaches to leishmaniasis. Current Opinion in Infectious Diseases 2003;16(5):397–401. Available from https://doi.org/10.1097/00001432-200310000-00005.

Bernhard SC, Nerima B, Mäser P, Brun R. Melarsoprol-and pentamidine-resistant Trypanosoma brucei rhodesiense populations and their cross-resistance. International Journal for Parasitology 2007;37(13):1443–8.

Bisser S, N'Siesi F-X, Lejon V, Preux P-M, Van Nieuwenhove S, Miaka Mia Bilenge C, et al. Equivalence trial of melarsoprol and nifurtimox monotherapy and combination therapy for the treatment of second-stage Trypanosoma brucei gambiense sleeping sickness. The Journal of Infectious Diseases 2007;195(3):322–9.

Braga SS. Multi-target drugs active against leishmaniasis: a paradigm of drug repurposing. European Journal of Medicinal Chemistry 2019;183:111660. Available from https://doi.org/10.1016/j.ejmech.2019.111660.

Breman JG. Ears of the hippopotamus: manifestations, determinants, and estimates of the malaria burden. In: Breman JG, Egan A, Keusch GT, editors. The Intolerable Burden of Malaria: A New Look at the Numbers: Supplement to Volume 64(1) of the American Journal of Tropical Medicine and Hygiene. Northbrook (IL): American Society of Tropical Medicine and Hygiene; 2001. Available from https://www.ncbi.nlm.nih.gov/books/NBK2615/.

Breman JG. Resistance to artemisinin-based combination therapy. The Lancet Infectious Diseases 2012;12(11):820–2. Available from https://doi.org/10.1016/S1473-3099(12)70226-8.

Bridges DJ, Gould MK, Nerima B, Mäser P, Burchmore RJ, de Koning HP. Loss of the high-affinity pentamidine transporter is responsible for high levels of cross-resistance between arsenical and diamidine drugs in African trypanosomes. Molecular Pharmacology 2007;71(4):1098–108.

Brun R, Blum J, Chappuis F, Burri C. Human african trypanosomiasis. Lancet 2010;375(9709):148–59.

Bryceson A. Current issues in the treatment of visceral leishmaniasis. Medical Microbiology and Immunology 2001;190(1):81–4.

Capela R, Moreira R, Lopes F. An overview of drug resistance in protozoal diseases. International Journal of Molecular Sciences 2019;20(22):5748. Available from https://doi.org/10.3390/ijms20225748.

Carter NS, Fairlamb AH. Arsenical-resistant trypanosomes lack an unusual adenosine transporter. Nature 1993;361(6408):173–6. Available from https://doi.org/10.1038/361173a0.

Cojean S, Houzé S, Haouchine D, Huteau F, Lariven S, Hubert V, et al. Leishmania resistance to miltefosine associated with genetic marker. Emerging Infectious Diseases 2012;18(4):704.

Cowman AF, Morry MJ, Biggs BA, Cross G, Foote SJ. Amino acid changes linked to pyrimethamine resistance in the dihydrofolate reductase-thymidylate synthase gene of Plasmodium falciparum. Proceedings of the National Academy of Sciences of the United States of America 1988;85(23):9109–13.

Croft SL, Coombs GH. Leishmaniasis - current chemotherapy and recent advances in the search for novel drugs. Trends in Parasitology 2003;19(11):502–8. Available from https://doi.org/10.1016/j.pt.2003.09.008.

Croft SL, Urbina JA, Brun R. Chemotherapy of human leishmaniasis and trypanosomiasis. In: Hide G, Moltram JC, Coombs GH, Holmes PH, editors. Trypanosomiasis and leishmaniasis: biology and control. CAB International: Wallingford; 1997. p. 245–58.

Croft SL, Barrett MP, Urbina JA. Chemotherapy of trypanosomiases and leishmaniasis. Trends in Parasitology 2005;21(11):508–12.

Croft SL, Sundar S, Fairlamb AH. Drug resistance in leishmaniasis. Clinical Microbiology Reviews 2006;19(1):111–26. Available from https://doi.org/10.1128/CMR.19.1.111-126.2006.

Daskum AM, Chessed G, Qadeer MA, Mustapha T. Antimalarial chemotherapy, mechanisms of action and resistance to major antimalarial drugs in clinical use: a review. Microbes and Infectious Diseases 2021;2(1):130–42. Available from https://doi.org/10.21608/mid.2020.43941.1064.

Date AA, Joshi MD, Patravale VB. Parasitic diseases: Liposomes and polymeric nanoparticles versus lipid nanoparticles. Advanced Drug Delivery Reviews 2007;59(6):505–21.

De Koning HP. Drug resistance in protozoan parasites. Emerging Topics in Life Sciences 2017;1(6):627–32. Available from https://doi.org/10.1042/ETLS20170113.

Delespaux V, Dekoning H. Drugs and drug resistance in African trypanosomiasis. Drug Resistance Updates 2007;10(1-2):30–50. Available from https://doi.org/10.1016/j.drup.2007.02.004.

Demarta-Gatsi C, Donini C, Duffy J, Sadler C, Stewart J, Barber JA, et al. Malarial PI4K inhibitor induced diaphragmatic hernias in rat: potential link with mammalian kinase inhibition. Birth Defects Research 2022;114(10):487–98. Available from https://doi.org/10.1002/bdr2.2012.

Dietze R, Carvalho S, Valli L, Berman J, Brewer T, Milhous W, et al. Phase 2 trial of WR6026, an orally administered 8-aminoquinoline, in the treatment of visceral leishmaniasis caused by Leishmania chagasi. The American Journal of Tropical Medicine and Hygiene 2001;65(6):685–9.

Djimdé A, Doumbo OK, Cortese JF, Kayentao K, Doumbo S, Diourté Y, et al. A molecular marker for chloroquine-resistant falciparum malaria. The New England Journal of Medicine 2001;344(4):257–63.

Dogra J, Saxena VN. Itraconazole and leishmaniasis: A randomised double-blind trial in cutaneous disease. International Journal for Parasitology 1996;26(12):1413–5. Available from https://doi.org/10.1016/S0020-7519(96)00128-2.

Chakravarty, J. and S. J. J. o. g. i. d. Sundar. Drug resistance in leishmaniasis. 2010;2(2):167-176.

Durand R, Jafari S, Vauzelle J, Delabre J-F, Jesic Z, Le Bras JJM. Analysis of pfcrt point mutations and chloroquine susceptibility in isolates of Plasmodium falciparum. Molecular and Biochemical Parasitology 2001;114(1):95–102.

Dziduch K, Greniuk D, Wujec M. The current directions of searching for antiparasitic drugs. Molecules 2022;27(5).

Egan TJ. Quinoline antimalarials. Expert Opinion on Therapeutic Patents 2001;11(2):185–209. Available from https://doi.org/10.1517/13543776.11.2.185.

Elammari NE, Sariti SR. Anti-Leishmanial drug Pentostam induced histological changes to liver and kidney in male BALB/c wild mice. Journal of International Medical Research & Health Sciences 2021;1(2):07–14.

Eltom EH, Alenezi BT, Soliman M, Jan M, Soliman A. Neglected tropical diseases: current treatment challenges and future therapeutic potentials. Prospects in Pharmaceutical Sciences 2025;23(2):1–9.

Fidock D. Mutations in the P. falciparum digestive vacuole transmembrane protein pfcrt and evidence for their role in chloroquine resistance. Molecular Cell 2000;6(4):861–71. Available from https://doi.org/10.1016/s1097-2765(00)00084-8.

Fidock DA, Nomura T, Talley AK, Cooper RA, Dzekunov SM, Ferdig MT, et al. Mutations in the P. falciparum digestive vacuole transmembrane protein PfCRT and evidence for their role in chloroquine resistance. Molecular Cell 2000;6(4):861–71.

Fitri LE, Widaningrum T, Endharti AT, Prabowo MH, Winaris N, Nugraha RYB. Malaria diagnostic update: From conventional to advanced method. Journal of Clinical Laboratory Analysis 2022;36(4):e24314.

Fletcher SM, Stark D, Harkness J, Ellis J. Enteric protozoa in the developed world: a public health perspective. Clinical Microbiology Reviews 2012;25(3):420–49.

García-Hernández R, Manzano JI, Castanys S, Gamarro F. Leishmania donovani develops resistance to drug combinations. PLoS Neglected Tropical Diseases 2012;6(12):e1974.

Ginsburg H, Krugliak M. Quinoline-containing antimalarials-mode of action, drug resistance and its reversal an update with unresolved puzzles. Biochemical Pharmacology 1992;43(1):63–70. Available from https://doi.org/10.1016/0006-2952(92)90662-3.

Goldgof GM, Durrant JD, Ottilie S, Vigil E, Allen KE, Gunawan F, et al. Comparative chemical genomics reveal that the spiroindolone antimalarial KAE609 (Cipargamin) is a P-type ATPase inhibitor. Sci Rep 2016;6(1):27806.

Greco A, Karki R, Gadiya Y, Deecke C, Zaliani A, Gul S. Pharmacological profiles of neglected tropical disease drugs. Artificial Intelligence in the Life Sciences 2024;6:100116.

Grimberg BT, Mehlotra RK. Expanding the antimalarial drug arsenal-now, but how? Pharmaceuticals 2011;4(5):681–712. Available from https://doi.org/10.3390/ph4050681.

Gujjari L, Kalani H, Pindiprolu SK, Arakareddy BP, Yadagiri G. Current challenges and nanotechnology-based pharmaceutical strategies for the treatment and control of malaria. Parasite Epidemiol Control 2022;17:e00244.

Handman E. Cell biology of Leishmania. Advances in Parasitology 1999;44:1–39. Available from https://doi.org/10.1016/s0065-308x(08)60229-8.

Hendrickx S, Beyers J, Mondelaers A, Eberhardt E, Lachaud L, Delputte P, et al. Evidence of a drug-specific impact of experimentally selected paromomycin and miltefosine resistance on parasite fitness in Leishmania infantum. The Journal of Antimicrobial Chemotherapy 2016;71(7):1914–21.

Iten M, Matovu E, Brun R, Kaminsky RJTM, Gesellschaft POOODT, Zusammenarbeit ODGFT. Innate lack of susceptibility of Ugandan Trypanosoma brucei rhodesiense to DL-alpha-difluoromethylornithine (DFMO). Tropical Medicine and Parasitology: Official Organ of Deutsche Tropenmedizinische Gesellschaft and of Deutsche Gesellschaft fur Technische Zusammenarbeit (GTZ) 1995;46(3):190–4.

Jhingran A, J A, Chawla BCB, Saxena SSS, Barrett M, Rentala Madhubala RM. Paromomycin: uptake and resistance in Leishmania donovani. Molecular and Biochemical Parasitology 2009;164(2):111–7.

Kamau E, Campino S, Amenga-Etego L, Drury E, Ishengoma D, Johnson K, et al. K13-propeller polymorphisms in Plasmodium falciparum parasites from sub-Saharan Africa. The Journal of Infectious Diseases 2015;211(8):1352–5.

Kansiime F, Adibaku S, Wamboga C, Idi F, Kato CD, Yamuah L, et al. A multicentre, randomised, non-inferiority clinical trial comparing a nifurtimox-eflornithine combination to standard eflornithine monotherapy for late stage Trypanosoma brucei gambiense human African trypanosomiasis in Uganda. Parasites & Vectors 2018;11(1):105.

Kennedy PGE. Clinical features, diagnosis, and treatment of human African trypanosomiasis (sleeping sickness). The Lancet Neurology 2013;12(2):186–94. Available from https://doi.org/10.1016/s1474-4422(12)70296-x.

Klein EY. Antimalarial drug resistance: a review of the biology and strategies to delay emergence and spread. International Journal of Antimicrobial Agents 2013;41(4):311–7. Available from https://doi.org/10.1016/j.ijantimicag.2012.12.007.

de Koning HP. Ever-increasing complexities of diamidine and arsenical crossresistance in African trypanosomes. Trends in Parasitology 2008;24(8):345–9. Available from https://doi.org/10.1016/j.pt.2008.04.006.

Koutinas AF, Saridomichelakis MN, Mylonakis ME, Leontides L, Polizopoulou Z, Billinis C, et al. A randomised, blinded, placebo-controlled clinical trial with allopurinol in canine leishmaniosis. Veterinary Parasitology 2001;98(4):247–61.

Laohasinnarong D. Chapter 6 - Sleeping sickness. In: Misra G, Srivastava V, editors. Molecular Advancements in Tropical Diseases Drug Discovery. Academic Press; 2020. p. 117–32. Available from https://doi.org/10.1016/B978-0-12-821202-8.00006-2.

Le Bras J, Durand R. The mechanisms of resistance to antimalarial drugs in Plasmodium falciparum. Fundamental & Clinical Pharmacology 2003;17(2):147–53.

Lopes A, Souto-Padrón T, Dias F, Gomes M, Rodrigues G, Zimmermann L, et al. Trypanosomatids: odd organisms, devastating diseases. Open Parasitol 2010;4:30–59.

Manaranche J, Laurent M, Tressieres R, Nguyen M, Salim M, Ouji M, et al. In vitro evaluation of ganaplacide/lumefantrine combination against Plasmodium falciparum in a context of artemisinin resistance. The Journal of Antimicrobial Chemotherapy 2024;79(11):2877–86.

Martin RJ. Therapeutic and diagnostic innovation for parasitology: grand challenges. Frontiers in Parasitology 2022;1. Available from https://doi.org/10.3389/fpara.2022.963671.

Maser P, Sutterlin C, Kralli A, Kaminsky RJS. A nucleoside transporter from Trypanosoma brucei involved in drug resistance. Science (New York, N.Y.) 1999;285(5425):242–4.

Mathews ES, Odom John AR. Tackling resistance: emerging antimalarials and new parasite targets in the era of elimination. F1000Research 2018;7:1170. Available from https://doi.org/10.12688/f1000research.14874.1.

Matovu E, Stewart ML, Geiser F, Brun R, Mäser P, Wallace LJ, et al. Mechanisms of arsenical and diamidine uptake and resistance in Trypanosoma brucei. Eukaryotic Cell 2003;2(5):1003–8.

Mitropoulos P, Konidas P, Durkin-Konidas M. New world cutaneous leishmaniasis: updated review of current and future diagnosis and treatment. Journal of the American Academy of Dermatology 2010;63(2):309–22.

Momeni A, Jalayer T, Emamjomeh M, Bashardost N, Ghassemi R, Meghdadi M, et al. Treatment of cutaneous leishmaniasis with itraconazole: randomized double-blind study. Archives of Dermatology 1997;6(4):244.

Mondelaers A, Sanchez-Cañete MP, Hendrickx S, Eberhardt E, Garcia-Hernandez R, Lachaud L, et al. Genomic and molecular characterization of miltefosine resistance in Leishmania infantum strains with either natural or acquired resistance through experimental selection of intracellular amastigotes. PLoS One 2016;11(4):e0154101.

Moolman C, Sluis RVD, Beteck RM, Legoabe LJJM. An update on development of small-molecule plasmodial kinase inhibitors. Molecules (Basel, Switzerland) 2020;25(21):5182.

Morizot G, Jouffroy R, Faye A, Chabert P, Belhouari K, Calin R, et al. Antimony to cure visceral leishmaniasis unresponsive to liposomal amphotericin B. PLoS Neglected Tropical Diseases 2016;10(1):e0004304.

Munoz-Calderon A, Díaz-Bello Z, Ramírez JL, Noya O, de Noya BA. Nifurtimox response of Trypanosoma cruzi isolates from an outbreak of chagas disease in Caracas, Venezuela. Journal of Vector Borne Diseases 2019;56(3):237–43.

Nassiri-Kashani M, Firooz A, Khamesipour A, Mojtahed F, Nilforoushzadeh M, Hejazi H, et al. A randomized, double-blind, placebo-controlled clinical trial of itraconazole in the treatment of cutaneous leishmaniasis. Journal of the European Academy of Dermatology and Venereology: JEADV 2005;19(1):80–3.

Ngwa CJ, Stratmann R, Musabyimana JP, Pannen K, Schöbel J-H, Frings M, et al. Evaluation of chiral organosulfur compounds on their activity against the malaria parasite Plasmodium falciparum. Tropical Medicine and Infectious Disease 2022;7(12):416. Available from https://doi.org/10.3390/tropicalmed7120416.

Nnamonu EI, Ndukwe-Ani PA, Imakwu CA, Okenyi CI, Ugwu FJ, Aniekwe MI, et al. Malaria: Trend of Burden and Impact of Control Strategies. International Journal of TROPICAL DISEASE & Health 2020;41(12):18–30. Available from https://doi.org/10.9734/ijtdh/2020/v41i1230338.

Ozawa S, Shankar R, Leopold C, Orubu S. Access to medicines through health systems in low- and middle-income countries. Health Policy and Planning 2019;34(Supplement_3):iii1–3.

Pandey BD, Pandey K, Kaneko O, Yanagi T, Hirayama K. Relapse of visceral leishmaniasis after miltefosine treatment in a nepalese patient. The American Journal of Tropical Medicine and Hygiene 2009;80(4):580–2. Available from https://doi.org/10.4269/ajtmh.2009.80.580.

Pandian SRK, Panneerselvam T, Pavadai P, Govindaraj S, Ravishankar V, Palanisamy P, et al. Nano based approach for the treatment of neglected tropical diseases. Frontiers in Nanotechnology 2021;Volume 3. Available from https://doi.org/10.3389/fnano.2021.665274.

Patterson S, Wyllie S. Nitro drugs for the treatment of trypanosomatid diseases: past, present, and future prospects. Trends in Parasitology 2014;30(6):289–98. Available from https://doi.org/10.1016/j.pt.2014.04.003.

Pedrique B, Strub-Wourgaft N, Some C, Olliaro P, Trouiller P, Ford N, et al. The drug and vaccine landscape for neglected diseases (2000-11): a systematic assessment. The Lancet Global Health 2013;1(6):e371. Available from https://doi.org/10.1016/S2214-109X(13)70078-0.

Pepin J, Milord F. The treatment of human African trypanosomiasis. Advances in Parasitology 1994;33:1–47. Available from https://doi.org/10.1016/s0065-308x(08)60410-8.

Peterson DS, Walliker D, Wellems TEJP. Evidence that a point mutation in dihydrofolate reductase-thymidylate synthase confers resistance to pyrimethamine in falciparum malaria. Proceedings of the National Academy of Sciences of the United States of America 1988;85(23):9114–8. Available from https://doi.org/10.1073/pnas.85.23.9114.

Plowe CV. Folate antagonists and mechanisms of resistance. In: Rosenthal PJ, editor. Antimalarial chemotherapy: mechanisms of action, resistance, and new directions in drug discovery. Totowa, NJ: Humana Press; 2001. p. 173–90. Available from https://doi.org/10.1007/978-1-59259-111-4_9.

Ponte-Sucre A, Gamarro F, Dujardin J-C, Barrett MP, López-Vélez R, García-Hernández R, et al. Drug resistance and treatment failure in leishmaniasis: A 21st century challenge. PLoS Neglected Tropical Diseases 2017;11(12):e0006052.

Purkait B, Kumar A, Nandi N, Sardar AH, Das S, Kumar S, et al. Mechanism of amphotericin B resistance in clinical isolates of Leishmania donovani. Antimicrobial Agents and Chemotherapy 2012;56(2):1031–41.

Qiu D, Pei JV, Rosling JE, Thathy V, Li D, Xue Y, et al. A G358S mutation in the Plasmodium falciparum Na+ pump PfATP4 confers clinically-relevant resistance to cipargamin. Nat Commun 2022;13(1):5746.

Rabie AM, Abd-Ellah OH, Abuelwafa EA, Abdelhameed R, Barakat AMAK. Nanotechnology and nanomedicine-based strategies in parasitic infection [a review article]. Egyptian Journal of Veterinary Sciences 2025:1–9.

Rai K, Cuypers B, Bhattarai NR, Uranw S, Berg M, Ostyn B, et al. Relapse after treatment with miltefosine for visceral leishmaniasis is associated with increased infectivity of the infecting Leishmania donovani strain. mBio 2013;4(5):00611–3. Available from https://doi.org/10.1128/mbio.

Rao SPS, Manjunatha UH, Mikolajczak S, Ashigbie PG, Diagana TT. Drug discovery for parasitic diseases: powered by technology, enabled by pharmacology, informed by clinical science. Trends in Parasitology 2023;39(4):260–71.

Rasmussen C, Alonso P, Ringwald P. Current and emerging strategies to combat antimalarial resistance. Expert Review of Anti-Infective Therapy 2022;20(3):353–72.

Raya Q. Drug resistance in parasitic infections: current status and future implications. Journal of Bacteriology & Parasitology 2024;S26:091.

Rijal S, Ostyn B, Uranw S, Rai K, Bhattarai NR, Dorlo TP, et al. Increasing failure of miltefosine in the treatment of Kala-azar in Nepal and the potential role of parasite drug resistance, reinfection, or noncompliance. Clinical Infectious Diseases: an Official Publication of the Infectious Diseases Society of America 2013;56(11):1530–8.

Rosenthal MR, Vijayrajratnam S, Firestone TM, Ng CL. Enhanced cell stress response and protein degradation capacity underlie artemisinin resistance in Plasmodium falciparum. mSphere 2024;9(11):e0037124.

Sanderson L, Dogruel M, Rodgers J, Bradley B, Thomas SA. The blood-brain barrier significantly limits eflornithine entry into Trypanosoma brucei brucei infected mouse brain. Journal of Neurochemistry 2008;107(4):1136–46.

Sankineni S, Chauhan S, Shegokar R, Pathak Y. Global health and malaria: past and present. In: Shegokar R, Pathak Y, editors. Malarial drug delivery systems: Advances in treatment of infectious diseases. Cham: Springer; 2023. p. 1–16. Available from https://doi.org/10.1007/978-3-031-15848-3_1.

Schmitt EK, Ndayisaba G, Yeka A, Asante KP, Grobusch MP, Karita E, et al. Efficacy of cipargamin (KAE609) in a randomized, phase II dose-escalation study in adults in sub-Saharan Africa with uncomplicated Plasmodium falciparum malaria. Clinical Infectious Diseases: an Official Publication of the Infectious Diseases Society of America 2022;74(10):1831–9.

Silva ACC, Brelaz-de-Castro MCA, Leite ACL, Pereira VRA, Hernandes MZ. Chagas disease treatment and rational drug discovery: a challenge that remains. Frontiers in Pharmacology 2019;Volume 10:873. Available from https://doi.org/10.3389/fphar.2019.00873.

Srivastava P, Prajapati VK, Rai M, Sundar SJ. Unusual case of resistance to amphotericin B in visceral leishmaniasis in a region in India where leishmaniasis is not endemic. Journal of Clinical Microbiology 2011;49(8):3088–91.

Srivastava S, Mishra J, Gupta AK, Singh A, Shankar P, Singh SJP. Laboratory confirmed miltefosine resistant cases of visceral leishmaniasis from India. Parasites & Vectors 2017;10(1):49.

Sundar S, More DK, Singh MK, Singh VP, Sharma S, Makharia A, et al. Failure of pentavalent antimony in visceral leishmaniasis in India: report from the center of the Indian epidemic. Clinical Infectious Diseases: an Official Publication of the Infectious Diseases Society of America 2000;31(4):1104–7.

Sundar S, Singh A, Rai M, Prajapati VK, Singh AK, Ostyn B, et al. Efficacy of miltefosine in the treatment of visceral leishmaniasis in India after a decade of use. Clinical Infectious Diseases: an Official Publication of the Infectious Diseases Society of America 2012;55(4):543–50.

Triglia T, Cowman AF. The mechanism of resistance to sulfa drugs in Plasmodium falciparum. Drug Resistance Updates 1999;2(1):15–9. Available from https://doi.org/10.1054/drup.1998.0060.

Tun KM, Imwong M, Lwin KM, Win AA, Hlaing TM, Hlaing T, et al. Spread of artemisinin-resistant Plasmodium falciparum in Myanmar: a cross-sectional survey of the K13 molecular marker. The Lancet Infectious Diseases 2015;15(4):415–21.

Valecha N, Srivastava P, Mohanty SS, Mittra P, Sharma SK, Tyagi PK, et al. Therapeutic efficacy of artemether-lumefantrine in uncomplicated falciparum malaria in India. Malaria Journal 2009;8(1):107.

Van den Kerkhof M, Sterckx YG-J, Leprohon P, Maes L, Caljon G. Experimental strategies to explore drug action and resistance in kinetoplastid parasites. Microorganisms 2020;8(6):950.

Vickerman K. Developmental cycles and biology of pathogenic trypanosomes. British Medical Bulletin 1985;41(2):105–14. Available from https://doi.org/10.1093/oxfordjournals.bmb.a072036.

Ward KE, Fidock DA, Bridgford JL. Plasmodium falciparum resistance to artemisinin-based combination therapies. Current Opinion in Microbiology 2022;69:102193.

Wellems TE, Walker-Jonah A, Panton LJ. Genetic mapping of the chloroquine-resistance locus on Plasmodium falciparum chromosome. Proceedings of the National Academy of Sciences of the United States of America 1991;88(8):3382–6. Available from https://doi.org/10.1073/pnas.88.8.3382.

Wernsdorfer W, Chongsuphajaisiddhi T, Salazar NP. A symposium on containment of mefloquine-resistant falciparum malaria in Southeast Asia with special reference to border malaria. The Southeast Asian Journal of Tropical Medicine and Public Health 1994;25(1):11–8.

White NJ. Assessment of the pharmacodynamic properties of antimalarial drugs in vivo. Antimicrobial Agents and Chemotherapy 1997;41(7):1413–22.

White NJ. Antimalarial drug resistance. Journal of Clinical Investigation 2004;113(8):1084–92. Available from https://doi.org/10.1172/JCI21682.

White NJ. Determinants of relapse periodicity in Plasmodium vivax malaria. Malaria Journal 2011;10. Available from https://doi.org/10.1186/1475-2875-10-297.

WHO. World Health Organization. Global report on neglected tropical diseases. 2023. Geneva: WHO; 2023. Available from https://www.who.int/teams/control-of-neglected-tropical-diseases/global-report-on-neglected-tropical-diseases-2023.

Wiedemar N, Hauser DA, Mäser P. 100 Years of Suramin. Antimicrobial Agents and Chemotherapy 2020;64(3).

Win KN, Manopwisedjaroen K, Phumchuea K, Suansomjit C, Chotivanich K, Lawpoolsri S, et al. Molecular markers of dihydroartemisinin-piperaquine resistance in northwestern Thailand. Malaria Journal 2022;21(1):352.

Wongsrichanalai C, Barcus MJ, Muth S, Sutamihardja A, Wernsdorfer WH. A review of malaria diagnostic tools: microscopy and rapid diagnostic test (RDT). Am J Trop Med Hyg 2007;77(6 Suppl):119–27.
Xiao Y, McCloskey DE, Phillips MAJEC. RNA interference-mediated silencing of ornithine decarboxylase and spermidine synthase genes in Trypanosoma brucei provides insight into regulation of polyamine biosynthesis. Eukaryotic Cell 2009;8(5):747–55.
Yadav GP, Arukha AP, Kothapalli Y, Singh US. Antimalarial drugs: discovery, mechanism of action, and drug resistance. Falciparum Malaria. Elsevier; 2024. p. 89–112.
Yu X, Wang C, Zhao Y, Tang J, Zhu M, Platon L, et al. Ring-stage growth arrest: Metabolic basis of artemisinin tolerance in Plasmodium falciparum. iScience 2023;26(1):105725.
Zhang H, Yan R, Liu Y, Yu M, He Z, Xiao J, et al. Progress in antileishmanial drugs: Mechanisms, challenges, and prospects. PLoS Neglected Tropical Diseases 2025;19(1):e0012735.

CHAPTER 3

Natural products in the fight against blood parasites

Rewaida Abdel-Gaber[1], Shaimaa M. Kasem[2], Omnia Hamed[3], and Mohamed Dkhil[3]
[1]Zoology Department, Faculty of Science, Cairo University, Cairo, Egypt,
[2]Zoology Department, Faculty of Science, Kafrelsheikh University, Kafr Elsheikh, Egypt,
[3]Department of Zoology and Entomology, Faculty of Science, Capital University, Cairo, Egypt

3.1 Introduction

Malaria, leishmaniasis, trypanosomiasis, and schistosomiasis are the major parasitic diseases that collectively pose an immense global health and socioeconomic burden, primarily in tropical and subtropical regions (Wang et al., 2025). *Plasmodium* parasites cause malaria and are transmitted by Anopheles mosquitoes; malaria persists as a significant global health issue. There has been a minor reduction in malaria-related deaths; however, the prevalence rate has seen a modest increase due to heightened international travel and migration, highlighting its ongoing threat to global health systems (Cui and Kim, 2024; World Health Organization, 2024). *Leishmania* species causes leishmaniasis via skin contact with infected female sandfly vectors during blood feeding. The illness impacts roughly 700,000 to 1 million individuals annually, with visceral leishmaniasis representing the most severe manifestation. Malnutrition, displacement, substandard housing, compromised immune systems, and economic stress represent significant risk factors (World Health Organization, 2025). African trypanosomiasis, also referred to as sleeping sickness, is caused by *Trypanosoma brucei.* is transmitted by the tsetse fly. It is focused on specific regions, primarily in sub-Saharan Africa. If not addressed, the illness is generally fatal. In the latest decades, the prevalence and appearance of this condition have diminished (Lejon et al., 2025; World Health Organization, 2025). *Trypanosoma cruzi* causes Chagas disease via touch with the feces or urine of diseased triatomine insects. The worldwide incidence is increasing, with the primary burden borne by Latin America. This ailment arises from intricate health conditions, and although a solution is feasible, urbanization, globalization, and new spread pathways have become a worldwide public health argue (de Sousa et al., 2024; World Health Organization, 2025). Schistosomiasis is caused by parasitic worms belonging to the genus *Schistosoma.* This disease disseminates chiefly through dermal contact with freshwater containing infectious cercariae, predominantly in Asia, Africa,

Innovative Strategies Against Blood Parasites
DOI: https://doi.org/10.1016/B978-0-443-48509-1.00003-3

and Latin America. The disease exhibits a significant prevalence, with almost 1 billion individuals worldwide at risk. Due to the intricate transmission cycle, elevated rates of reinfection, possible treatment resistance, constraints in identification methods, and socioeconomic obstacles, schistosomiasis considerably burdens global health incomes and is a substantial contributor to deprivation and its resurgence (Buonfrate et al., 2025; Shen and Luo, 2025).

The significant effect of human parasite infections has been exacerbated by the absence of effective vaccinations and harmless, inexpensive medications for their prevention and treatment (Capela et al., 2019). Antiparasitic medications have several adverse effects and possess a degree of toxicity. Furthermore, they frequently lack efficacy. The efficacy of existing pharmaceuticals is progressively jeopardized by the appearance of drug-resistant parasites (Dziduch et al., 2022). Additionally, host health affects infection transmission. People with immune systems that can tolerate parasite infections but not eradicate them become carriers and spread the infection. In high-prevalence areas, well-tolerated infections are rarely treated to remove the parasite because it would reduce immunity and increase reinfection (Capela et al., 2019). To reduce the global burden of parasitic infections in humans and cattle, innovative blood parasite treatment molecules must be safe, effective, and economical. In this context, studying naturally occurring antiparasitic chemicals, especially those from inexpensive and abundant plants, is intriguing. Traditional medicine has used plants for ages as a source of bioactive compounds (Ranasinghe et al., 2023). For example, artemisinin is a sesquiterpene lactone molecule (Fig. 3.1) characterized by a distinctive chemical structure originating from *Artemisia annua* L. (sweet wormwood plant). Since its development, it has emerged as the paramount and most efficacious antimalarial medication (Wang et al., 2019). Quinine (Fig. 3.1) was extracted from the bark of the

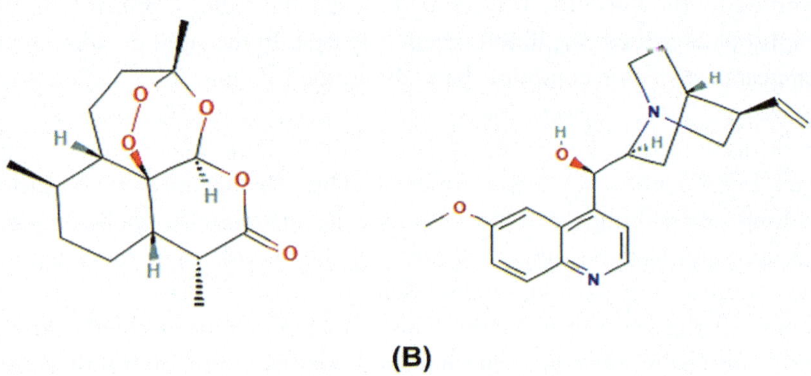

Figure 3.1 Chemical structure of (A) artemisinin. (B) quinine.

Peruvian Cinchona tree in the mid-1800s and rapidly emerged as the preferred remedy for irregular fever globally, serving as an antimalarial agent (Bohórquez et al., 2012).

3.2 Diversity of natural products as antiparasitic agents

3.2.1 Medicinal plants and ethnopharmacology

It is essential to emphasize that plants are used not only in traditional medicine for human problems but also in veterinary medicine to address various conditions in animals. Ethnoveterinary medicine is essential in several rural regions with restricted access to contemporary pharmaceuticals. Inhabitants of these isolated regions depend on conventional remedies for the treatment of domestic animals (Ranasinghe et al., 2023). Despite the historical efforts to avoid and treat parasitic diseases using medicinal plants in humans and animals, several such plants have not undergone rigorous scientific assessment of their efficacy, mechanisms of action, and active compounds. Recently, there has been a documented increase in controlled experimental investigations aimed at validating and quantifying the antiparasitic properties of plants and plant products used in traditional medicine (Ferreira et al., 2016). The conventional use of plants has resulted in the extraction of potential lead compounds from botanical sources and the development of novel pharmaceuticals (Ranasinghe et al., 2023). The usage of herbal medicines has a crucial role in the development of antimalarial chemotherapy. Among these, *Artemisia annua* has a long history and continues to be used clinically in China for malaria treatment. Artemisinin was first isolated from *A. annua* in 1971, and its derivatives, including dihydroartemisinin, artesunate, and artemether-lumefantrine, are now endorsed by the WHO for antimalarial therapy (Shang et al., 2025). Cinchona bark (quinine) has a long history of use in humans and continues to be employed clinically in Africa for malaria treatment. Quinine, the first antimalarial compound, was obtained from the bark of the Cinchona tree in 1820 and remains a widely used therapy against malaria (Gachelin et al., 2017). Also,(Rahmah et al., 2024) indicated that neem (*Azadirachta indica*) leaf extract, owing to its several antimalarial qualities, such as reducing parasitemia and inhibiting neuronal cell death, may serve as a substitute for medications for the ailment.

3.2.2 Marine-derived natural products

From 2011 to 2020, the main focus of discovering new chemicals from the sea shifted from sponges to microorganisms, especially fungi and bacteria that live in the ocean (Blunt et al., 2012). Also, sponges are still a major source of new chemicals, and there was growing recognition that the microbes living with sponges might actually be the real producers of these special chemicals (Reveillaud et al., 2014). The chemicals made by sponges are very varied and can be grouped into different types, such as nucleosides, terpenes, sterols, cyclic peptides, and alkaloids (Laport et al., 2009). A large quantity of alkaloids found in the sea have shown a strong ability to fight malaria. These include types such as β-carboline, indole, imidazole, and pyrrole. These alkaloids work in a unique way to fight different parts of the *Plasmodium* parasite (Negm et al., 2023). Two indole-based alkaloids called Didemnidines A (29) and B (30) were found in a type of sea squirt from New Zealand (Didemnidae). Didemnidine B had some effect against P. falciparum with an IC50 value of 0.047 mM (Finlayson et al., 2011). Manzamines are a group of complex alkaloids made up of seven to eight rings, and they contain a β-carboline part. Manzamine A was first found in a sponge from Okinawa called Haliclona (family Chalinidae). These compounds are important for fighting malaria (Kubota et al., 2020). Besides being safe for use in the body, manzamines are more effective than commonly used medicines such as artemisinin and chloroquine (Dai et al., 2018). β-carboline alkaloids work by stopping a key enzyme in malaria parasites called glycogen synthase kinase 3 (GSK-3) and stop DNA from working properly by fitting into the DNA strands (Negm et al., 2023). Imidazole-based alkaloids, such as girolline, which is a derivative of 2-aminoimidazole found in a sponge from the Caledonian region (Axinellidae), were found to be effective against the P. falciparum (FCM29) strain, with an IC50 of 0.13 mM. They also showed good results in animal tests using a model of *P. vinckei petteri*(Cheuka et al., 2017).

Marine sponges called *Spongia* sp. and *Ircinia* sp. found along the Turkish part of the Aegean Sea made some chemicals such as linear furanoterpenes, meroterpenes, di-terpenes, and triterpenes. These chemicals stopped the growth of a type of protozoan parasite (Orhan et al., 2010). One of the compounds, called 4-hydroxy-3-tetraprenyl-phenylacetic acid, worked best and most specifically against *T. b. rhodesiense*. It took 1.4 μm to stop the parasite's growth. Another compound named Heptaprenyl-p-quinol, which has a long chain of isoprene and a hydroquinone at the end, was also effective against *T.b. rhodesiense* with an IC50 of 5.9 μM. However, it was less effective against L6 cells (IC50 of 4.4 μM). Demethylfurospongin-4 was also effective against *T.b. rhodesiense* (IC50 of 11.8 μM). The diterpene 11β-acetoxyspongi-12-en-16-one had some effect on *T.b. rhodesiense* (IC50 of 11.5 μM) (Orhan et al., 2010). Many different trypanocidal compounds with variable levels of effectiveness have been found in *Agelas* sp. marine sponges. A sterol called 24-ethyl-cholest-5α-7-en-3-β-ol, taken from the n-hexane extract of the Turkish sponge *Agelas oroides*, had little effect on *T.b. rhodesiense* (IC50 of 34.2 μM) (Tasdemir et al., 2007).

Animal venom are regarded as a significant source of innovative antibacterial agents. Certain peptides derived from animal venoms possess amphipathic alpha-helix configurations. They impede pathogen proliferation by targeting membranes to create deadly holes, resulting in membrane rupture. Venom compounds typically exhibit immuno-modulatory characteristics and are helpful in the inhibition of harmful organisms (Yang et al., 2023). Subsequent research has demonstrated that animal venoms comprise a diverse array of bioactives, as indicated by proteomic studies. The components are intricate yet comparable across species, primarily comprising peptides and some proteins (Wu et al., 2023). Cationic peptides abundant in α-helix or β-sheet structures are intriguing options for battling diverse parasites (Li et al., 2014). BnSP-7 toxin is a homologous protein of Lys49 PLA2 derived from the venoms of *Bothrops pauloensis* (Soares et al., 2000) with antiparasitic activity (Siniavin et al., 2021). It can compromise the parasite's plasma membranes, resulting in alterations to membrane constitution and the extravasation of proteins. BnSP-7 exhibited anti-*Leishmania* action with a half maximum inhibitory concentration (IC50 58.7 μg/mL). It inhibited parasite multiplication and altered the membrane protein profile (Nunes et al., 2013). In *T. gondii*, BnSP-7 at varying concentrations (12.5–50 μg/mL) did not impede parasite death but diminished its attack and multiplication (Borges et al., 2016).

3.2.3 Microbial metabolites

Primary and secondary metabolism produce bioactive metabolites in plants, animals, fungi, and bacteria. They often function biologically. Secondary metabolites have unconventional chemical compositions and low molecular masses (Demain and Sanchez, 2009). Secondary metabolites, unlike primary metabolites, do not affect cell life cycles and characterize individual organisms. Numerous secondary microbial metabolites exhibit antibacterial, antifungal, and antiparasitic properties. They are frequently use in medical and veterinary practices (Solecka et al., 2012). Marine actinomycetes produce bioactive chemicals that inhibit *Leishmania major* and *T. brucei* (Pimentel-Elardo et al., 2010).

3.3 Mechanisms of action of natural products against blood parasites

Artemisinin-resistant parasites exhibit reduced oxidative stress and stronger antioxidant defenses, especially at the early ring stages, and this could improve antimalarial methods and understanding resistance mechanisms (Egwu et al., 2022). Quinolines inhibit hemozoin and enhance free hemin, which catalyzes peroxidative processes and cysteine protease inhibition in parasite digesting vacuoles with H_2O_2 (Herraiz et al., 2019). Berberine attributes its leishmanicidal action to over generating ROS, which boosts mitochondrial oxidative stress, depolarizes the mitochondrial transmembrane potential, and causes ATP depletion, leading to mitochondrial dysfunction (De Sarkar et al., 2019) as shown in Fig. 3.2. Many alkaloids modulate oxidative phosphorylation (OXPHOS) and ADP/ATP transport, involving sanguinarine, which opens the mitochondrial permeability transition pore (mPTP) and has mixed effects on Ca^{2+} loading. Capsaicin affects the mitochondrial electron transport chain and causes oxidative stress, and lamellarin-D decreases complex III activity and affects mPTP. Nicotine, a well-known alkaloid present in Solanaceae plants, inhibits OXPHOS machinery, thereby altering

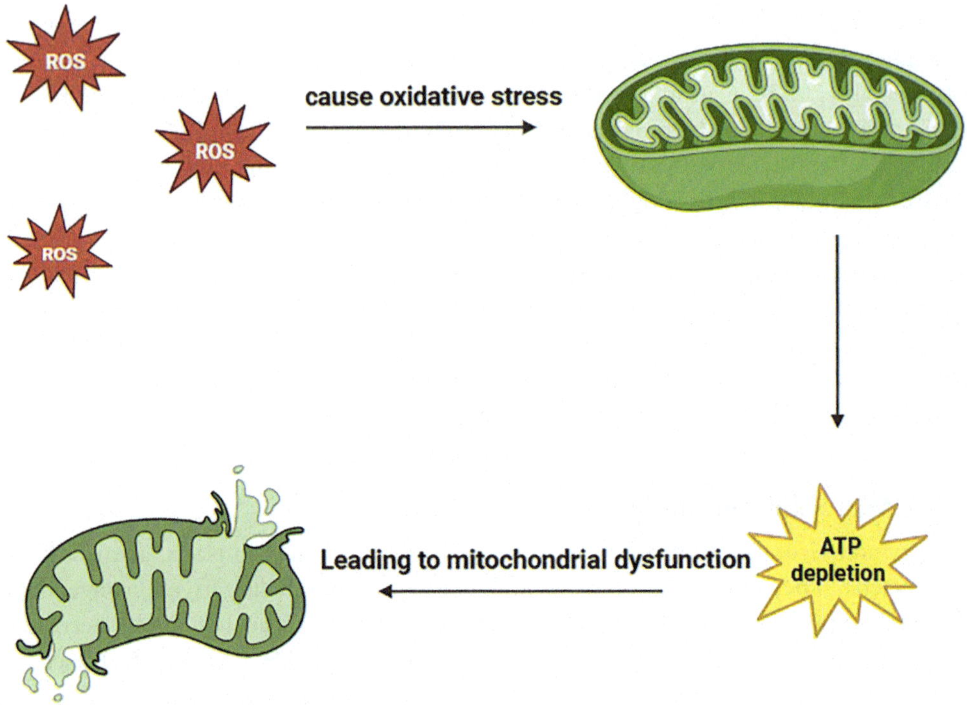

Figure 3.2 Schematic representation showing the over-generating of reactive oxygen species (ROS) by natural products induces oxidative stress in mitochondria, leading to mitochondrial dysfunction.

cell energy supply (Patalas-Krawczyk et al., 2021). Additionally, by obstructing the synthesis of β-hematin and the phagocytosis of parasite-infected erythrocytes, curcumin can enhance intracellular ROS production (Fig. 3.3). Furthermore, curcumin disrupts Plasmodium organelles, including microtubules, the apicoplast, and PfATP6 (Andromeda et al., 2020).

3.4 Synergistic effects and combination therapies

Chloroquine was the primary treatment for simple falciparum malaria, and its resistance indicators were discovered in 2001 (Djimdé et al., 2001). Maiga et al. (2021) stated that the main alternative to chloroquine is the artemisinin based combination therapy (ACT), which is the most effective therapy for simple falciparum malaria. Also, (Das et al., 2021) documented that the use of lupeol–amphotericin B combination significantly reduced the *Leishmania donovani* burden while restoring protective Th1-driven immunity in infected mice. This synergistic effect was linked to enhanced p38 mitogen-activated protein kinase (p38MAPK) activation and suppression of extra-cellular signal-related kinase (ERK) signaling.

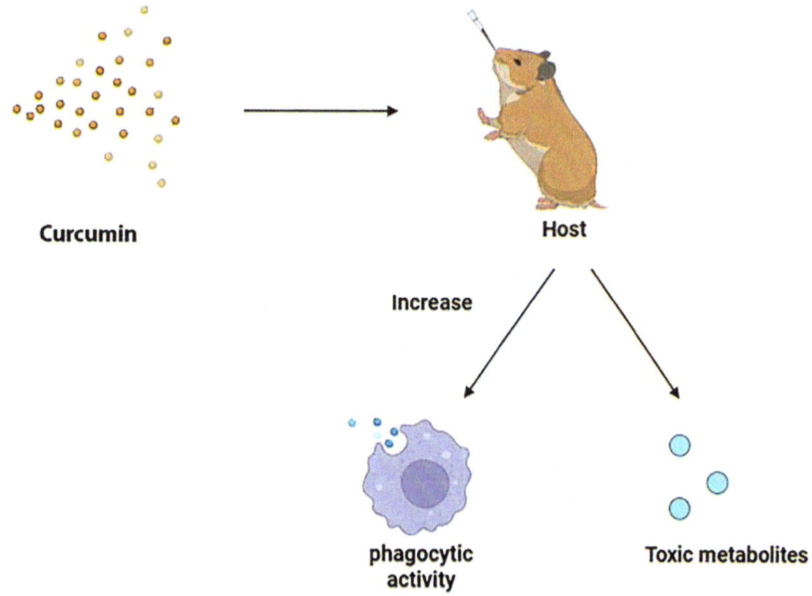

Figure 3.3 Schematic diagram indicating how curcumin induces an increase in phagocytic activity of immune cells.

3.5 Nanotechnology and natural products

The clinical performance of natural products remains limited because of poor solubility, rapid clearance, and low permeability, resulting in subtherapeutic drug levels. To surmount the obstacles encountered in the clinical use of natural products, a solution emerged by advancing novel nano-drug delivery systems (Lv et al., 2024). The solubility and pharmacological profile of active substances, including vaccines, have been improved by saponin-based NPs because of their immunostimulant and adjuvant qualities (Lokole et al., 2025). Alven and Aderibigbe (2020) showed that the therapeutic efficacy of nanoparticles encapsulating artemisinin and its derivatives in the treatment of malaria and leishmaniasis indicates their potential as treatments for the elimination of the specified disorders. Nanotechnology-based delivery of plant-derived schistosomicidal agents could greatly enhance their therapeutic potential by improving bioavailability, enabling targeted action, and ensuring sustained uptake by parasites, and this could support effective prophylaxis, particularly during the liver stage when schistosomula are most vulnerable (Eze et al., 2022).

3.6 Challenges and limitations

Botanical products show inherent variability in phytochemical composition because of differences in species, cultivation conditions, and processing methods. Multiple species or chemotypes can lead to significant variation in phytochemical content and therapeutic activity. Additionally, small-scale laboratory plants may not replicate the phytochemical profile observed in commercially cultivated crops because of environmental and agricultural factors (Adelusi et al., 2022). Despite promising in vitro and in vivo data, the translation of phytomedicine research into standardized clinical trials remains limited. Academic studies provide valuable pharmacological and toxicological insights, but their integration into mainstream clinical development is often slow and inconsistent (Ezeanochie et al., 2024). Despite their natural origin, phytochemicals can exhibit potent toxic effects, especially at high doses or in combination with other compounds. Preclinical toxicity screening is essential, with particular attention to hepatotoxicity, nephrotoxicity, and genotoxicity (Taiwo et al., 2024).

3.7 Future directions and perspectives

The rapid evaluation of large libraries of plant, marine, and microbial natural products for antiparasitic activity is enabled by advances in high-throughput screening technologies. This approach can accelerate the identification of novel lead compounds with potent efficacy and acceptable safety profiles, thereby streamlining early drug discovery. In addition, engineering microbial plant based production systems through synthetic biology offers a sustainable approach to produce natural compounds in large quantities. Such strategies can overcome limitations in natural supply, standardize active ingredient content, and reduce batch-to-batch variability. Moreover, artificial intelligence (AI) and machine learning tools can predict bioactivity, optimize compound structures, and identify synergistic combinations of natural products. These computational approaches can enhance efficiency, reduce experimental costs, and guide the rational design of antiparasitic agents. Leveraging traditional knowledge of medicinal plants and ethnoveterinary practices alongside modern pharmacological studies can uncover novel bioactive compounds. Combining ethnopharmacology with molecular and mechanistic insights can accelerate lead validation and facilitate culturally informed therapeutic development. Natural products with immunomodulatory properties present opportunities for vaccine adjuvants or immunotherapeutic agents. Exploring bioactive compounds that enhance host immunity or modulate parasite-induced immunosuppression may complement conventional chemotherapies and support long-term disease control.

3.8 Conclusion

In conclusion, natural products remain to serve as a cornerstone in the fight against major blood parasites, offering a rich source of bioactive constituents with potential antiparasitic activity and proven. Their integration with modern biotechnologies, including nanotechnology, synthetic biology, high-throughput screening, and AI-driven drug discovery, is crucial for overcoming challenges related to solubility, bioavailability, and clinical translation. Moving from laboratory research to effective clinical applications requires coordinated collaborative efforts among scientists, clinicians, and industry stakeholders to validate efficacy, ensure safety, and develop scalable interventions. Such multidisciplinary approaches hold promise for transforming traditional and natural remedies into safe, effective, and accessible therapies against malaria, leishmaniasis, trypanosomiasis, schistosomiasis, and other parasitic diseases.

AI disclosure

During the preparation of this work, the author(s) used ChatGpt in order to editing. After using this tool and /service, the author(s) reviewed and edited the content as needed and take(s) full responsibility for the content of the publication.

References

Adelusi BS, Ojika FU, Uzoka AC. A review of research on Artificial Neural Network for predictive maintenance of cooling devices. International Journal of Scientific Research in Civil Engineering 2022;8(2):1–13.

Alven S, Aderibigbe BA. Nanoparticles Formulations of Artemisinin and Derivatives as Potential Therapeutics for the Treatment of Cancer, Leishmaniasis and Malaria. Pharmaceutics 2020;12(8):748. Available from https://doi.org/10.3390/pharmaceutics12080748.

Andromeda, Ekawardhani S, Berbudi A. The role of Curcumin as an antimalarial agent. Systematic Reviews in Pharmacy 2020;11(7):18–25. Available from https://doi.org/10.31838/srp.2020.7.05.

Blunt JW, Copp BR, Keyzers RA, Munro MHG, Prinsep MR. Marine natural products. Natural Product Reports 2012;29(2):144–222. Available from https://doi.org/10.1039/c2np00090c.

Bohórquez EB, Chua M, Meshnick SR. Quinine localizes to a non-acidic compartment within the food vacuole of the malaria parasite Plasmodium falciparum. Malaria Journal 2012;11. Available from https://doi.org/10.1186/1475-2875-11-350.

Borges IP, Castanheira LE, Barbosa BF, De Souza DLN, Da Silva RJ, Mineo JR, et al. Anti-parasitic effect on Toxoplasma gondii induced by BnSP-7, a Lys49-phospholipase A 2 homologue from Bothrops pauloensis venom. Toxicon 2016;119:84–91. Available from https://doi.org/10.1016/j.toxicon.2016.05.010.

Buonfrate D, Ferrari TCA, Akim Adegnika A, Russell Stothard J, Gobbi FG. Human schistosomiasis. The Lancet 2025;405(10479):658–70. Available from https://doi.org/10.1016/S0140-6736(24)02814-9.

Capela R, Moreira R, Lopes F. An overview of drug resistance in protozoal diseases. International Journal of Molecular Sciences 2019;20(22):5748. Available from https://doi.org/10.3390/ijms20225748.

Cheuka P, Mayoka G, Mutai P, Chibale K. The role of natural products in drug discovery and development against neglected tropical diseases. Molecules (Basel, Switzerland) 2017;22(1):58. Available from https://doi.org/10.3390/molecules22010058.

Cui L, Kim K. Recent malaria outbreak in the USA: Risk of and response to malaria reintroduction in non-endemic regions. Decoding Infection and Transmission 2024;2:100018. Available from https://doi.org/10.1016/j.dcit.2024.100018.

Dai J, Dan W, Schneider U, Wang J. β-Carboline alkaloid monomers and dimers: occurrence, structural diversity, and biological activities. European Journal of Medicinal Chemistry 2018;157:622–56. Available from https://doi.org/10.1016/j.ejmech.2018.08.027.

Das A, Jawed JJ, Das MC, Parveen S, Ghosh C, Majumdar S, et al. Lupeol and amphotericin B mediate synergistic anti-leishmanial immunomodulatory effects in Leishmania donovani-infected BALB/c mice. Cytokine 2021;137. Available from https://doi.org/10.1016/j.cyto.2020.155319.

De Sarkar S, Sarkar D, Sarkar A, Dighal A, Staniek K, Gille L, et al. Berberine chloride mediates its antileishmanial activity by inhibiting Leishmania mitochondria. Parasitology Research 2019;118(1):335–45. Available from https://doi.org/10.1007/s00436-018-6157-3.

de Sousa AS, Vermeij D, Ramos AN, Luquetti AO. Chagas disease. The Lancet 2024;403(10422):203–18. Available from https://doi.org/10.1016/S0140-6736(23)01787-7.

Demain AL, Sanchez S. Microbial drug discovery: 80 Years of progress. Journal of Antibiotics 2009;62(1):5–16. Available from https://doi.org/10.1038/ja.2008.16.

Djimdé A, Doumbo OK, Cortese JF, Kayentao K, Doumbo S, Diourté Y, et al. A molecular marker for chloroquine-resistant falciparum malaria. New England Journal of Medicine 2001;344(4):257–63. Available from https://doi.org/10.1056/NEJM200101253440403.

Dziduch K, Greniuk D, Wujec M. The current directions of searching for antiparasitic drugs. Molecules (Basel, Switzerland) 2022;27(5):1534. Available from https://doi.org/10.3390/molecules27051534.

Egwu CO, Pério P, Augereau JM, Tsamesidis I, Benoit-Vical F, Reybier K. Resistance to artemisinin in falciparum malaria parasites: a redox-mediated phenomenon. Free Radical Biology and Medicine 2022;179:317–27. Available from https://doi.org/10.1016/j.freeradbiomed.2021.08.016.

Eze AA, Ogugofor MO, Ossai EC. Plant-derived compounds for the treatment of schistosomiasis. Nigerian Journal of Clinical Practice 2022;25(6):747–64. Available from https://doi.org/10.4103/njcp.njcp_1322_21.

Ezeanochie C, Akomolafe OO, Adeyemi C. Integrating phytomedicine research into clinical development pathways for novel therapies. Shodhshauryam, International Scientific Refereed Research Journal 2024;7(4):166–96. Available from https://doi.org/10.32628/SHISRRJ247158.

Ferreira LE, Benincasa BI, Fachin AL, França SC, Contini SSHT, Chagas ACS, et al. Thymus vulgaris L. essential oil and its main component thymol: Anthelmintic effects against Haemonchus contortus from sheep. Veterinary Parasitology 2016;228:70–6. Available from https://doi.org/10.1016/j.vetpar.2016.08.011.

Finlayson R, Pearce AN, Page MJ, Kaiser M, Bourguet-Kondracki ML, Harper JL, et al. Didemnidines A and B, indole spermidine alkaloids from the New Zealand ascidian didemnum sp. Journal of Natural Products 2011;74(4):888–92. Available from https://doi.org/10.1021/np1008619.

Gachelin G, Garner P, Ferroni E, Tröhler U, Chalmers I. Evaluating Cinchona bark and quinine for treating and preventing malaria. Journal of the Royal Society of Medicine 2017;110(1):31–40. Available from https://doi.org/10.1177/0141076816681421.

Herraiz T, Guillén H, González-Peña D, Arán VJ. Antimalarial Quinoline Drugs Inhibit β-Hematin and Increase Free Hemin Catalyzing Peroxidative Reactions and Inhibition of Cysteine Proteases. Scientific Reports 2019;9(1). Available from https://doi.org/10.1038/s41598-019-51604-z.

Kubota T, Kurimoto Si, Kobayashi J. The manzamine alkaloids. Alkaloids: Chemistry and Biology 2020;84:1–124. Available from https://doi.org/10.1016/bs.alkal.2020.03.001.

Laport M, Santos O, Muricy G. Marine Sponges: Potential Sources of New Antimicrobial Drugs. Current Pharmaceutical Biotechnology 2009;10(1):86–105. Available from https://doi.org/10.2174/138920109787048625.

Lejon V, Lindner AK, Franco JR. Human African trypanosomiasis. The Lancet 2025;405(10482):937–50. Available from https://doi.org/10.1016/S0140-6736(25)00107-2.

Li Z, Xu X, Meng L, Zhang Q, Cao L, Li W, et al. Hp1404, a New Antimicrobial Peptide from the Scorpion Heterometrus petersii. PLoS One 2014;9(5):e97539. Available from https://doi.org/10.1371/journal.pone.0097539.

Lokole PB, Byamungu GG, Mutwale PK, Ngombe NK, Mpuza MK, Mudogo V, et al. A review of saponin-based nanocarriers for drug delivery. Next Nanotechnology 2025;7. Available from https://doi.org/10.1016/j.nxnano.2024.100109.

Lv Y, Li W, Liao W, Jiang H, Liu Y, Cao J, et al. Nano-Drug Delivery Systems Based on Natural Products. International Journal of Nanomedicine 2024;19:541–69. Available from https://doi.org/10.2147/ijn.s443692.

Maiga FO, Wele M, Toure SM, Keita M, Tangara CO, Refeld RR, et al. Artemisinin-based combination therapy for uncomplicated Plasmodium falciparum malaria in Mali: a systematic review and meta-analysis. Malaria Journal 2021;20(1). Available from https://doi.org/10.1186/s12936-021-03890-0.

Negm WA, Ezzat SM, Zayed A. Marine organisms as potential sources of natural products for the prevention and treatment of malaria. RSC Advances 2023;13(7):4436–75. Available from https://doi.org/10.1039/d2ra07977a.

Nunes DCO, Figueira MMNR, Lopes DS, De Souza DLN, Izidoro LFM, Ferro EAV, et al. BnSP-7 toxin, a basic phospholipase A2 from Bothrops pauloensis snake venom, interferes with proliferation, ultrastructure and infectivity of Leishmania (Leishmania) amazonensis. Parasitology 2013;140(7):844–54. Available from https://doi.org/10.1017/S0031182013000012.

Orhan I, Şener B, Kaiser M, Brun R, Tasdemir D. Inhibitory Activity of Marine Sponge-Derived Natural Products against Parasitic Protozoa. Marine Drugs 2010;8(1):47–58. Available from https://doi.org/10.3390/md8010047.

Patalas-Krawczyk P, Malinska D, Walczak J, Kratzer G, Prill M, Michalska B, et al. Effects of plant alkaloids on mitochondrial bioenergetic parameters. Food and Chemical Toxicology 2021;154. Available from https://doi.org/10.1016/j.fct.2021.112316.

Pimentel-Elardo SM, Kozytska S, Bugni TS, Ireland CM, Moll H, Hentschel U. Anti-parasitic compounds from Streptomyces sp. strains isolated from Mediterranean sponges. Marine Drugs 2010;8(2):373–80. Available from https://doi.org/10.3390/md8020373.

Rahmah Z, Nirmala KC, Nashichuddin A, Riskiyana R, Milliana A, Indriana N, et al. Effect of neem leaf extract (Azadirachta indica) in reducing the degree of parasitemia and apoptosis in C57BL mice with cerebral malaria. Veterinary World 2024;17(7):1497–503. Available from https://doi.org/10.14202/vetworld.2024.1497-1503.

Ranasinghe S, Armson A, Lymbery AJ, Zahedi A, Ash A. Medicinal plants as a source of antiparasitics: an overview of experimental studies. Pathogens and Global Health 2023;117(6):535–53. Available from https://doi.org/10.1080/20477724.2023.2179454.

Reveillaud J, Maignien L, Eren MA, Huber JA, Apprill A, Sogin ML, et al. Host-specificity among abundant and rare taxa in the sponge microbiome. ISME Journal 2014;8(6):1198–209. Available from https://doi.org/10.1038/ismej.2013.227.

Shang X, Dai L, Cao X, Ma Y, Gulnaz I, Miao X, et al. Natural products in antiparasitic drug discovery: advances, opportunities and challenges. Natural Product Reports 2025;42(9):1419–58. Available from https://doi.org/10.1039/d5np00007f.

Shen Z, Luo H. The impact of schistosomiasis on the Global Disease Burden: a systematic analysis based on the 2021 Global Burden of Disease study. Parasite (Paris, France) 2025;32:12. Available from https://doi.org/10.1051/parasite/2025005.

Siniavin AE, Streltsova MA, Nikiforova MA, Kudryavtsev DS, Grinkina SD, Gushchin VA, et al. Snake venom phospholipase A2s exhibit strong virucidal activity against SARS-CoV-2 and inhibit the viral spike glycoprotein interaction with ACE2. Cellular and Molecular Life Sciences 2021;78(23):7777–94. Available from https://doi.org/10.1007/s00018-021-03985-6.

Soares AM, Guerra-Sá R, Borja-Oliveira CR, Rodrigues VM, Rodrigues-Simioni L, Rodrigues V, et al. Structural and functional characterization of BnSP-7, a Lys49 myotoxic phospholipase A2 homologue from Bothrops neuwiedi pauloensis venom. Archives of Biochemistry and Biophysics 2000;378(2):201–9. Available from https://doi.org/10.1006/abbi.2000.1790.

Solecka J, Zajko J, Postek M, Rajnisz A. Biologically active secondary metabolites from Actinomycetes. Open Life Sciences 2012;7(3):373–90. Available from https://doi.org/10.2478/s11535-012-0036-1.

Taiwo AE, Aduloju TD, Omolayo O, Olagoke-Komolafe O, Ayanwole AA. Quantum computing frameworks for real-time logistics optimization in smart supply chains. International Journal of Scientific Research in Science and Technology (IJSRST) 2024;9(4):554–64.

Tasdemir D, Topaloglu B, Perozzo R, Brun R, O'Neill R, Carballeira NM, et al. Marine natural products from the Turkish sponge Agelas oroides that inhibit the enoyl reductases from Plasmodium falciparum, Mycobacterium tuberculosis and Escherichia coli. Bioorganic and Medicinal Chemistry 2007;15(21):6834–45. Available from https://doi.org/10.1016/j.bmc.2007.07.032.

Wang C-C, Zhang W-X, He Y, Liu J-H, Ju C-S, Wu Q-L, et al. Global epidemiology of vector-borne parasitic diseases: burden, trends, disparities, and forecasts (1990–2036). Pathogens 2025;14(9):844. Available from https://doi.org/10.3390/pathogens14090844.

Wang J, Xu C, Wong YK, Li Y, Liao F, Jiang T, et al. Artemisinin, the magic drug discovered from traditional Chinese medicine. Engineering 2019;5(1):32–9. Available from https://doi.org/10.1016/j.eng.2018.11.011, http://www.journals.elsevier.com/engineering/.

World Health Organization. World Malaria Report 2024: Addressing Inequity in the Global Malaria Response. World Health Organization; Geneva, Switzerland: 2024.

World Health Organization Chagas Disease (Also Known as American Trypanosomiasis)[(accessed on 20 April 2025)]. Available online: https://www.who.int/news-room/fact-sheets/detail/chagas-disease-(american-trypanosomiasis%EF%BC%89.

World Health Organization Leishmaniasis. [(accessed on 20 April 2025)]. Available online: https://www.who.int/news-room/fact-sheets/detail/leishmaniasis.

World Health Organization Trypanosomiasis, Human African (Sleeping Sickness)[(accessed on 20 April 2025)]. Available online: https://www.who.int/news-room/fact-sheets/detail/trypanosomiasis-human-african-(sleeping-sickness%EF%BC%89.

Wu X, Chen Y, Liu H, Kong X, Liang X, Zhang Y, et al. The molecular composition of peptide toxins in the venom of spider lycosa coelestis as revealed by cDNA library and transcriptomic sequencing. Toxins 2023;15(2):143. Available from https://doi.org/10.3390/toxins15020143.

Yang D, Liu X, Li J, Xie J, Jiang L. Animal venoms: a novel source of anti-Toxoplasma gondii drug candidates. Frontiers in Pharmacology 2023;14. Available from https://doi.org/10.3389/fphar.2023.1178070.

CHAPTER 4

Mechanisms of action of natural antiparasitic agents

Felwa A. Thagfan[1], Huda A. Alqahtani[2], Omnia Hamed[3], and Mohamed Dkhil[3]
[1]Department of Biology, College of Science, Princess Nourah Bint Abdulrahman University, Riyadh, Saudi Arabia,
[2]Department of Zoology, College of Science, King Saud University, Riyadh, Saudi Arabia,
[3]Department of Zoology and Entomology, Faculty of Science, Capital University, Cairo, Egypt.

4.1 Introduction

Major blood parasites including, *Plasmodium spp.* (causing malaria), *trypanosoma spp.* (causing trypanosomiasis/chagas disease/sleeping sickness), *babesia spp.* (causing babesiosis), and *leishmania donovani* (causing visceral leishmaniasis) collectively pose a significant global health burden, particularly in tropical and subtropical regions, contributing to approximately 9 million disability adjusted life years (DALYs) worldwide (Sargsyan et al., 2025). Malaria is responsible for hundreds of thousands of deaths annually, with *Plasmodium falciparum* causing acute febrile illness by destroying red blood cells (Cholewiński et al., 2015; Sargsyan et al., 2025). Trypanosomiasis includes African sleeping sickness and American Chagas disease; the latter's chronic stage involves severe cardiac and alimentary system disorders in 20% to 40% of infected individuals (Cholewiński et al., 2015). Babesiosis involves blood cell destruction by tick-borne *Babesia* parasites and can be life-threatening, particularly in immunocompromised patients (Cholewiński et al., 2015; Sargsyan et al., 2025). Lastly, *leishmania donovani* causes visceral leishmaniasis (kala-azar), the most severe form of leishmaniasis, which is characterized by fever, splenomegaly, and anemia, and is typically fatal if left untreated, remaining one of the most neglected tropical diseases globally (Cholewiński et al., 2015; Sargsyan et al., 2025).

Current treatments for parasitic diseases face significant limitations (Kimeli et al., 2025), mainly because of the emergence of drug resistance (Tenorio, 2025), which is compounded by financial constraints, poor compliance in mass drug administration (MDA) programs, and inappropriate use of drugs, leading to the selection of resistant parasites (Kimeli et al., 2025; Tenorio, 2025). This challenge underscores the critical importance of understanding molecular mechanisms, as resistance is often attributed to mutations in target proteins including the β-tubulin gene for benzimidazoles, ligand-gated chloride channels for ivermectin, or alterations in binding sites for praziquantel that compromise drug efficacy and binding (Tenorio, 2025). By focusing on these mechanisms, molecular assessments can identify resistance associated mutations and

Innovative Strategies Against Blood Parasites
DOI: https://doi.org/10.1016/B978-0-443-48509-1.00001-X

inform mitigation strategies before current control and elimination programs are undermined by widespread resistance (Tenorio, 2025).

4.2 Targeting parasite metabolism

Blood borne parasites continue to impose a heavy global health burden, especially in tropical and low-resource settings where they contribute substantially to morbidity and mortality. The selection of therapy depends on the causative species, patterns of drug resistance, and clinical severity. Treatment strategies rely on a wide range of antiparasitic agents that compromise parasite viability by interfering with essential metabolic processes, neuromuscular signaling, membrane stability, or reproductive capacity (Campbell & Soman-Faulkner, 2023).

Malaria, caused by *Plasmodium* spp., illustrates the need for species- and region-specific therapeutic regimens. Chloroquine remains useful for most non-falciparum species (*P. vivax, P. malariae, P. ovale*, and *P. knowlesi*), yet widespread resistance has limited its effectiveness against *P. falciparum* (World Health Organization, 2015). Artemisinin-based combination therapies such as artemether-lumefantrine or atovaquone-proguanil have therefore become central to managing chloroquine-resistant infections (Hill et al., 2023). Artemisinin derivatives—including artesunate, artemether, and dihydroartemisinin—offer rapid parasite clearance and are typically paired with longer-acting agents such as lumefantrine (Meshnick, 2002; Ribbiso et al., 2021). Quinine continues to play a role in severe malaria and during pregnancy, while mefloquine, primaquine, doxycycline, and atovaquone-proguanil are frequently used for prophylaxis (World Health Organization, 2015; Hill et al., 2023).

Other hemoparasitic infections also require targeted pharmacological approaches. Babesiosis is managed with atovaquone plus azithromycin or with clindamycin–quinine combinations in severe illness (Vannier et al., 2008). Chagas disease therapy relies on benznidazole or nifurtimox (Campbell & Soman-Faulkner, 2023). African trypanosomiasis is treated according to disease stage: pentamidine is preferred for early *T. brucei gambiense* infection, suramin for early *T. brucei rhodesiense*, eflornithine for CNS involvement in gambiense disease, and melarsoprol for CNS-stage rhodesiense disease (Thomas et al., 2018; Fairlamb & Horn, 2018). Leishmaniasis therapy commonly begins with sodium stibogluconate, although alternatives such as amphotericin B, paromomycin, pentamidine, and meglumine antimoniate are used for resistant or visceral cases (Sundar & Singh, 2018; Aflatoonian et al., 2019).

A major metabolic vulnerability of *Plasmodium* lies in its digestion of hemoglobin within erythrocytes. As the parasite degrades hemoglobin for amino acids, it releases free heme, a highly reactive and toxic molecule (Herraiz et al., 2019). To avoid self-damage, the parasite converts heme into the inert crystalline pigment hemozoin. Numerous antimalarials exploit this step. Chloroquine, amodiaquine, and other 4-aminoquinolines block heme polymerization, causing lethal accumulation of free heme (Herraiz et al., 2019). Artemisinin compounds are activated by heme and generate reactive radicals that alkylate critical parasite proteins, especially within the digestive vacuole (Meshnick, 2002; Ribbiso et al., 2021). Mutations that reduce heme reactivity or alter redox processes contribute to artemisinin resistance (Luo et al., 2023). Amino alcohols such as lumefantrine, quinine, and mefloquine further impair heme detoxification and are used either independently or in combination with artemisinins (Hill et al., 2023).

Folate metabolism represents another strategic target. Parasites require reduced folate cofactors for nucleotide and amino acid biosynthesis, produced mainly via dihydrofolate reductase (DHFR) and pteridine reductase 1 (PTR1) (Vickers and Beverley, 2011; Sehrawat et al., 2024). Because PTR1 can compensate for DHFR inhibition, effective therapy often requires simultaneous targeting of both enzymes (Pohner et al., 2022). In trypanosomatids, DHFR is part of a bifunctional DHFR-thymidylate synthase complex (DHFR-TS) that converts dUMP to dTMP, making it an exceptionally attractive drug target (Gibson et al., 2016; Francesconi et al., 2024). Potent inhibitors—including nolatrexed, 2-amino triazino benzimidazoles, and 2-guanidino benzimidazoles—have shown strong antitrypanosomal activity (Francesconi et al., 2024). Classical DHFR/DHPS-targeting regimens such as pyrimethamine–sulfadiazine remain effective against toxoplasmosis, *P. jirovecii* pneumonia, and chloroquine-resistant malaria (Shamshad et al., 2022; Campbell & Soman-Faulkner, 2023).

The parasite mitochondrion has become a central focus of therapeutic development because of its importance in ATP production, the maintenance of redox homeostasis, pyrimidine synthesis, and heme metabolism, as well as its biochemical divergence from the host's mitochondria (Goodman et al., 2017; Vaidya and Mather, 2009). Inhibiting components of the mitochondrial electron transport chain collapses membrane potential, halts DHOD-dependent pyrimidine biosynthesis, and precipitates irreversible death pathways (Painter et al., 2007; Nixon et al., 2013). This makes the organelle a promising anchor for multistage antimalarial strategies (Greco et al., 2025).

Overall, effective antiparasitic therapy reflects sophisticated exploitation of weak metabolic points. By disrupting hemoglobin degradation, folate utilization, mitochondrial function, or other essential pathways, modern drugs achieve high selectivity for parasites over host cells. Nevertheless, the continuous emergence of resistance demands new therapeutics that target multiple pathways simultaneously (Singh and Tripathi, 2023; Zuzarte-Luís and Mota, 2018).

Pentamidine, an aromatic diamidine, exemplifies such pathway-targeted therapy. It primarily disrupts mitochondrial membrane potential in protozoan parasites (Thomas et al., 2018; Biagiotti et al., 2017). It is the first line treatment for early-stage *T. brucei gambiense* infection and is also used as an alternative to sodium stibogluconate in visceral leishmaniasis, in addition to its activity against *P. jirovecii* (Campbell & Soman-Faulkner, 2023).

Melarsoprol, a trivalent organic arsenical, is reserved for second-stage *T. brucei rhodesiense* infections with CNS involvement. Its high lipid solubility enables penetration of the blood–brain barrier. The drug kills parasites by inhibiting trypanothione reductase, thereby disrupting the organism's redox balance (Fairlamb & Horn, 2018).

Atovaquone, a hydroxynaphthoquinone, is the first licensed antimalarial designed specifically to inhibit the *Plasmodium* mitochondrion. Acting as a ubiquinone mimic, it binds the quinol oxidation site of complex III (cytochrome b), interrupting electron transport and energy production (Goodman et al, 2017). It is widely used in combination with proguanil (Malarone) for malaria treatment and prophylaxis, demonstrating excellent safety even in children and pregnant women (Nixon et al., 2013). The rapid emergence of resistance, however, underscores the need for next-generation mitochondrial inhibitors (Greco et al., 2025).

4.3 Drugs disrupting parasite membrane integrity

Numerous antiparasitic agents exert their effects by disrupting the metabolic pathways and redox homeostasis that parasites rely on for survival in the bloodstream. Blood parasites, particularly *Plasmodium spp.*, are highly dependent on hemoglobin digestion and oxidative metabolism within the intraerythrocytic environment, making metabolic enzymes and redox-sensitive systems essential drug targets.

4.3.1 Artemisinin and its derivatives

Artemisinin, isolated from *Artemisia annua*, and its semisynthetic derivatives—including dihydroartemisinin (DHA), artesunate, artemether, and arteether—form the cornerstone of artemisinin-based combination therapy (ACT), the standard first-line treatment for uncomplicated *Plasmodium falciparum* malaria (Jin et al., 2023; Shi et al., 2022). These compounds provide rapid parasite clearance and remain among the most effective antiparasitic therapies available globally (Bassi et al., 2017).

4.3.1.1 Mechanism of action

The activity of artemisinin is mediated by its unique **endoperoxide bridge**, which undergoes activation by ferrous iron (Fe^{2+}) released from hemoglobin digestion in the parasite's food vacuole. This reaction generates **reactive carbon-centered radicals** that cause extensive damage to parasite biomolecules(Shi et al., 2022). The mechanism include:

- Radical-mediated **alkylation of parasite proteins**, including those involved in glycolysis and stress response
- **Redox disruption**, overwhelming parasite antioxidant systems
- **Lipid peroxidation**, damage parasite membranes and organelles

- Potential interaction with **PfATP6**, a parasite SERCA-type Ca^{2+} ATPase (a proposed mechanism)

Proteomic studies confirm artemisinin's **multitarget mechanism**, as the drug modifies a wide range of proteins involved in essential metabolic functions (Cowell and Winzeler, 2019).

4.3.1.2 Clinical effectiveness and resistance

While ACTs remain highly effective, **partial artemisinin resistance**, characterized by slower parasite clearance, has emerged in Southeast Asia and Africa. This phenotype is associated with mutations in the *Pfkelch13* gene that modulate the parasite's response to oxidative damage (World Health Organization, 2024). Ongoing genomic surveillance is necessary to protect ACT efficacy.

4.4 Molecular interference with DNA replication and protein synthesis in blood parasites

Blood parasites such as *Plasmodium*, *Babesia*, and *Trypanosoma* rely on precisely regulated pathways controlling DNA replication, chromatin remodeling, and protein synthesis. These pathways are essential for parasite proliferation inside erythrocytes and represent critical targets for antiparasitic drug development. This section summarizes major mechanisms by which drugs disrupt genome maintenance and translational processes in blood parasites.

4.4.1 Inhibition of DNA replication and repair pathways

4.4.1.1 Replication protein a inhibition

Replication Protein A (RPA) is the principal single stranded DNA-binding complex essential for replication fork stability and coordination of the DNA damage response. Blocking RPA-DNA interactions induces fork collapse and replication stress. Natural inhibitors such as rupesin E have been shown to bind selectively to RPA1, destabilizing the complex and impairing DNA synthesis in blood-stage parasites (Gomes et al., 2022).

4.4.1.2 Targeting replication fork progression and polymerases

Blood parasites use specialized polymerases and helicases to sustain rapid intracellular replication. Molecules interfering with polymerase δ/ε or the MCM helicase complex reduce DNA chain elongation and suppress origin firing, severely impairing schizogony and merozoite formation (Patel et al., 2023). These disruptions ultimately prevent completion of the parasite cell cycle.

4.4.2 Disruption of chromatin remodeling and epigenetic regulation

4.4.2.1 The PfMYST/PfNuA4 histone acetyltransferase complex

The PfMYST (PfNuA4) complex controls histone H4 acetylation and promotes an open chromatin configuration required for replication initiation and transcription. Inhibiting of PfMYST results in chromatin condensation, downregulation of replication-associated genes, and impaired DNA repair capacity (Kalamuddin et al., 2024). Because PfMYST also influences antigenic variation and stress responses, its inhibition affects multiple survival pathways.

4.4.2.2 Epigenetic modulators

Histone acetyltransferase and methyltransferase inhibitors reduce parasite proliferation thereby suppressing transcriptional programs essential for erythrocytic growth (Gupta et al., 2017). Reduced acetylation correlates with weakened replication and diminished adaptability to host stress environments.

4.4.3 Inhibition of organellar DNA replication

4.4.3.1 Apicoplast DNA polymerase inhibitors

The apicoplast contains a small circular genome that is replicated by a plant-like DNA polymerase (apPOL). Selective apPOL inhibitors such as pepstatin derived molecules interfere with apicoplast DNA replication, producing the characteristic "delayed-death" phenotype of apicoplast-targeting agents (Kaur et al., 2022). Because apPOL shares minimal sequence identity with human polymerases, it represents an attractive drug target.

4.4.3.2 Disrupting apicoplast replication machinery

Additional apicoplast enzymes, such as gyrase, primase, and helicases, show bacterial ancestry, making them selectively susceptible to antibiotics that target prokaryotic replication. Drugs affecting these enzymes disrupt essential metabolic pathways, such as fatty acid and isoprenoid synthesis, eventually causing parasite death (Ralph et al., 2004; Tang Girdwood et al., 2015).

4.4.4 Inhibition of homologous recombination and DNA repair

4.4.4.1 RAD51 inhibition

Homologous recombination (HR) is required for the accurate repair of replication-associated DNA breaks. RAD51 facilitates homology search and strand exchange.

Small molecules that prevent RAD51 filament formation compromise genome repair and increase sensitivity to replication stress (Kelso et al., 2017). In *Plasmodium* and *Trypanosoma*, impaired RAD51 activity leads to reduced viability and enhanced drug susceptibility.

4.4.4.2 Other DNA repair pathways

Agents that indirectly overwhelm base excision (BER), nucleotide-excision (NER), or mismatch repair (MMR) pathways can induce lethal DNA damage when combined with replication stress. Some antiparasitic drugs exploit this by generating excess oxidative or alkylating lesions that exceed repair capacity (Huang et al., 2014).

4.4.5 Inhibition of protein synthesis

4.4.5.1 Apicoplast translation inhibitors

The apicoplast ribosome resembles a bacterial 70 S ribosome. Tetracyclines (e.g., doxycycline) inhibit the 30 S subunit, whereas clindamycin and related agents target the 50 S subunit, thereby blocking peptide elongation. By preventing the translation of apicoplast-encoded proteins, these drugs disrupt essential biosynthetic pathways and produce a delayed-death phenotype (Dahl et al., 2006; Mamudu et al., 2024).

4.4.5.2 Mitochondrial translation inhibitors

Some antiparasitic agents selectively impair mitochondrial ribosomes, thereby reducing the synthesis of respiratory chain components and leading to ATP depletion and oxidative stress (Elaagip et al., 2022). This effect is particularly detrimental during blood-stage development.

4.4.5.3 Cytosolic protein synthesis disruption

Aminoacyl-tRNA synthetase inhibitors block tRNA charging, thereby halting cytosolic translation (Verhoef et al., 2021). Artemisinin and related endoperoxides alkylate multiple translation-associated proteins and stress-response regulators, thereby contributing to rapid parasite killing (Wang et al., 2018).

4.4.6 Combined effects on replication and translation

Many antiparasitic agents simultaneously disrupt DNA replication and protein synthesis. Reduced translation limits the availability of replication factors, while replication stress increases the requirement for repair proteins. When both pathways are inhibited, parasites accumulate irreparable DNA lesions and fail to complete erythrocytic development.

4.5 Disruption of membrane integrity by amphotericin B derivatives and silver nanoparticles

A second major class of antiparasitic agents acts by damaging parasite membranes. Blood parasites depend on intact and highly regulated plasma and organelle membranes for nutrient uptake, ionic balance, and interaction with host cells. Agents that compromise membrane integrity rapidly lead to parasite dysfunction and death.

4.5.1 Amphotericin B derivatives (A21)

Amphotericin B, a polyene macrolide with potent sterol-binding properties, has inspired several derivatives with activity against protozoan blood parasites. A21, a semisynthetic derivative, shows strong efficacy against *Trypanosoma cruzi*, the causative agent of Chagas disease (Martínez et al., 2024).

4.5.1.1 Mechanism of action

A21 acts by binding to **ergosterol**, the major sterol in the *T. cruzi* membrane, forming transmembrane pores that lead to leakage of intracellular contents and disruption of membrane stability. Additional effects include:

- Morphological alterations of parasite cells
- Damage to plasma and organelle membranes
- Reduction of mitochondrial membrane potential
- Increased generation of **reactive oxygen species**

In vivo studies using a mouse model of acute Chagas disease demonstrated that A21 combined with benznidazole significantly reduced parasitemia and prevented mortality caused by a virulent strain of *T. cruzi* (Martínez et al., 2024).

4.5.2 Silver nanoparticles (AgNPs)

Silver nanoparticles (AgNPs) have emerged as versatile antiparasitic agents because of their ability to disrupt parasite membranes and interfere with metabolic function. Their activity has been demonstrated against *Plasmodium* and *Leishmania* species (Zhang et al., 2023).

4.5.2.1 Mechanism of action

AgNPs primarily act through the **release of silver ions (Ag^{+})**, which interact with phospholipids and membrane-associated proteins as in Fig. 4.1, leading to:

- Loss of membrane integrity and fluidity
- Increased permeability and leakage of cellular contents

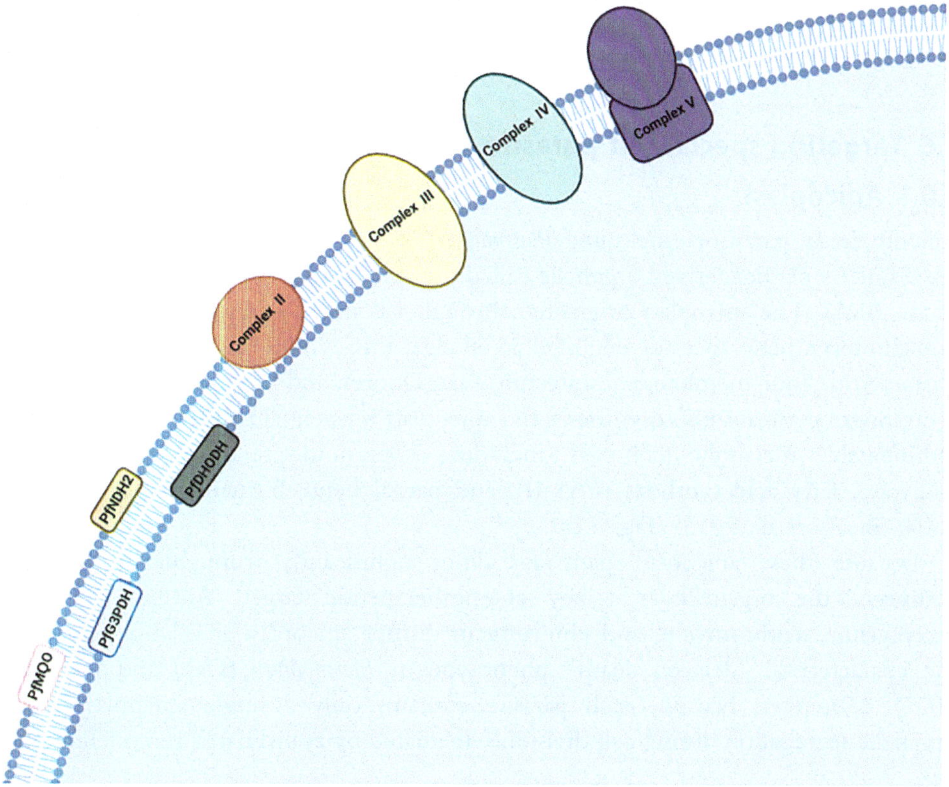

Figure 4.1 Shows how different parts of the mitochondrial electron transport chain are affected by antimalarial drugs. Endochin-like quinolones include HDQ, MPQ, CK-2–68, SL-2–64, SL-2–25, RYL-552, RYL-581, RKA066, WJM228, ELQ-300, ELQ-331, ELQ-596, ELQ-598, and ELQ-400. Naphthoquinones include plumbagin, nepodin, and atovaquone. Terpene compounds include siccanin and dobikin K (Greco et al., 2025).

- Disruption of ion gradients
- Structural membrane damage due to nanoparticle deposition

Furthermore, AgNPs affect parasite metabolism by targeting key enzymes and inducing oxidative stress (Zhang et al., 2023).

4.5.2.2 Examples of plant-derived AgNPs

Green-synthesized AgNPs derived from *Moringa oleifera*, *Zingiber officinale* (ginger), and *Teucrium stocksianum* have demonstrated:

- Inhibition of malaria parasite growth
- Potent antileishmanial activity
- Improved biocompatibility compared with chemically synthesized nanoparticles

These properties highlight AgNPs as promising membrane-targeting agents for future therapeutic development.

4.6 Targeting specialized parasite organelles

4.6.1 Apicoplast

Apicomplexan parasites—including *Plasmodium falciparum* and *Toxoplasma gondii*—possess a unique plastid-derived organelle called the apicoplast (Ralph et al., 2004; Verhoef et al., 2021). The apicoplast originated through secondary endosymbiosis, in which a non-photosynthetic ancestor engulfed a red alga; this evolutionary history explains its characteristic four-membrane architecture (van Dooren and Striepen, 2013). Although it no longer performs photosynthesis, the apicoplast is essential because it houses several indispensable metabolic pathways, including isoprenoid precursor synthesis (MEP pathway), fatty acid synthesis (FAS-II), and partial heme biosynthesis (Ralph et al., 2004; Shears et al., 2015) (Fig. 4.2).

Because these apicoplast pathways differ significantly from human metabolic pathways, the organelle is a key chemotherapeutic target. Antibiotics such as doxycycline, azithromycin, and clindamycin disrupt apicoplast translation, producing the characteristic "delayed death" phenotype in *Plasmodium* (Dahl and Rosenthal, 2007). Moreover, because each parasite contains only a single apicoplast, proper organelle segregation during cell division—mediated by coordinated remodeling of the

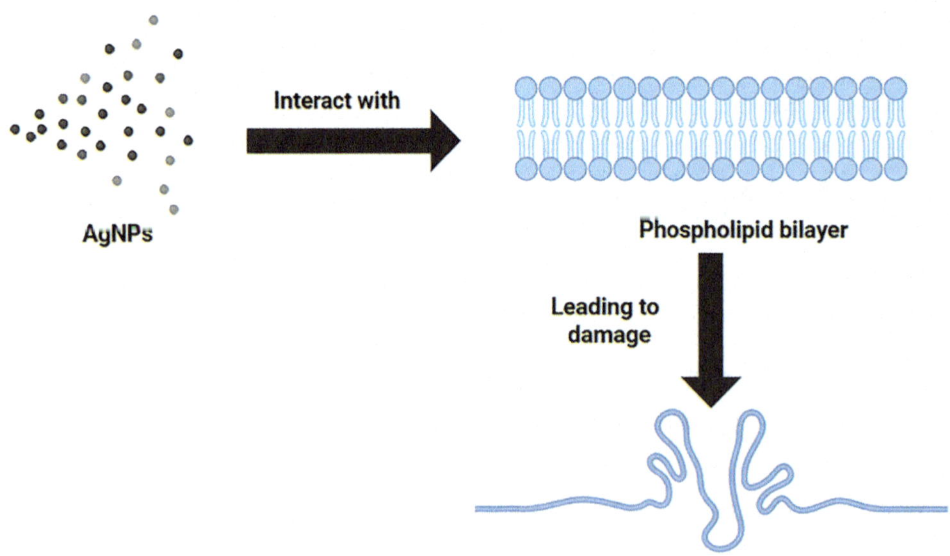

Figure 4.2 The effect of AgNPs on phospholipid bilayer.

parasite's actin and microtubule cytoskeleton—is crucial for parasite replication (Verhoef et al., 2021; van Dooren et al., 2009). These singular features make the apicoplast a validated and highly attractive antiparasitic target.

4.6.2 Acidic food vacuole (digestive vacuole)

Many protozoan parasites rely on acidic, lysosome-like compartments to digest macromolecules acquired from the host. *Plasmodium* species, for example, possess a specialized digestive vacuole that functions as the primary site of hemoglobin degradation, generating amino acids required for parasite growth (Ginsburg, 2010; Wiser, 2024). This vacuole provides a unique biochemical microenvironment, acidic pH, high heme concentration, and active proteases, that forms the basis of several potent antimalarial chemotherapies.

Classical quinoline antimalarials, including chloroquine, quinine, and amodiaquine, exert their activity by preventing the detoxification of heme into hemozoin, leading to toxic heme accumulation and parasite death (Egan, 2008). The vacuole also serves as the target of artemisinin activation, which depends on ferrous iron released during hemoglobin breakdown. Beyond *Plasmodium*, other protozoa maintain analogous acidic organelles: *Trypanosoma cruzi* possesses reservosomes used for endocytosed nutrient storage, while *Leishmania* species contain megasomes, large acidic vacuoles critical for protein degradation (Wiser, 2024; Motta et al., 2019). These digestive compartments thus provide multiple opportunities for selective therapeutic intervention across several parasite lineages.

4.6.3 Glycosomes in trypanosomes

Glycosomes are specialized peroxisome-like organelles found in kinetoplastid parasites, including *Trypanosoma brucei* and *Trypanosoma cruzi*. Their defining feature is the compartmentalization of the majority of glycolytic enzymes, a unique adaptation because these parasites rely heavily on glycolysis for ATP production, particularly in the bloodstream form of *T. brucei* (Michels et al., 2006; Quiñones et al., 2020). In some stages, glycolytic enzymes constitute over 90% of total glycosomal protein content, highlighting the organelle's central metabolic role.

Glycosomes also contain enzymes involved in β-oxidation, purine salvage, and ether lipid synthesis, illustrating their multifunctional nature (Haanstra et al., 2014). Because glycosomal pathways require precise regulation, continual metabolite exchange between the glycosome and cytosol is essential for maintaining metabolic flux. This exchange is mediated by membrane transporters, including homologs of the ATP-binding cassette (ABC) and mitochondrial carrier family (MCF) transporters (Quiñones et al., 2020).

The structural and functional distinctiveness of the glycosome makes it an extremely promising drug target. Inhibitors of glycosomal protein import (PEX proteins), glycolytic enzymes, or glycosomal membrane transporters have shown strong trypanocidal potential (Colasante et al., 2018; Haanstra et al., 2014). Because glycosome disruption rapidly collapses energy metabolism, this organelle remains at the forefront of kinetoplastid drug discovery efforts.

4.7 Immune-modulating mechanisms

4.7.1 Macrophage activation

Macrophages play a central role in controlling blood parasites by phagocytosing infected cells and producing reactive nitrogen and oxygen species (Munder, 2020). Several natural compounds and microbial products enhance macrophage activity, thereby promoting antiparasitic defense. For example, propolis stimulates macrophage activation, thereby improving host defense against intracellular pathogens (Nuzzo et al., 2022). Similarly, gut commensals such as *Lactobacillus rhamnosus* GG can modulate macrophage function through the release of lipoteichoic acid, which enhances tissue protection during infections (Yin et al., 2023). *Parabacteroides distasonis* has been reported to induce M2 macrophage polarization, which contributes to the resolution of inflammation and may assist in limiting parasite-induced tissue damage (Yin et al., 2023). Additionally, specific peptidoglycan fragments, such as iE-DAP and FK-156, modulate macrophage activation, enhancing their antimicrobial and immunoregulatory functions (Yin et al., 2023). These mechanisms can be leveraged to improve host responses against blood parasites such as *Plasmodium*, *Trypanosoma*, and *Leishmania*.

4.7.2 Cytokine modulation

Cytokines orchestrate the immune response to parasitic infections, influencing both innate and adaptive immunity. T regulatory (Treg) cells suppress excessive inflammation via cytokines such as IL-10, IL-35, and TGF-β, which prevent tissue damage during parasitic infections (Smyth et al., 2013). In contrast, proinflammatory cytokines such as IFN-γ and IL-12 are essential for Th1 responses, promoting the activation of cytotoxic T lymphocytes and macrophages that control intracellular parasites (Nuzzo et al., 2022). Certain natural products modulate these cytokine pathways; for instance, triptolide inhibits proinflammatory mediators IL-1, TNF-α, and IL-6, whereas propolis enhances anti-inflammatory IL-10 production (Nuzzo et al., 2022). Adenosine signaling on activated T cells also suppresses proinflammatory cytokines such as IL-2 and IFN-γ and promotes Treg differentiation through TGF-β induction, thereby contributing to immune homeostasis during parasitic infections (Smyth et al., 2013;

Antonioli et al., 2013). Such modulation is crucial for balancing effective parasite clearance while preventing host tissue damage.

4.7.3 Extracellular vesicle and nanoparticle effects

Extracellular vesicles (EVs), including exosomes, are nanosized membrane vesicles (50–150 nm) that mediate intercellular communication and immune modulation (Smyth et al., 2013). Parasite- or host-derived EVs can influence immune responses by modulating macrophage function, cytokine production, and T cell activity. For example, Treg-derived exosomes expressing CD73 produce adenosine, thereby suppressing effector T-cell proliferation and cytokine secretion (Smyth et al., 2013). Recent studies suggest that engineered nanoparticles may mimic these effects, offering a promising strategy to deliver immunomodulatory compounds that enhance host defense against blood parasites (Bottini et al., 2021).

4.7.4 Natural product–based immunomodulation

Natural products remain a major source of immunomodulatory agents that can enhance host defense against parasitic infections. Compounds such as andrographolide, derived from *Andrographis paniculata*, stimulate both antigen-specific and nonspecific immune responses, improving parasite clearance (Nuzzo et al., 2022). Curcumin, a polyphenol from *Curcuma longa*, exhibits anti-inflammatory and immunostimulatory effects by modulating cytokine production and enhancing macrophage activity (Hewlings and Kalman, 2017; Nuzzo et al., 2022). Peptidoglycan molecules from gut commensals also contribute to immune remodeling, promoting macrophage and dendritic cell responses that support antiparasitic immunity (Yin et al., 2023). Together, these natural immunomodulators represent promising adjuncts to therapeutic strategies targeting blood parasites.

4.8 Mechanisms of drug resistance

4.8.1 Genetic mutations

Genetic alterations can occur rapidly, allowing parasites such as *Leishmania* to survive under pharmacological strain (Bharadava et al., 2024). Resistance in *P. falciparum* to the antimalarial fosmidomycin (FSM) was found to require a loss-of-function mutation in HAD2 (Guggisberg et al., 2018). This HAD2 mutation resulted in a truncated (R157X) protein variant (Guggisberg et al., 2018). The use of a screen for suppression of drug resistance also uncovered hypomorphic suppressor mutations in the PFK9 locus (Guggisberg et al., 2018). Mutations in critical genes in *Leishmania* can lead to resistance against antileishmanial medicines (Bharadava et al., 2024).

4.8.2 Drug efflux pumps

Resistance in pathogens such as *Leishmania* is frequently linked to enhanced efflux of the drug from the parasite (Bharadava et al., 2024). Acquired resistance mechanisms can be linked to changes in drug efflux or sequestration (Bharadava et al., 2024). The Multidrug resistance protein (MRPA), an ABC transporter, is associated with increased drug efflux (Bharadava et al., 2024). ABC transporters are a well-known family of proteins that use ATP hydrolysis to eliminate numerous kinds of substances across cell membranes (Bharadava et al., 2024). These ABC transporters an important activity in resistance and have been widely investigated and linked to treatment resistance in various *Leishmania* species (Bharadava et al., 2024).

4.8.3 Metabolic reprogramming

A key resistance mechanism in parasites is the development of alternative metabolic pathway (Bharadava et al., 2024). Loss of the HAD2 protein in *P. falciparum* dysregulates glycolysis, which misroutes metabolites toward the MEP pathway, conferring drug resistance (Guggisberg et al., 2018). In the malaria parasite, FSM resistance is achieved by increased steady-state levels of MEP pathway and glycolytic intermediates (Guggisberg et al., 2018). Study of *P. falciparum* drug resistance revealed PFK9 as a novel site of genetic metabolic plasticity in the parasite (Guggisberg et al., 2018). In *Leishmania*, resistance to miltefosine involves the alteration in alkyl-lipid metabolism and phospholipid biosynthesis (Bharadava et al., 2024). Changes in drug metabolism are a mechanism of drug resistance, involving proteins like Pteridine reductase 1 (PTR1) in *Leishmania* (Bharadava et al., 2024).

4.9 Novel and emerging therapeutic strategies

4.9.1 Natural products as multi target agents

Natural products, particularly plant-derived compounds, have long served as a source of therapeutic agents because of their chemical diversity and multitarget properties (Makhoba et al., 2020; Newman and Cragg, 2020). Historically, medicinal plants were screened for activity against infectious diseases, including malaria, trypanosomiasis, and leishmaniasis (Liu et al., 2021). For instance, quinine from *Cinchona* species and artemisinin from *Artemisia annua* are prime examples of plant-derived antimalarials that target multiple stages of the parasite lifecycle (Tu, 2016; Liu et al., 2021). Other compounds, such as curcumin and andrographolide, have been reported to modulate both parasite metabolism and host immune responses, demonstrating their potential for **multitarget therapy** against blood parasites (Raj et al., 2020; Nuzzo et al., 2022).

The multitarget approach is particularly advantageous in tackling **drug-resistant parasites**, as compounds acting on multiple biochemical pathways reduce the likelihood of resistance development (Zhang et al., 2022). Additionally, integrating natural products with conventional therapies has shown promise for enhancing efficacy and mitigating toxicity (Zhang et al., 2022; Raj et al., 2020).

4.9.2 AI-based drug discovery

Artificial intelligence (AI) and machine learning (ML) have emerged as powerful tools to accelerate drug discovery against blood parasites such as *Plasmodium falciparum* and *Trypanosoma* species (Stokes et al., 2020; Keshavarzi Arshadi et al., 2020; Winkler, 2021). For example, the DeepMalaria system uses graph convolutional neural networks trained on over 13,000 antiplasmodial compounds to predict inhibitory activity and cytotoxicity, successfully identifying all nanomolar-active compounds and discovering new chemical scaffolds (Keshavarzi Arshadi et al., 2020).

Beyond malaria, AI-driven virtual screening and drug repurposing have been applied to *Trypanosoma cruzi* and *Leishmania* to identify compounds targeting parasite metabolism, membrane integrity, or organelle-specific pathways (Gentile et al., 2022; Wang et al., 2023). Transfer learning, reinforcement learning, and generative models allow the prediction of active molecules even with limited experimental data, thereby accelerating the identification of novel therapeutics (Stokes et al., 2020; Gentile et al., 2022). Integrating AI with natural product databases provides a promising strategy for combine traditional knowledge with cutting-edge computational drug discovery for blood parasites.

4.10 Conclusion

Major blood parasites, cause a significant global health burden, contributing to approximately 9 million Disability-Adjusted Life Years (DALYs) worldwide as *plasmodium* spp. (Malaria), *trypanosoma* spp. (trypanosomiasis), *babesia* spp. (babesiosis), and *leishmania donovani* (Visceral Leishmaniasis). These parasites are responsible for devastating conditions, like the acute illness from red blood cell destruction by *P. falciparum*, the severe cardiac and alimentary system disorders in chronic Chagas disease, life-threatening babesiosis, particularly in immunocompromised patients, and fatal Visceral Leishmaniasis if left untreated. Current treatments face major limitations, primarily due to the emergence of drug resistance, which is compounded by financial constraints and poor compliance in mass drug administration programs, underscoring the critical need to understand the molecular mechanisms of action and resistance for developing effective new therapies.

References

Antonioli L, Blandizzi C, Pacher P, Haskó G. Immunity, inflammation and cancer: a leading role for adenosine. Nature Reviews. Cancer 2013;13(12):842–57. Available from https://doi.org/10.1038/nrc3613.

Aflatoonian MR, Sharifi I, Aflatoonian B, Bamorrovat M, Heshmatkhah A, Babaei Z, et al. Associated-risk determinants for anthroponotic cutaneous leishmaniasis treated with meglumine antimoniate: A cohort study in Iran. PLoS Neglected Tropical Diseases 2019;13(6):e0007423. Available from https://doi.org/10.1371/journal.pntd.0007423.

Bassi PU, Abubakar A, Abdullahi MI, Abubakar U. Efficacy of artemisinin-based combination antimalarial therapy for uncomplicated Plasmodium falciparum malaria in Africa: a systematic review and meta-analysis. Malaria Journal 2017;16. Available from https://doi.org/10.1186/s12936-017-2108-8.

Bharadava K, Upadhyay TK, Kaushal RS, Ahmad I, Alraey Y, Siddiqui S, et al. Genomic insight of leishmania parasite: in-depth review of drug resistance mechanisms and genetic mutations. ACS Omega 2024;9(11). Available from https://doi.org/10.1021/acsomega.3c09400.

Biagiotti M, Dominguez S, Yamout N, Zufferey R. Lipidomics and anti-trypanosomatid chemotherapy. Clinical and Translational Medicine 2017;6(1):27.

Bottini M, Bosi S, Carrega P. Nanoparticle-mediated immunomodulation in infectious diseases. Frontiers in Immunology 2021;12:676550. Available from https://doi.org/10.3389/fimmu.2021.676550.

Campbell S, Soman-Faulkner K. Antiparasitic drugs. Treasure Island (FL): StatPearls Publishing; 2023. Available from http://www.ncbi.nlm.nih.gov/books/NBK544251/.

Cholewiński M, Derda M, Hadaś E. Parasitic diseases in humans transmitted by vectors. Annals of parasitology 2015;61(3):137–57. Available from https://doi.org/10.17420/ap6103.01.

Colasante C, Voncken F, Manful T, Ruppert T, Tielens AGM, van Hellemond JJ. Proteomic analysis of glycosomes from *Trypanosoma brucei* reveals novel metabolic functions. Journal of Biological Chemistry 2018;293(15):5458–75. Available from https://doi.org/10.1074/jbc.RA117.001099.

Cowell AN, Winzeler EA. The genomic architecture of antimalarial drug resistance. Briefings in Functional Genomics 2019;18(5):314–28. Available from https://doi.org/10.1093/bfgp/elz008.

Dahl EL, Rosenthal PJ. Multiple antibiotics exert delayed effects against the Plasmodium falciparum apicoplast. Antimicrobial Agents and Chemotherapy 2007;51(10):3485–90. Available from https://doi.org/10.1128/AAC.00527-07.

Dahl EL, Shock JL, Shenai BR, Gut J, DeRisi JL, Rosenthal PJ. Tetracyclines specifically target the apicoplast of Plasmodium falciparum. Antimicrobial Agents and Chemotherapy 2006;50(9):3124–31. Available from https://doi.org/10.1128/AAC.00394-06.

Egan TJ. Haemozoin formation. Molecular and Biochemical Parasitology 2008;157(2):127–36. Available from https://doi.org/10.1016/j.molbiopara.2007.11.005.

Elaagip A, Absalon S, Florentin A. Apicoplast dynamics during plasmodium cell cycle. Frontiers in Cellular and Infection Microbiology 2022;12. Available from https://doi.org/10.3389/fcimb.2022.864819.

Fairlamb AH, Horn D. Melarsoprol Resistance in African Trypanosomiasis. Trends in Parasitology 2018;34(6):481–92. Available from https://doi.org/10.1016/j.pt.2018.04.002.

Francesconi V, Rizzo M, Pozzi C, Tagliazucchi L, Konchie Simo CU, Saporito G, et al. Identification of innovative folate inhibitors leveraging the amino dihydrotriazine motif from cycloguanil for their potential as anti-trypanosoma brucei agents. ACS Infectious Diseases 2024;10(8):2755–74. Available from https://doi.org/10.1021/acsinfecdis.4c00113.

Gentile F, Agostino M, Brancale A. Artificial intelligence in neglected tropical disease drug discovery. Drug Discovery Today 2022;27(9):2330–42. Available from https://doi.org/10.1016/j.drudis.2022.06.011.

Gibson MW, Dewar S, Ong HB, Sienkiewicz N, Fairlamb AH. Trypanosoma brucei DHFR-TS revisited: characterisation of a bifunctional and highly unstable recombinant dihydrofolate reductase-thymidylate synthase. PLoS Neglected Tropical Diseases 2016;10(5). Available from https://doi.org/10.1371/journal.pntd.0004714.

Ginsburg H. Progress in in silico functional genomics: the malaria metabolic pathway database. Trends in Parasitology 2010;26(3):85–8. Available from https://doi.org/10.1016/j.pt.2009.12.005.

Gomes ARQ, Cunha N, Varela ELP, Brígido HPC, Vale VV, Dolabela MF, et al. Oxidative stress in malaria: potential benefits of antioxidant therapy. International Journal of Molecular Sciences 2022;23(11):5949.

Goodman CD, Buchanan HD, McFadden GI. Is the mitochondrion a good malaria drug target? Trends in Parasitology 2017;33(3):185–93. Available from https://doi.org/10.1016/j.pt.2016.10.002.

Greco S, Assalve G, Lunetti P, Kayentao K, Dara A, Scaramuzzi D, et al. Targeting Mitochondrial function in Plasmodium falciparum: insight into antimalarial drugs and the emerging role of Saccharomyces cerevisiae as a model system. International Journal of Molecular Sciences 2025;26(18):9150. Available from https://doi.org/10.3390/ijms26189150.

Guggisberg AM, Frasse PM, Jezewski AJ, Kafai NM, Gandhi AY, Erlinger SJ, et al. Suppression of drug resistance reveals a genetic mechanism of metabolic plasticity in malaria parasites. mBio 2018;9(6). Available from https://doi.org/10.1128/mbio.01193-18.

Gupta AP, Zhu L, Tripathi J, Kucharski M, Patra A, Bozdech Z. Histone 4 lysine 8 acetylation regulates proliferation and host–pathogen interaction in Plasmodium falciparum. Epigenetics & Chromatin 2017;10(1). Available from https://doi.org/10.1186/s13072-017-0147-z.

Haanstra JR, González-Marcano EB, Gualdrón-López M, Michels PAM. Biogenesis, maintenance and dynamics of glycosomes in trypanosomatid parasites. Biochimica et Biophysica Acta (BBA) - Molecular Cell Research 2014;1843(9):1617–28. Available from https://doi.org/10.1016/j.bbamcr.2014.03.010.

Herraiz T, Guillén H, González-Peña D, Arán VJ. Antimalarial quinoline drugs inhibit β-hematin and increase free hemin catalyzing peroxidative reactions and inhibition of cysteine proteases. Scientific Reports 2019;9(1):15398.

Hewlings SJ, Kalman DS. Curcumin: a review of its effects on human health. Foods 2017;6(10). Available from https://doi.org/10.3390/foods6100092.

Hill SR, Thakur RK, Sharma GK. Antimalarial medications. 2023 Aug 8. In: StatPearls [Internet]. Treasure Island (FL): StatPearls Publishing; 2025 Jan–. PMID: 29261925.

Huang F, Mazin AV, Korolev S. A small molecule inhibitor of human RAD51 potentiates breast cancer cell killing by therapeutic agents in mouse xenografts. PLoS One 2014;9(6):e100993. Available from https://doi.org/10.1371/journal.pone.0100993.

Jin Q, Liu T, Chen D, Yang L, Mao H, Ma F, et al. Therapeutic potential of artemisinin and its derivatives in managing kidney diseases. Frontiers in Pharmacology 2023;14. Available from https://doi.org/10.3389/fphar.2023.1097206.

Kalamuddin, M, Shakri, AR, Wang, C, Min, H, Li, X, Cui, L, et al. MYST regulates DNA repair and forms a NuA4-like complex in the malaria parasite Plasmodium falciparum. mSphere, 2024;9(4):e0014024. Available from https://doi.org/10.1128/msphere.00140-24.

Kaur S, Nieto NS, McDonald P, Beck JR, Honzatko RB, Roy A, et al. Discovery of small molecule inhibitors of Plasmodium falciparum apicoplast DNA polymerase. Journal of Enzyme Inhibition and Medicinal Chemistry 2022;37(1):1320–6. Available from https://doi.org/10.1080/14756366.2022.2070909.

Keshavarzi Arshadi A, Salem M, Collins J, Yuan JS, Chakrabarti D. DeepMalaria: Artificial Intelligence driven discovery of potent antiplasmodials. Frontiers in pharmacology 2020;10:1526. Available from https://doi.org/10.3389/fphar.2019.01526.

Kelso AA, Waldvogel SM, Luthman AJ, Sehorn MG. Homologous recombination in protozoan parasites and recombinase inhibitors. Frontiers in Microbiology 2017;8. Available from https://doi.org/10.3389/fmicb.2017.01716.

Kimeli P, Mwacalimba K, Tiernan R, Mijten E, Miroshnychenko T, Poulsen Nautrup B. Important diseases of small ruminants in Sub-Saharan Africa: A review with a focus on current strategies for treatment and control in smallholder systems. Animals 2025;15(5):706. Available from https://doi.org/10.3390/ani15050706.

Liu C, Zhang J, Zhou W. Natural products as multi-target therapeutics for parasitic infections. Frontiers in Pharmacology 2021;12:685294. Available from https://doi.org/10.3389/fphar.2021.685294.

Luo AP, Giannangelo C, Siddiqui G, Creek DJ. Promising antimalarial hits from phenotypic screens: a review of recently-described multi-stage actives and their modes of action. Frontiers in Cellular and Infection Microbiology 2023;13. Available from https://doi.org/10.3389/fcimb.2023.1308193.

Makhoba XH, Viegas C, Mosa RA, Viegas FPD, Pooe OJ. Potential impact of the multi-target drug approach in the treatment of some complex diseases. Drug Design, Development and Therapy 2020;14:3235–49. Available from https://doi.org/10.2147/DDDT.S257494.

Mamudu CO, Tebamifor ME, Sule MO, Dokunmu TM, Ogunlana OO, Iheagwam FN. Apicoplast-resident processes: exploiting the chink in the armour of Plasmodium falciparum parasites. Advances in Pharmacological and Pharmaceutical Sciences 2024;2024. Available from https://doi.org/10.1155/2024/9940468.

Martínez I, Rivera-Santiago L, Rodríguez-Hernández KD, Galván-Hernández A, Rodríguez-Fragoso L, Díaz-Peralta L, et al. A promising amphotericin B derivative induces morphological alterations, mitochondrial damage, and oxidative stress in vitro and prevents mice from death produced by a virulent strain of Trypanosoma cruzi. Microorganisms 2024;12(6). Available from https://doi.org/10.3390/microorganisms12061064.

Meshnick SR. Artemisinin: Mechanisms of action, resistance and toxicity. International Journal for Parasitology 2002;32(13):1655–60. Available from https://doi.org/10.1016/S0020-7519(02)00194-7.

Michels PAM, Bringaud F, Herman M, Hannaert V. Metabolic functions of glycosomes in trypanosomatids. Biochimica et Biophysica Acta - Molecular Cell Research 2006;1763(12):1463–1477. Available from https://doi.org/10.1016/j.bbamcr.2006.08.019.

Motta MCM, Yoshida N, Soares MJ. The reservosome: An endocytic compartment of *Trypanosoma cruzi* that stores proteins and glycoconjugates. International Journal for Parasitology 2019;49(7):501–10. Available from https://doi.org/10.1016/j.ijpara.2019.02.002.

Munder M. Macrophage biology in parasitic infections. Frontiers in Immunology 2020;11:580728. Available from https://doi.org/10.3389/fimmu.2020.580728.

Newman DJ, Cragg GM. Natural products as sources of new drugs over the nearly four decades from 01/1981 to 09/2019. Journal of Natural Products 2020;83(3):770–803. Available from https://doi.org/10.1021/acs.jnatprod.9b01285.

Nixon GL, Pidathala C, Shone AE, Antoine T, Fisher N, O'Neill PM, et al. Targeting the mitochondrial electron transport chain of Plasmodium falciparum: New strategies towards the development of improved antimalarials for the elimination era. Future Medicinal Chemistry 2013;5(13):1573–91. Available from https://doi.org/10.4155/fmc.13.121.

Nuzzo G, Senese G, Gallo C, Albiani F, Romano L, d'Ippolito G, et al. Antitumor potential of immunomodulatory natural products. Marine Drugs 2022;20(6):386.

Painter HJ, Morrisey JM, Mather MW, Vaidya AB. Specific role of mitochondrial electron transport in blood-stage Plasmodium falciparum. Nature 2007;446(7131):88–91. Available from https://doi.org/10.1038/nature05572.

Patel A, Patel J, Patel R, Patidar V. Nanotechnology in Malaria Diagnosis. In Infectious Diseases Drug Delivery Systems. Cham: Springer International Publishing; 2023. pp. 77–99.

Pohner I, Quotadamo A, Panecka-Hofman J, Luciani R, Santucci M, Linciano P, et al. Multitarget, selective compound design yields potent inhibitors of a kinetoplastid pteridine reductase 1. Journal of Medicinal Chemistry 2022;65(13):9011–33.

Quiñones W, Acosta H, Gonçalves CS, Motta MCM, Gualdrón López M, Michels PA. Structure, properties, and function of glycosomes in Trypanosoma cruzi. Frontiers in Cellular and Infection Microbiology 2020;10:25.

Raj V, Ramasamy K, Sundar S. Plant-derived compounds as immunomodulators in parasitic diseases. Parasite Immunology 2020;42(12):e12770. Available from https://doi.org/10.1111/pim.12770.

Ralph SA, van Dooren GG, Waller RF, Crawford MJ, Fraunholz MJ, Foth BJ, et al. Tropical infectious diseases: metabolic maps and drug targets of the apicoplast. Nature Reviews. Microbiology 2004;2(3):203–16. Available from https://doi.org/10.1038/nrmicro843.

Ribbiso KA, Heller LE, Taye A, Julian E, Willems AV, Roepe PD. Artemisinin-based drugs target the plasmodium falciparum heme detoxification pathway. Antimicrobial Agents and Chemotherapy 2021;65(4). Available from https://doi.org/10.1128/AAC.02137-20.

Sargsyan T, Stepanyan L, Tsaturyan A, Palumbo R, Vicidomini C, Roviello GN. Intracellular parasitic infections caused by Plasmodium falciparum, Leishmania spp., Toxoplasma gondii, Echinococcus multilocularis, Among key pathogens: Global burden, transmission dynamics, and vaccine advances-A narrative review with contextual insights from Armenia. Vaccines 2025;13(11):1082. Available from https://doi.org/10.3390/vaccines13111082.

Sehrawat R, Rathee P, Khatkar S, Akkol E, Khayatkashani M, Nabavi SM, et al. Dihydrofolate reductase (DHFR) inhibitors: a comprehensive review. Current Medicinal Chemistry 2024;31(7):799–824. Available from https://doi.org/10.2174/0929867330666230310091510.

Shamshad H, Bakri R, Mirza AZ. Dihydrofolate reductase, thymidylate synthase, and serine hydroxy methyltransferase: successful targets against some infectious diseases. Molecular Biology Reports 2022;49(7):6659–91. Available from https://doi.org/10.1007/s11033-022-07266-8.

Shears MJ, Botté CY, McFadden GI. Fatty acid metabolism in Plasmodium falciparum: New targets for drug discovery. Trends in Parasitology 2015;31(1):30–9. Available from https://doi.org/10.1016/j.pt.2014.11.004.

Shi M, Wu Y, Yang J, Yang X, Li X, Liu Z. Artemisinin derivatives: An overview of their biological activity, mechanism of action, and pharmacological properties. European Journal of Medicinal Chemistry 2022;247:115000.

Singh K, Tripathi RP. Carbohydrate derivatives fight against malaria parasite as anti-plasmodial agents. Carbohydrate Research 2023;531:108887. Available from https://doi.org/10.1016/j.carres.2023.108887.

Smyth LA, Ratnasothy K, Tsang JYS, Boardman D, Warley A, Lechler R, et al. CD73 expression on extracellular vesicles derived from CD4+CD25+Foxp3+ T cells contributes to their regulatory function. European Journal of Immunology 2013;43(9):2430–40. Available from https://doi.org/10.1002/eji.201242909.

Stokes JM, Yang K, Swanson K, Jin W, Cubillos-Ruiz A, Donghia NM, et al. A deep learning approach to antibiotic discovery. Cell 2020;180(4):688. Available from https://doi.org/10.1016/j.cell.2020.01.021.

Sundar S, Singh A. Chemotherapeutics of visceral leishmaniasis: present and future developments. Parasitology 2018;145(4):481–9. Available from https://doi.org/10.1017/S0031182017002116.

Tang Girdwood SC, Nenortas E, Shapiro TA. Targeting the gyrase of Plasmodium falciparum with topoisomerase poisons. Biochemical Pharmacology 2015;95(4):227–37. Available from https://doi.org/10.1016/j.bcp.2015.03.018.

Tenorio JC. Drug resistance in parasites: A review of mechanisms, drivers, and mitigation strategies. Microbes and Infectious Diseases 2025;6(3):6152–60.

Thomas JA, Baker N, Hutchinson S, Dominicus C, Trenaman A, Glover L, et al. Insights into antitrypanosomal drug mode-of-action from cytology-based profiling. PLoS Neglected Tropical Diseases 2018;12(11):e0006980. Available from https://doi.org/10.1371/journal.pntd.0006980.

Tu Y. Artemisinin—a gift from traditional Chinese medicine to the world (nobel lecture). Angewandte Chemie - International Edition 2016;55(35):10210–26. Available from https://doi.org/10.1002/anie.201601967.

van Dooren GG, Striepen B. The apicoplast: biogenesis, maintenance, and functions in apicomplexan parasites. Annual Review of Microbiology 2013;67:211–33. Available from https://doi.org/10.1146/annurev-micro-092412-155620.

van Dooren GG, Su V, D'Ombrain MC, McFadden GI. Development of the endoplasmic reticulum, mitochondrion and apicoplast during the *Plasmodium falciparum* life cycle. International Journal for Parasitology 2009;40(4):427–38. Available from https://doi.org/10.1016/j.ijpara.2009.10.012.

Vaidya AB, Mather MW. Mitochondrial evolution and functions in malaria parasites. Annual Review of Microbiology 2009;63:249–67. Available from https://doi.org/10.1146/annurev.micro.091208.073424.

Vannier E, Gewurz BE, Krause PJ. Human babesiosis. Infectious Disease Clinics of North America 2008;22(3):469–88. Available from https://doi.org/10.1016/j.idc.2008.03.010.

Verhoef JM, Meissner M, Kooij TW. Organelle dynamics in apicomplexan parasites. MBio 2021;12(4):10–1128.

Vickers TJ, Beverley SM. Folate metabolic pathways in Leishmania. Essays in Biochemistry 2011;51(1):63–80. Available from https://doi.org/10.1042/BSE0510063.

Wang X, Ahmad S, Zhang Z, Côté J, Cai G. Architecture of the *Saccharomyces cerevisiae* NuA4/TIP60 complex. Nature Communications 2018;9(1):1147. Available from https://doi.org/10.1038/s41467-018-03504-5.

Wang X, Li Y, Chen Y. AI-based screening of natural products for antitrypanosomal activity. Computational Biology and Chemistry 2023;104:107845. Available from https://doi.org/10.1016/j.compbiolchem.2023.107845.

Winkler DA. Use of artificial intelligence and machine learning for discovery of drugs for neglected tropical diseases. Frontiers in Chemistry 2021;9:614073.

Wiser MF. The digestive vacuole of the malaria parasite: a specialized lysosome. Pathogens 2024;13(3):182.

World Health Organization. (2015). Guidelines for the treatment of malaria (3rd ed.). World Health Organization.

World Health Organization. (2024). World malaria report 2024. WHO Press.

Yin R, Wang T, Dai H, Han J, Sun J, Liu N, et al. Immunogenic molecules associated with gut bacterial cell walls: chemical structures, immune-modulating functions, and mechanisms. Protein & cell 2023;14(10):776–85. Available from https://doi.org/10.1093/procel/pwad016.

Zhang H, Liu X, Zhang L. Multi-target natural compounds against malaria and other parasitic diseases. Phytotherapy Research 2022;36(10):4260–75. Available from https://doi.org/10.1002/ptr.7630.

Zhang P, Gong J, Jiang Y, Long Y, Lei W, Gao X, et al. Application of silver nanoparticles in parasite treatment. Pharmaceutics 2023;15(7):1783. Available from https://doi.org/10.3390/pharmaceutics15071783.

Zuzarte-Luís V, Mota MM. Parasite sensing of host nutrients and environmental cues. Cell Host and Microbe 2018;23(6):749–58. Available from https://doi.org/10.1016/j.chom.2018.05.018.

CHAPTER 5

Medicinal and analogue chemistry of natural products

Simeon Santourlidis[1], Youssef A. El-Sayed[2], Khalid Awad Elkareem Ahmed[3], Rania Ali El-Hadi Mohamed[4], and Mohamed Dkhil[5]

[1]Epigenetics Laboratory for Human Health and Longevity, Institute of Transplantation Diagnostics and Cell Therapeutics, Medical Faculty, Heinrich Heine University Duesseldorf, Duesseldorf, Germany,
[2]Genetic Engineering and Biotechnology Program, Faculty of Science, Helwan National University, Helwan, Egypt,
[3]Tropical Medicine Research Institute, National Centre for Research, Ministry of Science & Technology, Khartoum, Sudan,
[4]Department of Biology, Faculty of Science, Princess Nourah bint Abdulrahman University, Riyadh, Saudi Arabia,
[5]Department of Zoology and Entomology, Faculty of Science, Capital University, Cairo, Egypt

5.1 Introduction

5.1.1 Blood parasites and their public health significance

Blood parasites are a broad category of helminthic and protozoan organisms that infiltrate and proliferate in the bloodstream or related tissues of vertebrate hosts, frequently resulting in serious morbidity and death in both humans and animals. *Plasmodium* spp. (malaria), *Trypanosoma* spp. (African sleeping sickness and Chagas disease), *Leishmania* spp. (visceral and cutaneous leishmaniasis), and *Schistosoma* spp. (schistosomiasis) are some of the most important cases (Hotez et al., 2015). These infections pose a serious threat to public health, especially in tropical and subtropical areas where endemic circulation is encouraged by vector transmission, inadequate sanitation, and a lack of health care facilities (World Health Organization (WHO), 2023).

Approximately 249 million clinical cases and over 600,000 fatalities are caused by malaria alone each year, with pregnant women and children under five years old being the most vulnerable (World Health Organization (WHO), 2023). Similar to this, leishmaniasis is still endemic in more than 98 countries, whereas trypanosomatid illnesses, including African trypanosomiasis and Chagas disease, together afflict over 20 million people globally (Burza et al., 2018). Because they cause chronic anemia, hepatosplenic illness, and impaired cognitive development, helminthic blood parasites such as *Schistosoma mansoni*, *S. haematobium*, and *S. japonicum* continue to have a substantial socioeconomic impact (Colley et al., 2014).

Beyond their direct consequences on health, blood parasite infections also contribute to poverty cycles by lowering educational attainment, raising health care expenditures, and decreasing productivity in endemic areas (King, 2010). The crisis is made worse by resistance to current chemotherapeutics, such as Artemisinin resistance in *Plasmodium falciparum* and growing tolerance to benznidazole in Trypanosoma cruzi. This highlights

Innovative Strategies Against Blood Parasites
DOI: https://doi.org/10.1016/B978-0-443-48509-1.00002-1

the critical need for new antiparasitic agents made from natural products (Chatelain and Ioset, 2011; Ashley et al., 2014).

Therefore, a foundation for logical medication design and optimization of natural product-based therapies is provided by knowledge of the biology, epidemiology, and molecular adaptability of blood parasites. A critical multidisciplinary strategy to combat growing resistance and enhance global health outcomes is the merging of medicinal chemistry, semisynthetic analogue creation, and gene-level analysis.

5.1.2 Nature-derived antiparasitic agents

The development of antiparasitic medicines has traditionally relied heavily on natural compounds obtained from microorganisms, plants, and marine organisms. They frequently have good safety profiles and can target blood parasites selectively according to their structural diversity and innate biological activity (Shang et al., 2025). Classic examples are artemisinin, a sesquiterpene lactone from Artemisia annua that is still used as a first-line treatment for *Plasmodium falciparum*, and quinine, an alkaloid from Cinchona bark that transformed the treatment of malaria (Ashley et al., 2014; Haynes, 2001).

Natural product research continues to produce new scaffolds with distinct modes of action, such as the disruption of kinetoplastid mitochondrial activity or the inhibition of heme detoxification in malaria parasites (Borst and Ouellette, 1995). Peptides and polyketides, which are produced from marine sources and frequently offer chemical templates not found in terrestrial sources, have also shown promise as leads against trypanosomatids and schistosomes (Cheng et al., 2025). In addition to their direct antiparasitic activities, natural compounds provide flexible chemical frameworks that can be modified semisynthetically to optimize pharmacokinetic characteristics, decrease toxicity, and improve efficacy (Shang et al., 2025). Their dual function as a chemical scaffolds and bioactive agents highlights their ongoing significance in the search for and creation of cutting-edge treatments for blood parasites.

5.1.3 The contribution of analogue-based medicinal chemistry to drug discovery

The conversion of naturally occurring bioactive chemicals into therapeutically useful antiparasitic medications is largely dependent on medicinal chemistry. Although natural compounds offer biologically active scaffolds, their direct use is sometimes constrained by low solubility, chemical instability, off-target toxicity, or inferior pharmacokinetic characteristics (Newman and Cragg, 2020). Medicinal chemists improve the effectiveness, selectivity, and bioavailability of these natural scaffolds through methodical structural modification, such as functional group alteration, hybridization, and semisynthesis (Ding and Xue, 2024).

The effective use of medicinal chemistry to overcome the drawbacks of parent natural compounds is demonstrated by semisynthetic analogs, such as synthetic quinoline analogs or dihydroartemisinin derivatives (artesunate, artemether) (Ashley et al., 2014; Haynes, 2001). By focusing on parasite-specific metabolic pathways or modifying drug-target interactions at the molecular level, these alterations not only enhance pharmacological performance but also enable the avoidance of developing drug resistance.

Additionally, a logical framework for lead optimization is provided by the combination of computational modeling, gene-level analysis, and medicinal chemistry. The development of analogs with improved potency, decreased toxicity, and optimized selectivity profiles is guided by structure-activity relationship (SAR) studies, which are informed by both chemical and genetic insights (Shang et al., 2025). In order to bridge the gap between the discovery of natural products and the creation of next-generation treatments for blood parasite illnesses, medicinal and analogue chemistry is essential (Burrows et al., 2013).

By combining knowledge from chemical modification, semisynthetic analogue production, and gene-level analysis, this chapter seeks to give a thorough overview of the medicinal and analogue chemistry of natural compounds employed against blood parasites. In order to overcome pharmacokinetic constraints, improve selectivity, and combat the emergence of drug resistance in important blood parasites such as *Plasmodium, Trypanosoma, Leishmania, and Schistosoma* species, natural scaffolds are optimized (Shang et al., 2025; Newman and Cragg, 2020).

The structure-activity relationship (SAR) concept for logically designing analogs with enhanced potency and safety profiles is extensively explored in this chapter. It also examines how genetic and molecular methods can be used to validate therapeutic targets, comprehend mechanisms of action, and direct medicinal chemistry approaches. This chapter offers a roadmap for the creation of next-generation natural product-based antiparasitic medicines by integrating chemical, biological, and computational methods.

In general, the scope covers everything from traditional natural product discovery to contemporary methods in gene-guided drug development, SAR-driven design, and semisynthetic optimization, showcasing case studies where these interdisciplinary approaches have produced clinically significant results.

5.1.4 Chemical classes of natural products with activity against blood parasites

The antiparasitic potential of natural compounds is directly related to their amazing chemical diversity. Alkaloids, terpenoids, flavonoids, sterols, and peptides are the main families of bioactive substances that combat blood parasites, and each has unique chemical structures and modes of action (Nweze et al., 2021).

Quinine from *Cinchona* bark and similar synthetic counterparts are examples of alkaloids that mainly work against *Plasmodium* by obstructing heme detoxification routes in the parasite's digestive vacuole (Druilhe et al., 1988). Terpenoids, such as artemisinin and its derivatives, produce reactive oxygen species that quickly eradicate *Plasmodium falciparum* by targeting several cellular components (Ashley et al., 2014).

By altering redox balance and enzymatic activity, flavonoids and polyphenolic chemicals, which are extensively found in medicinal plants, have inhibitory effects on helminthic and protozoan parasites (Cushnie and Lamb, 2005). While peptides, especially those derived from marine organisms, exert selective cytotoxicity by permeabilizing parasite membranes or targeting intracellular organelles, sterols and sterol-like compounds disrupt membrane integrity in kinetoplastid parasites, such as *Trypanosoma* spp. and *Leishmania* spp. (Cheng et al., 2025).

In addition to offering several pharmacophores for direct antiparasitic action, this chemical diversity acts as a scaffold for semisynthetic modification, allowing the creation of analogs with enhanced pharmacokinetic profiles, potency, and selectivity (Shang et al., 2025).

5.1.5 Examples of bioactive compounds and their natural sources

Natural products continue to be a significant source of bioactive substances that fight blood parasites and provide a variety of chemical scaffolds for the development of new drugs. Many other natural chemicals have shown considerable antiparasitic promise, although traditional compounds such as quinine from Cinchona bark and artemisinin from Artemisia annua laid the groundwork for contemporary antimalarial medicine (Druilhe et al., 1988; Ashley et al., 2014).

By intercalating into parasite DNA and preventing replication, alkaloids other than quinine, including cryptolepine from *Cryptolepis sanguinolenta*, demonstrate strong antimalarial and antitrypanosomal efficacy (Mensah et al., 2019). By interfering with mitochondrial activity, isoquinoline alkaloids, such as berberine from *Berberis* species, have demonstrated inhibitory effects on *Trypanosoma* spp. and *Leishmania* spp. (De Sarkar et al., 2019).

Azadirachta indica (neem) and *Andrographis paniculata* contain terpenoids and limonoids that act on a variety of parasitic targets, hindering the growth and survival of helminthic and protozoan parasites (Wylie and Merrell, 2022). *Trypanosoma* and *Schistosoma* species' cell membranes or organelles are preferentially disrupted by marine-derived peptides and polyketides, such as didemnin B from tunicates, which are promising leads for therapeutic development (Cheng et al., 2025).

Furthermore, luteolin and epigallocatechin gallate from plant and tea extracts are examples of flavonoids and polyphenols that block oxidative pathways and parasitic enzymes, lowering parasite viability (Cushnie and Lamb, 2005; Jomova et al., 2025).

When taken as a whole, these instances demonstrate the chemical variety of natural compounds, which offer scaffolding for semisynthetic optimization in addition to direct medicinal effects.

5.1.6 Common molecular features influencing antiparasitic activity

A wide variety of antiparasitic compounds can be found in natural products and their derivatives. Medicinal chemists can optimize potency, selectivity, and pharmacokinetic characteristics by using specific molecular properties that are common to highly active drugs despite their chemical variety (Shang et al., 2025; Marchant et al., 2018). Designing semisynthetic analogs and increasing scaffold efficiency require an understanding of these characteristics.

Nitrogen-containing heterocycles are common molecular motifs found in a variety of alkaloids, including quinolines, benzylisoquinolines, and aporphines. These structures allow for binding to receptors, nucleic acids, or parasite enzymes. For instance, through DNA intercalation and replication process inhibition, cryptolepine and other isoquinoline derivatives have antitrypanosomal and antimalarial activity (Marchant et al., 2018). Bioactivity and parasite selectivity are strongly influenced by substitution patterns on these heterocycles.

The existence of aromatic scaffolds and π-conjugated systems, which improve interactions with protein targets and nucleic acids, is another recurrent characteristic. In trypanosomatids and *Plasmodium* species, polyphenols, flavonoids, and lignans use prolonged conjugation to interfere with redox homeostasis, inhibit enzymes, and alter mitochondrial function (Soto-Sánchez, 2022). These structures' planarity and aromaticity influence biological specialization and binding affinity.

The importance of lipophilic moieties is equal. Terpenoids, sterols, and other hydrophobic chains increase the permeability of membranes, making it easier for intracellular parasite targets to enter. These characteristics make it possible for substances to build up in lipid-rich organelles, compromise the integrity of membranes, and interfere with vital metabolic processes (Orosco et al., 2024). Optimizing lipophilicity during semisynthetic modification frequently improves bioavailability and efficacy.

Another important characteristic is the presence of electrophilic centers and redox-active functional groups, including hydroxyquinones, endoperoxides, and imidazole moieties. Rapid cytotoxic effects can result from these groups' ability to produce reactive species or alkylate parasite biomolecules (Ashley et al., 2014). For example, artemisinin derivatives damage many parasite targets in *Plasmodium falciparum* by using their endoperoxide bridge to generate reactive oxygen species.

Heterocycles, conjugated aromatic systems, lipophilic chains, and electrophilic/redox-active groups are common molecular characteristics that together offer a logical framework for drug development. In order to target *Plasmodium* spp., *Trypanosoma* spp., *Leishmania* spp., and *Schistosoma* spp., they direct the design of semisynthetic analogs, optimize pharmacological properties, and identify scaffolds (Shang et al., 2025; Marchant et al., 2018; Soto-Sánchez, 2022). Transforming natural product variety into clinically successful antiparasitic treatments requires an understanding of these characteristics.

5.1.7 Antiparasitic activities across *Plasmodium* spp., *Trypanosoma* spp., *Leishmania* spp., and *Schistosoma spp.*

When it comes to major blood and tissue parasites, natural products exhibit different and occasionally overlapping modes of action that reflect both their structural diversity and the biochemical distinctiveness of each parasite. For example, redox-active substances such as artemisinin and quinine derivatives, which work by producing reactive oxygen species and interfering with heme detoxification pathways, are very harmful to *Plasmodium* spp. (Tu, 2011; Vangapandu et al., 2007).

On the other hand, *Trypanosoma* species are extremely susceptible to substances that disrupt trypanothione metabolism and mitochondrial respiration, which are vital processes for preserving redox equilibrium. Sesquiterpene lactones and naphthoquinones, which cause oxidative stress and hinder ATP generation, are prime examples of this process (Santos et al., 2023; González-Montero et al., 2024).

By suppressing topoisomerase, collapsing mitochondrial potential, and modifying macrophage immunological functions, flavonoids and alkaloids such as quercetin, berberine, and betulinic acid have significant antileishmanial effects (Marquis et al., 2003; Kar et al., 2022). Similar to this, *Schistosoma* species react aggressively to substances like curcumin, saponins, and analogs of Praziquantel that disrupt calcium homeostasis and tegument integrity, causing the worms to become paralyzed and eventually die (Marchant et al., 2018; Rashed et al., 2021).

A comparative summary of these mechanisms and their representative natural compounds is shown in Table 5.1 (Tu, 2011; Vangapandu et al., 2007; Santos et al., 2023; Kar et al., 2022; Marchant et al., 2018). This table illustrates how each compound class's chemical makeup determines both its mode of action and target location across many parasite taxa, exposing convergent vulnerabilities that may inform future analog design.

5.2 Strategies for optimization of natural leads

5.2.1 Medicinal chemistry principles in lead modification

The basis for converting natural compounds into optimized drug leads with better pharmacological characteristics is provided by medicinal chemistry. Natural scaffolds' intrinsic complexity provides a wealth of bioactivity, but in order to improve potency,

Table 5.1 comparative activities of natural products (NPs) against major blood parasites.

Parasite	Major active NPs	Mechanism of action	Biological effect
Pla smodium spp.	Artemisinin, quinine	Generates ROS; interferes with heme detoxification	Rapid parasiticidal effect; inhibition of hemoglobin digestion
Trypanosoma spp.	Naphthoquinones, sesquiterpene lactones	Disrupts mitochondrial function; inhibits trypanothione metabolism	Oxidative stress and parasite death
Leishmania spp.	Quercetin, berberine, betulinic acid	Inhibits topoisomerase; induces mitochondrial depolarization; modulates macrophage response	Apoptosis-like death; immune modulation
Schistosoma spp.	Curcumin, saponins, praziquantel analogs	Disrupts tegument; affects calcium channels	Paralysis; tegument damage; immune clearance

Marchant, J.S., Harding, W.W., & Chan, J.D. (2018). Structure-activity profiling of alkaloid natural product pharmacophores against a Schistosoma serotonin receptor. International Journal for Parasitology: Drugs and Drug Resistance, 8(3), 550–558. https://doi.org/10.1016/j.ijpddr.2018.09.001.

selectivity, and pharmacokinetic behavior, these compounds frequently need structural modification (Harvey et al., 2015). Functional group optimization, isosteric substitution, and scaffold hopping are important lead modification techniques that attempt to increase target affinity while reducing toxicity (Koehn and Carter, 2005).

A basic principle is to identify the pharmacophore—the essential structural elements important for biological activity and then change peripheral substituents to fine-tune electronic and steric properties (Patrick, 2017). For example, converting natural artemisinin into semisynthetic derivatives such as artesunate and artemether increased solubility and bioavailability while maintaining significant antimalarial activity (Tu, 2011). Similarly, alkaloid frameworks such as quinine have acted as templates for analogs with improved antiplasmodial selectivity and lower neurotoxicity (Olliaro and Wells, 2009).

Medicinal chemists also use structure-activity relationship (SAR) and quantitative structure-activity relationship (QSAR) analyses to link certain structural properties to biological outcomes, allowing for the rational design of analogs with predictable efficacy (Houghton et al., 2007). Computational methods such as molecular docking and pharmacophore modeling are increasingly being used in the optimization process, allowing for more efficient lead refining while reducing experimental burden (Kitchen et al., 2004).

Finally, applying these medicinal chemistry concepts to natural materials ensures a balance between biological potency and drug-like characteristics acceptable for clinical usage, transforming intriguing natural scaffolds into feasible therapeutic options.

5.2.2 Semisynthesis and derivatization for enhanced potency and selectivity

Semisynthesis is critical in converting natural products into optimal therapeutic candidates because it allows specific structural alterations that would be difficult or impossible to obtain through whole synthesis. This method retains the biologically validated core scaffold while modifying individual functional groups to improve potency, selectivity, pharmacokinetics, or safety (Newman and Cragg, 2020). Because many natural compounds have significant structural complexity and many stereocenters, semisynthesis is an effective technique to modify their structures while preserving crucial pharmacophoric features (Harvey et al., 2015).

A typical example is the semisynthetic production of Artemisinin derivatives. Although artemisinin has powerful antimalarial activity, its poor solubility and restricted oral bioavailability led to the semisynthetic production of artemether, artesunate, and dihydroartemisinin. These compounds attain higher lipid or water solubility, faster onset of action, and superior therapeutic profiles while retaining the critical endoperoxide bridge crucial for antiplasmodial activity (Tu, 2011).

Similarly, quassinoids, naphthoquinones, and indole alkaloids have been rationally derivatized to increase selectivity against *Trypanosoma* spp. and *Leishmania* spp. (Menna-Barreto et al., 2009) found that converting lapachol to β-lapachone increased its redox cycling characteristics and cytotoxicity against trypanosomatids. In the instance of *Leishmania* spp., derivatization of betulinic acid at the C-28 carboxyl group produced amide and ester analogs with significantly higher activity and lower host-cell toxicity (Cunha et al., 2021).

Semisynthesis also allows for the fine control of physicochemical features such as lipophilicity and metabolic stability, both of which have a direct impact on distribution into parasite-infected tissues. Introducing halogen atoms, forming ether or carbonate linkages, and changing glycosidic patterns are common derivatization techniques for modulating membrane permeability and enzymatic susceptibility (Majhi and Das, 2021). These approaches work together to optimize natural product leads in ways that balance efficacy and desirable drug-like characteristics.

5.2.3 Physicochemical optimization

Optimizing physicochemical characteristics is a critical step in moving marine natural materials from potential hits to effective antiparasitic medication candidates. Many marine-derived compounds have limited aqueous solubility, owing to their hard or very hydrophobic scaffolds. Introducing ionizable groups or lowering excess hydrophobicity can greatly improve solubility and absorption after oral administration (Zaid et al., 2010).

Lipophilicity must also be carefully controlled. While moderate lipophilicity increases passive membrane permeability and allows for access into intracellular parasites, too lipophilic compounds exhibit high nonspecific protein binding and quick metabolic clearance. Medicinal chemists frequently modify logP/logD values by introducing heteroatoms or lowering bulky hydrophobic segments (Leeson and Springthorpe, 2007; Lipinski and Hopkins, 2004).

Chemical and metabolic instability represent an additional significant challenge. Marine natural products usually contain reactive or labile functional groups, that breakdown under physiological conditions. Bioisosteric replacement, steric shielding of weak bonds, and increasing structural rigidity through restricted conformations are all ways for improving stability (Kerns and Li, 2008; Gleeson, 2008).

These physicochemical optimizations improve pharmacokinetic behavior by increasing bioavailability, prolonging half-life, and lowering toxicity, increasing the likelihood that complex marine-derived molecules will successfully progress through the drug development pipeline (Zaid et al., 2010).

5.2.4 Hybrid & conjugated molecules in drug design

By merging two bioactive pharmacophores into a single chemical entity, hybrid molecule creation has become a successful method for increasing the antiparasitic activity of natural medicinal products. This strategy seeks to limit resistance development, enhance selectivity, and produce dual or synergistic modes of action. Because many blood parasite species have complicated life cycles and are resistant to single-target treatments, hybridization is especially beneficial for these parasites (Muregi et al., 2011).

Conjugating a natural product scaffold with a recognized antiparasitic pharmacophore is a popular tactic. For instance, artemisinin–quinoline combinations have demonstrated significantly increased effectiveness against *Plasmodium falciparum*, taking use of both hemozoin interference and endoperoxide-mediated oxidative damage pathways (Wang et al., 2015). Similarly, because the redox-active ferrocene core improves intracellular accumulation within parasite-infected erythrocytes, ferroquine–-natural product hybrids have increased antimalarial action (Biot et al., 2011).

Additionally, molecular conjugation can enhance pharmacokinetic characteristics by reducing metabolic inactivation, improving membrane permeability, and optimizing distribution. For example, by taking advantage of parasite-specific transporter uptake processes, peptide–natural product conjugates have been designed to improve selectivity for *Leishmania* (Robledo et al., 2023).

Additionally, hybrid design provides a platform to address multidrug resistance. The molecule can overcome single-pathway alterations and lessen the possibility of resistance formation by combining two pathways into a single framework (Muregi et al., 2011). Because of this, hybrid molecules represent a viable avenue for natural product leads originating from plants and marine sources that target leishmaniasis, schistosomiasis, trypanosomiasis, and malaria.

5.2.5 Prodrug design and formulation advances

A potent tactic to get around the inherent drawbacks of many natural medications used to combat blood parasites is prodrug creation. Prodrug conversion can deliberately conceal undesirable functional groups to improve pharmacokinetic performance, as natural scaffolds frequently have poor solubility, limited membrane permeability, quick metabolism, or systemic toxicity (Testa, 2009).

The main goal of prodrug methods for marine- and plant-derived antiparasitic medicines has been to increase oral bioavailability. One of the most popular chemical techniques is esterification. For instance, converting hydroxyl-rich natural products into ester prodrugs improves lipophilicity and promotes passive intestinal absorption, which is followed by systemic circulation enzymatic activation (Rautio et al., 2008). This technique has been used to enhance the delivery of phenolic compounds with intrinsic antimalarial activity and sesquiterpene lactones.

Improving target-site delivery is another important purpose. Improved water solubility in phosphate prodrugs of weakly soluble natural compounds enables greater and more consistent systemic exposure. This idea is comparable to the successful creation of fosmidomycin analogs, where the phosphate moiety significantly boosted solubility and enhanced antimalarial efficacy (Fernandes et al., 2015).

Another important factor is formulation science. Lipid carrier systems and encapsulation based on nanoparticles can prolong circulation time, prevent premature degradation of structurally delicate natural products, and encourage targeted accumulation in tissues infested with parasites. In order to improve the transport of hydrophobic antileishmanial and antimalarial natural chemicals, lipid nanoparticles and polymeric carriers have demonstrated great promise (Ghasemiyeh and Mohammadi-Samani, 2018).

2.6 By facilitating better absorption, distribution, metabolic stability, and controlled activation at the site of infection, prodrug strategies combined with formulation innovations greatly increase the therapeutic potential of natural products and ultimately support their development into clinically viable antiparasitic candidates (Rautio et al., 2008; Ghasemiyeh and Mohammadi-Samani, 2018).

5.2.6 Synthetic biology and metabolic engineering approaches

The development of metabolic engineering and synthetic biology has made it possible to produce natural molecules with antiblood parasite properties in a sustainable manner. Because of the exceptionally low natural yields of many antiparasitic chemicals obtained from plants and marine life, chemical extraction is challenging and environmentally unsustainable. A scalable substitute that permits structural diversification through pathway engineering is to reconstruct their biosynthetic pathways in microbial hosts such as *Saccharomyces cerevisiae* or *Escherichia coli* (Nielsen and Keasling, 2016).

The microbial synthesis of artemisinin precursors, which was accomplished by introducing the Artemisia annua biosynthetic genes into modified yeast, is a significant achievement in the field of research. According to (Ro et al., 2006; Paddon et al., 2013), this platform made it possible to synthesize artemisinic acid at a high yield, making artemisinin-based antimalarials more dependable and affordable. Alkaloids, polyketides, and triterpenoids with antileishmanial or antimalarial properties have all been treated using similar tactics.

Additionally, pathway remodeling to produce semisynthetic counterparts is made possible by metabolic engineering. Researchers can create novel analogs with enhanced potency or pharmacokinetic characteristics by adjusting enzyme selectivity, changing cofactor supply, or introducing mutant tailoring enzymes—something that is frequently difficult with standard synthetic chemistry (Keasling, 2008). Using this method, improved sesquiterpene and polyketide compounds that are effective against *Leishmania* and *Plasmodium* have been produced.

Furthermore, previously inaccessible natural product scaffolds with possible anti-parasitic efficacy can be revealed through the heterologous expression of cryptic biosynthetic gene clusters made possible by synthetic biology. Promoter engineering or global regulator manipulation can activate silent clusters seen in many marine creatures and symbiotic microorganisms (Ziemert et al., 2016).

The discovery of next-generation treatments for parasitic diseases can be accelerated by combining synthetic biology and metabolic engineering, which provide a potent platform for enhancing accessibility, structural diversity, and the drug-like optimization of leads derived from natural products (Keasling, 2008).

5.3 Structure-activity relationship (SAR) analysis

Medicinal chemists can logically optimize natural product leads against blood parasites by using structure-activity relationship (SAR) analysis, which examines how particular structural characteristics inside a molecule affect its biological activity. Because many natural compounds have complex scaffolds where minor changes can significantly alter potency, selectivity, metabolic stability, and toxicity, SAR is crucial in the search for antiparasitic drugs (Lemmer & Soloviev, 2013).

Pharmacophores are the basic structural components needed for activity, and SAR analysis helps identify them and separate them from regions that can be changed. When optimizing natural products with rigid or polycyclic frameworks, such as terpenoids or marine polyketides, this distinction is essential (Huggins et al., 2012).

SAR enables more targeted and effective lead optimization for parasitic diseases like leishmaniasis, trypanosomiasis, and malaria by revealing how structural motifs interact with particular biological targets, such as heme, topoisomerases, redox enzymes, or membrane components (Müller and Hemphill, 2016). By ensuring that potency gains are in line with acceptable physicochemical and pharmacokinetic profiles, SAR-driven iteration also reduces attrition.

Finally, SAR is essential for converting natural compounds into therapies that are clinically useful because it provides the analytical framework that links structure to molecular mechanism and antiparasitic efficacy (Lemmer & Soloviev, 2013; Huggins et al., 2012).

To comprehend how molecular changes impact antiparasitic potency, structure-activity relationship (SAR) investigations use both computational and experimental methods. *In vitro* tests against *Plasmodium*, *Leishmania*, or *Trypanosoma* species are used to create and assess natural product analogs experimentally. This allows for the direct observation of how structural alterations affect efficacy, cytotoxicity, and selectivity (Van den Kerkhof et al., 2020). Computational modeling is based on these empirical data.

By modeling activity trends before synthesis, computational techniques greatly speed up SAR interpretation. Molecular characteristics including hydrophobicity, steric bulk, and electronic properties, are correlated with biological activity through quantitative structure-activity relationship (QSAR) models. For natural product scaffolds with complicated chemistry, QSAR models are frequently used to prioritize analogue design (Cherkasov et al., 2014).

By modeling the interaction between the drug and its biological target, such as heme, cysteine proteases, topoisomerases, or redox enzymes, molecular docking enhances QSAR. Docking offers information about important intermolecular interactions, binding poses, and structural elements that improve affinity (Pagadala et al., 2017). This is particularly useful for antiparasitic targets that have distinct active areas.

More sophisticated methods such as comparative Molecular similarity indices analysis (CoMSIA) and comparative molecular field analysis (CoMFA) provide 3D contour maps that highlight areas where steric or electrostatic changes are expected to boost activity. Terpenoids, quinoline derivatives, and marine polyketides that are effective against blood parasites have all been successfully treated with these 3D-QSAR techniques (Nantasenamat et al., 2009).

Combining computational QSAR, docking, and CoMFA techniques with experimental bioassays offers a comprehensive approach to comprehending SAR trends, minimizing synthetic workload, and directing logical optimization of natural antiparasitic leads (Cherkasov et al., 2014).

5.3.1 Key SAR findings in major compound classes

5.3.1.1 Artemisinin and derivatives

The primary source of artemisinin's antimalarial action is its 1,2,4-trioxane endoperoxide bridge, which is cleaved by iron in *Plasmodium*-infected erythrocytes to produce cytotoxic radicals that alkylate parasite membranes and proteins (Meshnick et al., 1991). Its non-negotiable pharmacophoric significance in pharmacological action is demonstrated by structure–activity experiments, which repeatedly reveal that disrupting, decreasing, or substituting this peroxide leads in total loss of activity (O'Neill et al., 2010).

3.1.2. Clinically relevant semisynthetic derivatives like dihydroartemisinin, artemether, and artesunate have been made possible by peripheral changes, especially at the C-10 position. These alterations improve solubility, metabolic stability, and bioavailability while keeping the peroxide-dependent process (Klayman, 1985; Sun et al., 2025). In order to maximize pharmacokinetic behavior, SAR data thus highlight preserving the peroxide while adjusting lipophilicity and polarity.

5.3.1.2 Quinine and quinolone analogs

The planar quinoline aromatic system, which binds firmly to ferriprotoporphyrin IX and inhibits hemozoin synthesis in the parasite digesting vacuole, is the distinguishing SAR component of quinoline antimalarials (Foley and Tilley, 1997). Chloroquine's increased effectiveness over previous analogs can be explained by substituents at the 7-position, particularly electron-withdrawing groups such as chlorine, which significantly increase heme affinity and accumulation within the acidic vacuole (Ridley, 2002).

The basic side chain is also important; in order to facilitate effective proton trapping within the vacuole, it must have the ideal length and pKa. Vacuolar accumulation and activity are decreased by changing the chain length or decreasing its basicity (Wellems and Plowe, 2001). As an example of how SAR-guided alteration can restore therapeutic efficacy, more recent analogs such as amodiaquine and piperaquine have structural characteristics that circumvent PfCRT-mediated resistance (Cooper et al., 2005).

5.3.1.3 Alkaloids and terpenoid scaffolds

Strong interactions with parasite enzymes and nucleic acids are made possible by the heterocyclic nitrogen atoms and rigid aromatic or bicyclic frameworks found in many alkaloids (Gohil et al., 2012). Indole alkaloids maintain the indole ring as a crucial pharmacophore; N-alkylation can enhance absorption but occasionally reduce receptor binding, while substituents at C-3 modify potency by changing electron density and steric accessibility (Gul and Hamann, 2005).

Terpenoid scaffolds, particularly sesquiterpenes and triterpenoids, display SAR interactions controlled by stereochemistry and oxygenation patterns. By facilitating hydrogen bonding or boosting electrophilicity, important locations such as the C-3 hydroxyl and epoxides increase potency (Rocha et al., 2005). For maximum bioactivity, polarity and lipophilicity must be balanced, as excessive oxygenation may decrease permeability (del Carmen Recio et al., 1995).

5.3.1.4 Marine natural products

Marine natural products have distinctive SAR characteristics because of polyether frameworks, halogenation, and macrocyclic stiffness. The presence of halogen atoms (Br, Cl, and I) in metabolites obtained from sponges increases their lipophilicity and strengthens their interactions with parasite ion channels and enzymes; removal of these halogens usually results in decreased activity (Carroll et al., 2019). For macrocyclic marine chemicals to attach to biological targets effectively, severe conformational rigidity is frequently necessary.

The ability of polyether metabolites, such as ionophoric marine polyketides, to disturb ionic homeostasis in parasites is determined by their SAR patterns, which are characterized by the orientation and spacing of ether links (Blunt et al., 2018). Potency is significantly influenced by hydroxylation patterns and oxidation states; some hydroxyl configurations improve solubility and protein binding, whereas excessive oxygenation lowers membrane permeability (Jiang et al., 2025).

5.3.2 Linking molecular structure to target engagement and potency

A key component of antiparasitic medicinal chemistry is the conversion of chemical structure into biological effect: certain functional groups and three-dimensional configurations dictate whether a molecule will interact with a particular parasitic biomolecule with enough affinity and selectivity to yield a therapeutic effect. For instance, iron-dependent radical production that alkylates parasite proteins is directly made possible by the endoperoxide motif in artemisinin. This mechanism connects a distinct chemical functionality to strong parasiticidal potency (Meshnick et al., 1991); (O'Neill et al., 2010). As an illustration of how aromaticity and planarity map onto a different biological target and outcome, planar heteroaromatic systems such as quinolines achieve potency through strong π–π stacking with ferriprotoporphyrin IX in the food vacuole rather than covalent reactivity (Foley and Tilley, 1997).

Physicochemical characteristics such as lipophilicity and basicity influence intracellular localization and, thus, the effective concentration at the target site in addition to individual pharmacophores. Vacuolar trapping of quinoline derivatives is made possible by protonatable side chains with an ideal pKa, which raises local drug levels and strengthens heme binding-driven potency; on the other hand, vacuolar accumulation and efficacy are decreased by incorrect pKa or excessive polarity (Wellems and Plowe, 2001). Terpenoids and alkaloids must also have balanced lipophilicity in order to penetrate membranes; adequate hydrophobicity facilitates cellular uptake and access to mitochondrial or membrane targets, but excessive lipophilicity increases nonspecific binding and toxicity, demonstrating the correlation between bulk physicochemical parameters and both potency and safety (Young, 2014; Huggins et al., 2012).

When the biological target has a defined three-dimensional pocket, stereochemistry and structural rigidity often influence target fit and, consequently, potency. Macrocyclic marine metabolites and polycyclic terpenoids exemplify this principle: their locked geometries position key functional groups precisely for interaction with enzyme active sites or ion channels, and even small changes in ring size or chiral configuration dramatically reduce activity (Carroll et al., 2019; Zhang et al., 2021). Because of this stereochemical dependence, many lead-optimizations focus on preserving core geometry while adjusting peripheral substituents to adjust ADME characteristics without affecting target engagement.

Furthermore, the relationship between reactive functionality and target class highlights trade-offs that medicinal chemistry must manage: halogenation can enhance binding and membrane interactions but may increase lipophilicity beyond desirable limits; redox-active groups (peroxides, quinones) deliver rapid and potent parasite killing by generating damaging species, but they also risk host toxicity and metabolic instability (Meshnick et al., 1991; Carroll et al., 2019). When converting natural scaffolds into clinical candidates, it is possible to rationally prioritize modifications that maximize potency and selectivity while minimizing liabilities by identifying these correlations, which map particular structural motifs to parasite targets, localization mechanisms, and pharmacokinetic consequences (Müller and Hemphill, 2016; Huggins et al., 2012).

5.3.3 Semi-synthetic analogs of natural antiparasitics artemisinin analogs: dihydroartemisinin, artesunate, artemether

Artemisinin was modified semisynthetically to get overcome the parent compound's limitations with solubility, bioavailability, and metabolic stability. All clinically used analogs retain the central pharmacophore, the 1,2,4-trioxane endoperoxide, which is crucial for the production of iron-mediated radicals and the destruction of parasites (Meshnick et al., 1991). Although its instability in acidic settings restricts its direct therapeutic usage, dihydroartemisinin (DHA), the principal active metabolite of most derivatives, shows higher potency because of greater peroxide reactivity (Haynes et al., 2013).

In order to overcome artemisinin's solubility issues, artesunate was created. It has a hemisuccinate ester that significantly improves water solubility and permits intravenous, intramuscular, and rectal administration. Because of its ability to quickly reach therapeutic plasma concentrations, artesunate is the recommended treatment for severe malaria globally (White, 1994). Because the ester is quickly hydrolyzed to DHA, the active species benefits from better pharmacokinetics while maintaining the mechanistic characteristics of artemisinin.

A lipophilic methyl ether derivative of DHA, artemether increases oral and intramuscular absorption as well as membrane permeability. Because of its greater lipophilicity, it converts to DHA more slowly, resulting in a longer prolonged pharmacokinetic profile that is appropriate for combination therapy with long-acting partner medications (White et al., 2014). When taken as a whole, these analogs show how peripheral alteration of the lactone and C-10 sections can maximize drug transport, stability, and clinical application while maintaining the crucial peroxide pharmacophore.

5.3.4 Quinine derivatives and synthetic quinolines

The modification of the quinoline core and side chain to improve heme binding, lower toxicity, and overcome resistance has long been the focus of the semisynthetic and synthetic evolution of quinoline antimalarials. By offering a more straightforward and powerful framework that can effectively accumulate in the parasite digesting vacuole, chloroquine, a synthetic 4-aminoquinoline, improves upon quinine's intricate natural architecture (Foley and Tilley, 1997). Strong heme binding and vacuolar trapping require structural adjustment at the C-7 position and terminal amine chain optimization (Ridley, 2002).

However second-generation analogs such as amodiaquine and piperaquine were developed in response to widespread resistance caused by PfCRT mutations. In order to increase retention at the vacuolar target site and decrease efflux susceptibility, these compounds include hydroxylated side chains, bis-quinoline frameworks, or Mannich bases (Cooper et al., 2005). Their structural development demonstrates how specific semisynthetic modifications can help resistant parasite populations regain their potency.

Ferrocene groups or peroxide bridges are examples of extra pharmacophores that are included into modern synthetic quinolines, such as ferroquine and trioxaquines, to enable dual modes of action. These developments show how the quinoline scaffold is becoming more and more versatile, with synthetic alterations offering improved potency, stability, and action against resistant *Plasmodium* strains (Biot et al., 2011).

5.3.5 Ivermectin and avermectin modifications

Ivermectin, a semisynthetic derivative with greatly increased safety and efficacy, was created by chemically optimizing avermectins, which were first obtained from *Streptomyces avermitilis*. The C-22=C-23 double bond is hydrogenated to produce ivermectin, which lowers toxicity while retaining high affinity for parasite glutamate-gated chloride channels

(Crump, 2017). This structural alteration improves therapeutic compatibility with human use while maintaining the macrocyclic lactone core.

The C-23 substituent and methoxime groups have been altered in subsequent analogs, such as moxidectin, to enhance metabolic stability and prolong half-life (Prichard et al., 2012). Moxidectin is very useful in mass drug administration programs for onchocerciasis because of these characteristics, which allow for extended antiparasitic efficacy.

The macrolide framework is being functionalized as part of ongoing chemical optimization efforts to improve selectivity for parasite channels, restrict transit through the blood–brain barrier, and lessen neurotoxicity. The goal of these SAR-driven approaches is to produce safer next-generation endectocides that can combat helminth and ectoparasite resistance (Ashour, 2019).

5.3.6 Miltefosine and related phospholipid analogs

Miltefosine, which was initially developed as an antineoplastic alkylphosphocholine, was subsequently employed as the first oral drug to successfully treat leishmaniasis. It can be introduced into parasite membranes and disrupt signaling cascades and lipid metabolism because of its structural resemblance to membrane phospholipids (Dorlo et al., 2012). SAR studies highlight the importance of alkyl chain length and the phosphocholine head group, which together regulate membrane affinity and antiparasitic efficacy.

Perifosine and edelfosine are examples of semisynthetic phospholipid analogs that alter lipid saturation, side-chain branching, or headgroup polarity to increase membrane contacts or selectivity for protozoan parasites (Ahmed et al., 2020). While lowering gastrointestinal toxicity and teratogenicity, these compounds seek to preserve miltefosine's membrane-disruptive action.

In order to address resistance seen in *Leishmania donovani*, recent efforts concentrate on creating analogs that avoid parasite efflux pumps and show better oral stability. The phospholipid scaffold is a promising platform for the development of next-generation antiparasitic drugs because of its tunability (Pérez-Victoria et al., 2006).

5.3.7 Recent marine-derived analogs with novel scaffolds

Many semisynthetic analogs have been developed as a result of the structurally diverse scaffolds found in marine natural products, including macrolides, polyketides, peptides, and terpenoids. In order to increase stability and decrease cytotoxicity while retaining efficacy against blood parasites, recent studies have concentrated on altering brominated terpenoids and macrocyclic lactones (Carroll et al., 2019). These changes frequently target reactive functional groups, macrocycle conformation, or halogenation patterns.

In order to enhance membrane penetration and lessen metabolic degradation, semisynthetic analogs of marine polyethers and depsipeptides have been created. Analogs with increased effectiveness against *Plasmodium* and *Trypanosoma* species have been produced through modifications in polyether chain length, stereochemistry, or macrocyclic stiffness (Blunt et al., 2018).

Marine natural products' characteristic three-dimensional structures make them particularly ideal for SAR-driven modification, resulting in new scaffolds with mechanisms different from those of traditional antiparasitic medications. Their chemical variety is still being used in ongoing research to find novel therapeutic targets (Zhang et al., 2021).

5.3.8 Comparative pharmacological and toxicological profiles

The pharmacokinetic and safety characteristics of semisynthetic analogs are frequently better than those of their natural counterparts. Examples are moxidectin, whose longer half-life improves long-acting antiparasitic effects, and artesunate, which offers quick systemic exposure because of enhanced solubility (White, 1994; Prichard et al., 2012).

By reducing membrane disruption, decreasing interactions with off-target channels, and enhancing metabolic stability, chemical refining also lessens toxicity. For example, certain changes in phospholipid analogs and quinolines reduce gastrointestinal and cardiotoxic symptoms while preserving antiparasitic efficacy (White, 2007; Dorlo et al., 2012).

5.4 Gene analysis and molecular mechanisms

5.4.1 Genomic, transcriptomic and Proteomic approaches to identify drug targets

Gene analysis is necessary to determine whether a biological pathway is essential for parasite life and, therefore, a promising therapeutic target. Assays for knockout, knockdown, and overexpression are examples of functional genetic techniques that demonstrate if changing a gene prevents differentiation, slows development, or disrupts metabolic balance. These results have largely contributed to the validation of PfATP4 and DHODH, two antimalarial targets that have been shown to be crucial for blood-stage proliferation (Gamo et al., 2010; Phillips et al., 2017). These techniques prevent paths in drug discovery pipelines that are overly redundant or unnecessary from proceeding.

Additionally, gene expression profiling aids in determining if a prospective target is expressed in sufficient quantities and during pertinent life-cycle stages to be pharmacologically actionable. Many metabolic enzymes and transporters are stage-specific in *Plasmodium* and kinetoplastid parasites, which affects when and how medications work

(Le Roch et al., 2003). This is revealed by transcriptome investigations. By combining expression-based and functional evidence, medicinal chemistry efforts are guaranteed to concentrate on targets that are both clinically significant and biologically verified.

High-resolution maps of parasite gene content are made possible by whole-genome sequencing, which makes it possible to identify crucial metabolic nodes, transporter families, and distinct biochemical pathways that are not present in humans. Mutations in important loci including pfcrt, mdr1, and kelch13 have been found by comparative genomics of drug-sensitive and resistant strains, exposing molecular vulnerabilities and connecting genetic diversity with drug response (Miotto et al., 2015). A structural foundation for understanding pharmacological processes and resistance is established by these databases.

After drug exposure, dynamic changes in gene expression are captured using transcriptomic methods such as RNA-seq. Short-term transcriptional responses frequently reveal pathways that are directly affected by drug action, such as the suppression of purine salvage following quinoline exposure or the activation of oxidative stress genes following artemisinin treatment (Wicht et al., 2020). These fingerprints help identify primary targets and differentiate them from secondary stress reactions.

4.2. Proteomic analyses complement genomic and transcriptomic data by quantifying drug-induced changes in protein abundance, turnover, and modification states. Cowell et al. (2018) state that mass spectrometry-based "chemical proteomics" can directly identify proteins that are covalently bound by bioactive natural compounds or destabilized upon inhibition. When transcriptomics, proteomics, and genomes are combined, they provide a multilayered systems biology perspective that guides analog optimization and supports mechanism-of-action research.

5.4.2 Genetic determinants of drug resistance and functional genomics

Resistance genetic markers provide important information on how parasites adjust to chemical stress. The K13 propeller domain in *Plasmodium falciparum* is the most studied example; point mutations such as C580Y and R539T diminish susceptibility to artemisinin by decreasing ring-stage clearance and changing ubiquitin-dependent stress responses (Ariey et al., 2014). Global policy on artemisinin combination medicines is currently guided by surveillance of K13 mutations.

Other notable markers include mutations in pfmdr1, where amplification events influence susceptibility to quinolines and aryl-amino alcohols, and pfcrt, which causes chloroquine resistance through altered digestive-vacuole transport (Fidock et al., 2000). While changes in mitochondrial genes lead to miltefosine resistance, amplification of ABC transporters, such as MRPA in *Leishmania*, decreases intracellular antimonial accumulation in kinetoplastids (Sundar and Singh, 2018). Chemists can create analogs that can circumvent or reverse resistance mechanisms by identifying these markers.

Target discovery in kinetoplastids has been revolutionized by functional genomics. Essential genes in sterol biosynthesis, mitochondrial RNA editing, and redox control have been identified in *Trypanosoma brucei* by genome-wide RNA interference screens; several of these genes lack human homologs, making them particularly desirable for selective inhibition (Alsford et al., 2011). Additionally, these screens examine chemical-genetic interactions, pinpointing pathways that alter susceptibility to frontline drugs such as nifurtimox and eflornithine.

In *Leishmania* spp., the use of CRISPR-Cas9 has permitted the exact production of knockouts and gene addbacks, allowing for mechanistic investigation of drug response. Studies have identified genes involved in antimonial resistance, such as those that govern thiol metabolism, metal transport, and trypanothione pathways (Zhang and Matlashewski, 2015). Integrating transcriptome data from altered strains reveals additional compensatory metabolic circuits. These findings show potential vulnerabilities in lipid metabolism, redox defense, and membrane homeostasis.

5.4.3 Integrating genetic data with structural design: SAR-genomic correlations

Combining SAR with genomic and transcriptome profiling allows researchers to better understand how structural variations in analogs affect biological responses. Drug-induced transcriptional signatures frequently correspond to specific chemical motifs; for example, peroxide-containing analogs consistently activate pathways associated with proteotoxic and oxidative stress, whereas quinoline analogs modulate heme metabolism and vacuolar transport genes (Mok et al., 2021). Such information reveals if a tweak increases on-target potency, changes the mechanism, or creates off-target hazards.

Additionally, structural characteristics that produce selective versus pleiotropic responses are identified using comparative transcriptomics among analogue series. While broad stress-related alterations may indicate non-specific toxicity, narrow, well-conserved expression patterns suggest particular target engagement. Thus, by identifying which chemical changes enhance route specificity and which should be avoided, integration of SAR-genomics data speeds up optimization (Mok et al., 2021; Cowell et al., 2018).

Analogue design is increasingly influenced by genetic research, which identifies pharmacological target residues or domains that are susceptible to mutation. Chemists can improve substituents to preserve interactions with conserved residues and prevent contacts that select for resistance by mapping resistance-associated mutations onto structural models (Le Bras and Durand, 2003). Next-generation inhibitors that target PfATP4, DHODH, and kinetoplastid sterol pathways have been designed using this approach.

Chemical-genetic interaction profiling is also useful for mechanistic elucidation, as hypersensitivity or resistance patterns across mutant libraries show if a substance targets a specific enzyme or pathway. In kinetoplastids, such methods have elucidated the action of sterol demethylase inhibitors and redox-active naphthoquinones (Westrop et al., 2015). In *Plasmodium* spp., combining K13-mediated phenotypes with transcriptomics has enhanced understanding of artemisinin activation and downstream damage responses.

Ultimately, combining SAR data with genetic and functional information produces a feedback loop that continually refines analogue design. This synergy confirms gene analysis as a fundamental component of contemporary natural product-based medicinal chemistry and speeds up the discovery of powerful, selective, and resistance-evading antiparasitic medicines.

5.5 Computational and integrative approaches

5.5.1 Molecular modeling and docking for target prediction

Molecular modeling has become critical for predicting how natural chemicals and analogs interact with proven therapeutic targets. Docking techniques replicate ligand-receptor binding geometries, allowing researchers to identify advantageous orientations, binding energies, and important intermolecular interactions such as hydrogen bonds, hydrophobic contacts, and metal coordination (Morris et al., 2009). These computational predictions aid in the prioritization of analogs with excellent complementarity to parasite enzymes, membrane proteins, or transporters, hence minimizing experimental screening efforts.

Docking studies may provide information on how structural changes affect affinity and selectivity since natural products frequently have intricate, inflexible scaffolds. For example, docking-based investigations have clarified how quinoline derivatives interact with the hemozoin crystal surface and how artemisinin analogs interact with PfATP6 and heme. Chemists can modify substituents that improve binding strength while avoiding steric conflicts or unfavorable desolvation penalties by combining docking predictions with SAR. Prior to laboratory validation, this computational method enhances mechanistic theories and speeds up the construction of reasonable analogs (Hadni and Elhallaoui, 2019).

5.5.2 Machine learning and cheminformatics in analog design

The application of machine learning (ML) models for predicting the bioactivity, ADMET traits, and resistance risk of analogs generated from natural products is growing. In order to identify key qualities that influence activity, quantitative structure-activity relationship (QSAR) models employ molecular descriptors such as topology, electrostatics, and physicochemical features. By simulating the screening of hundreds of potential analogs, these models greatly reduce the amount of chemical space needed for synthesis (Cherkasov et al., 2014).

This method is expanded by deep-learning frameworks, which use massive chemical datasets to learn non-linear structure-function connections. *Plasmodium* spp. growth inhibition, ligand–target interactions, and physicochemical liabilities including cytotoxicity or metabolic instability have all been successfully predicted using neural networks in antiparasitic research. Cheminformatics techniques such as fragmentation analysis, substructure mining, and similarity mapping are used to find pharmacophores and toxicophores that are important for optimization. When combined, machine learning and cheminformatics offer scalable, predictive platforms that improve the accuracy and efficiency of analog design (Stokes et al., 2020).

5.5.3 Integration of genomic data with chemical databases

Compounds that target particular parasite vulnerabilities can be systematically identified by connecting genetic data with chemical libraries. Integrative systems link drug activity profiles from extensive phenotypic screens to genomic markers, such as resistance-associated mutations or essential-gene signatures. This method helps differentiate between on-target and off-target interactions and reveals chemical scaffolds that are effective against genetically verified targets (Subramanian et al., 2017).

Combining chemical sensitivity statistics with transcriptome data in malaria research has identified drugs whose effectiveness correlates with particular transcriptional modules, allowing for hypothesis-driven analogue refinement. Similarly, metabolic circuits that are preferentially targeted by natural product analogs have been found by combining drug-response profiles with *Trypanosoma* and *Leishmania* CRISPR datasets. This paradigm for gene-chemical linkage improves compound prioritization and helps create analogs that take advantage of genetically specified vulnerabilities (Gao et al., 2021).

5.5.4 Systems biology and network pharmacology for multi-target natural products

Single-protein tests are insufficient to properly understand the multi-target or pathway-level impacts of many natural compounds. Researchers can examine how disruptions spread through interconnected pathways by reconstructing parasite metabolic and signaling networks using systems biology models. Central nodes, synthetic lethal connections, and metabolic bottlenecks affected by natural product scaffolds are identified by mapping compound-induced alterations onto these networks (Forth, 2012).

In order to anticipate synergistic interactions, assess probable toxicity resulting from wide pathway modification, and identify likely target constellations, network pharmacology combines chemical characteristics with multi-omic information. For instance, systems-level investigations have shown that derivatives of artemisinin jointly interfere with hemoglobin digestion, protein damage responses, and redox homeostasis. For increased therapeutic resilience, these findings guide the design of analogs with higher selectivity, decreased pleiotropy, or deliberate multi-target action (Wang et al., 2015).

5.6 Challenges, future perspectives, and conclusions

There are still many scientific and technological challenges in the process of natural product-based discoveries. Because of the great structural complexity of many metabolites, large-scale analogue production or complete synthesis is difficult and resource-intensive. Furthermore, many scaffolds exhibit metabolic instability, quick chemical degradation, or low aqueous solubility, all of which impede their optimization into therapeutically viable leads (Harvey et al., 2015). Iterative cycles in medicinal chemistry are frequently slowed down by these inherent constraints.

Biological challenges also contribute to decreased translation efficiency. *In vitro* antiparasitic assays usually fail to capture stage-specific biology, immunological interactions, and pharmacokinetic behavior *in vivo*, confounding the prediction of therapeutic utility. Furthermore, natural compounds with multi-target or pleiotropic effects complicate mechanism of action research, necessitating coordinated chemical, genomic, and biochemical techniques to minimize misunderstanding (Barba-Ostria et al., 2022). These challenges underscore the importance of more standardized, multi-layered evaluation frameworks.

5.6.1 Overcoming supply and synthesis barriers

For many natural product-based medicines, especially those made from uncommon plants, marine organisms, or uncultivable microorganisms, availability problems remain to be a major bottleneck. By rebuilding biosynthetic pathways in microbial hosts, advances in synthetic biology have overcome this problem and made it possible to produce chemicals like artemisinin and other polyketides in a stable and scalable manner (Paddon et al., 2013). These heterologous platforms lessen reliance on biomass sources that are seasonal or endangered.

In synthetic chemistry, techniques such as pharmacophore extraction, modular assembly, and scaffold simplification have made it possible for chemists to build analogue families without depending on intricate natural templates. These methods increase synthetic accessibility, lower production costs, and maintain the key bioactive characteristics. They offer a strong way to get over persistent supply limitations when paired with metabolic engineering (Newman and Cragg, 2020).

5.6.2 Addressing resistance through rational analogue design

The long-term efficacy of antiparasitic treatments is increasingly threatened by drug resistance, which makes rational analogue design crucial. By reducing reliance on mutation-prone interactions, it is possible to create medicines that avoid recognized resistance pathways by utilizing genomic markers, such as K13 mutations in *Plasmodium*, pfcrt variations associated with chloroquine resistance, or ABC transporter amplification in *Leishmania* spp. (Le Bras and Durand, 2003). These genetic discoveries help medicinal chemists develop more resilient inhibitors.

The deliberate creation of multi-target analogs is a second tactic that lessens the possibility of single-step resistance mutations by simultaneously applying pressure on various biological pathways. In order to overcome traditional resistance mechanisms, hybrid compounds, synergistic combinations, and dual-pharmacophore constructions have demonstrated promise (Shibeshi et al., 2020). The importance of incorporating evolutionary and genomic ideas into chemical optimization pathways is shown by these findings.

5.6.3 The future of gene-guided medicinal chemistry

The optimization of natural product analogs is changing because of gene-guided medicinal chemistry. New methods that offer high-resolution insights into target essentiality, pathway vulnerability, and resistance mechanisms include transcriptome perturbation analysis, proteomic interaction mapping, and CRISPR fitness profiling (Rocamora and Winzeler, 2020). Chemists can use these datasets to create changes that increase potency without creating risks related to compensatory pathways or stress reactions.

Predictive analogue design will be increasingly driven by machine learning algorithms that incorporate phenotypic, chemical, and genetic data. These integrative approaches greatly speed up discovery by predicting resistance trajectories, toxicity risks, and multi-target interaction patterns prior to synthesis. An important step toward more accurate and durable antiparasitic drugs is the combination of chemical biology and genome-scale data (Stokes et al., 2020).

5.6.4 Final remarks and research outlook

Antiparasitic drug discovery is entering a new phase because of the integration of natural product chemistry, genomics, systems biology, and computational modeling. Even while supply constraints, resistance, and structural complexity are still major obstacles, contemporary technology provide effective ways to overcome them. According to (Newman and Cragg, 2020), natural products continue to offer unparalleled chemical diversity, and genomic and computational technologies enable further in-depth investigation of their processes and optimization pathways.

Future research will require cross-disciplinary integration, which includes gene-guided analogue design, multitarget modeling, sustainable production strategies, and predictive computational frameworks. By combining chemical innovation with biological accuracy, the sector is well positioned to produce the next generation of effective, safe, and resistant antiparasitic medicines.

AI disclosure

During the preparation of this work the author(s) used quillbot and chatGpt in order to for editing. After using this tool/service, the author(s) reviewed and edited the content as needed and take(s) full responsibility for the content of the publication.

References

Ahmed H, Carter KC, Williams RAM. Structure and antiparasitic activity relationship of alkylphosphocholine analogues against *Leishmania donovani*. Microorganisms 2020;8(8):1–17. Available from https://doi.org/10.3390/microorganisms8081117.

Alsford S, Turner DJ, Obado SO, Sanchez-Flores A, Glover L, Berriman M, et al. High-throughput phenotyping using parallel sequencing of RNA interference targets in the African trypanosome. Genome Research 2011;21(6):915–24. Available from https://doi.org/10.1101/gr.115089.110.

Ariey F, Witkowski B, Amaratunga C, Beghain J, Langlois AC, Khim N, et al. A molecular marker of artemisinin-resistant *Plasmodium falciparum* malaria. Nature 2014;505(7481):50–5. Available from https://doi.org/10.1038/nature12876.

Ashley EA, Dhorda M, Fairhurst RM, Amaratunga C, Lim P, Suon S, et al. Spread of artemisinin resistance in *Plasmodium falciparum* malaria. The New England Journal of Medicine 2014;371(5):411–23. Available from https://doi.org/10.1056/NEJMoa1314981.

Ashour DS. Ivermectin: from theory to clinical application. International Journal of Antimicrobial Agents 2019;54(2):134–42. Available from https://doi.org/10.1016/j.ijantimicag.2019.05.003.

Barba-Ostria C, Carrera-Pacheco SE, Gonzalez-Pastor R, Heredia-Moya J, Mayorga-Ramos A, Rodríguez-Pólit C, et al. Evaluation of biological activity of natural compounds: current trends and methods. Molecules 2022;27(14). Available from https://doi.org/10.3390/molecules27144490.

Biot C, Nosten F, Fraisse L, Ter-Minassian D, Khalife J, Dive D. The antimalarial ferroquine: from bench to clinic. Parasite 2011;18(3):207–14. Available from https://doi.org/10.1051/parasite/2011183207.

Blunt JW, Carroll AR, Copp BR, Davis RA, Keyzers RA, Prinsep MR. Marine natural products. Natural Product Research 2018;35(1):8–53. Available from https://doi.org/10.1039/c7np00052a.

Borst P, Ouellette M. New mechanisms of drug resistance in parasitic protozoa. Annual Review of Microbiology 1995;49(1):427–60. Available from https://doi.org/10.1146/annurev.mi.49.100195.002235.

Burrows JN, Hooft Van Huijsduijnen R, Möhrle JJ, Oeuvray C, Wells TN. Designing the next generation of medicines for malaria control and eradication. Malaria Journal 2013;12:187. Available from https://doi.org/10.1186/1475-2875-12-187.

Burza S, Croft SL, Boelaert M. Leishmaniasis. Lancet 2018;392(10151):951–70. Available from https://doi.org/10.1016/S0140-6736(18)31204-2.

Carroll AR, Copp BR, Davis RA, Keyzers RA, Prinsep MR. Marine natural products. Natural Product Research 2019;36(1):122–73. Available from https://doi.org/10.1039/c8np00092a.

Chatelain E, Ioset JR. Drug discovery and development for neglected diseases: The DNDi model. Drug Design, Development and Therapy 2011(5):175–81. Available from https://doi.org/10.2147/DDDT.S16381.

Cheng W, Huang Y, Gao H, Bold B, Zhang T, Yang D. Marine natural products as novel treatments for parasitic diseases. Handbook of Experimental Pharmacology 2025;287:325–93. Available from https://doi.org/10.1007/164_2024_712.

Cherkasov A, Muratov EN, Fourches D, Varnek A, Baskin II, Cronin M, et al. QSAR modeling: where have you been? Where are you going to? Journal of Medicinal Chemistry 2014;57(12):4977–5010. Available from https://doi.org/10.1021/jm4004285.

Colley DG, Bustinduy AL, Secor WE, King CH. Human schistosomiasis. Lancet 2014;383(9936):2253–64. Available from https://doi.org/10.1016/S0140-6736(13)61949-2.

Cooper RA, Hartwig CL, Ferdig MT. pfcrt is more than the plasmodium falciparum chloroquine resistance gene: a functional and evolutionary perspective. Acta Tropica 2005;94(3):170–80. Available from https://doi.org/10.1016/j.actatropica.2005.04.004.

Cowell AN, Istvan ES, Lukens AK, Gomez-Lorenzo MG, Vanaerschot M, Sakata-Kato T, et al. Mapping the malaria parasite druggable genome by using in vitro evolution and chemogenomics. Science 2018;359(6372):191–9. Available from https://doi.org/10.1126/science.aan4472.

Crump A. Ivermectin: enigmatic multifaceted 'wonder' drug continues to surprise and exceed expectations. Journal of Antibiotics 2017;70(5):495–505. Available from https://doi.org/10.1038/ja.2017.11.

Cunha AB, Batista R, Castro MÁ, David JM. Chemical strategies towards the synthesis of betulinic acid and its more potent antiprotozoal analogues. Molecules 2021;26(4). Available from https://doi.org/10.3390/molecules26041081.

Cushnie TPT, Lamb AJ. Antimicrobial activity of flavonoids. International Journal of Antimicrobial Agents 2005;26(5):343–56. Available from https://doi.org/10.1016/j.ijantimicag.2005.09.002.

del Carmen Recio M, Giner R, Máñez S, Ríos J. Structural requirements for the antiinflammatory activity of natural triterpenoids. Planta Medica 1995;61(2):182–5. Available from https://doi.org/10.1055/s-2006-958045.

De Sarkar S, Sarkar D, Sarkar A, Dighal A, Staniek K, Gille L, et al. Berberine chloride mediates its antileishmanial activity by inhibiting Leishmania mitochondria. Parasitology Research 2019;118(1):335–45. Available from https://doi.org/10.1007/s00436-018-6157-3.

Ding Y, Xue X. Medicinal chemistry strategies for the modification of bioactive natural pProducts. Molecules 2024;29(3):689. Available from https://doi.org/10.3390/molecules29030689.

Dorlo TPC, Balasegaram M, Beijnen JH, de Vries PJ. Miltefosine: a review of its pharmacology and therapeutic efficacy in the treatment of leishmaniasis. Journal of Antimicrobial Chemotherapy 2012;67(11):2576–97. Available from https://doi.org/10.1093/jac/dks275.

Druilhe P, Brandicourt O, Chongsuphajaisiddhi T, Berthe J. Activity of a combination of three cinchona bark alkaloids against Plasmodium falciparum in vitro. Antimicrobial Agents Chemotherapy 1988;32(2):250–4. Available from https://doi.org/10.1128/aac.32.2.250.

Fernandes JF, Lell B, Agnandji ST, Obiang RM, Bassat Q, Kremsner PG, et al. Fosmidomycin as an antimalarial drug: a meta-analysis of clinical trials. Future Microbiology 2015;10(8):1375–90. Available from https://doi.org/10.2217/FMB.15.60.

Fidock DA, Nomura T, Talley AK, Cooper RA, Dzekunov SM, Ferdig MT, et al. Mutations in the P. falciparum digestive vacuole transmembrane protein PfCRT and evidence for their role in chloroquine resistance. Molecular Cell 2000;6(4):861–71. Available from https://doi.org/10.1016/S1097-2765(05)00077-8.

Foley M, Tilley L. Quinoline antimalarials: mechanisms of action and resistance. International Journal for Parasitology 1997;27(2):231–40. Available from https://doi.org/10.1016/S0020-7519(96)00152-X.

Forth T. Metabolic Systems Biology of the Malaria Parasite. University of Leeds; 2012.

Gamo FJ, Sanz LM, Vidal J, De Cozar C, Alvarez E, Lavandera JL, et al. Thousands of chemical starting points for antimalarial lead identification. Nature 2010;465(7296):305–10. Available from https://doi.org/10.1038/nature09107.

Gao JF, Lv QB, Mao RF, Sun YY, Chen YY, Qiu YY, et al. Integrative transcriptomics and proteomics analyses to reveal the developmental regulation of metorchis orientalis: a neglected trematode with potential carcinogenic implications. Frontiers in Cellular and Infection Microbiology 2021;11. Available from https://doi.org/10.3389/fcimb.2021.783662.

Ghasemiyeh P, Mohammadi-Samani S. Solid lipid nanoparticles and nanostructured lipid carriers as novel drug delivery systems: applications, advantages and disadvantages. Research in Pharmaceutical Sciences 2018;13(4):288–303. Available from https://doi.org/10.4103/1735-5362.235156.

Gleeson MP. Generation of a set of simple, interpretable ADMET rules of thumb. Journal of Medicinal Chemistry 2008;51(4):817–34. Available from https://doi.org/10.1021/jm701122q.

Gohil VM, Brahmbhatt KG, Loiseau PM, Bhutani KK. Synthesis and anti-leishmanial activity of 1-aryl-β-carboline derivatives against Leishmania donovani. Bioorganic & Medicinal Chemistry Letters 2012;22(12):3905–7. Available from https://doi.org/10.1016/j.bmcl.2012.04.115.

González-Montero MC, Andrés-Rodríguez J, García-Fernández N, Pérez-Pertejo Y, Reguera RM, Balaña-Fouce R, et al. Targeting trypanothione metabolism in trypanosomatids. Molecules 2024;29(10). Available from https://doi.org/10.3390/molecules29102214.

Gul W, Hamann MT. Indole alkaloid marine natural products: an established source of cancer drug leads with considerable promise for the control of parasitic, neurological and other diseases. Life Sciences 2005;78(5):442–53. Available from https://doi.org/10.1016/j.lfs.2005.09.007.

Hadni H, Elhallaoui M. Molecular docking and QSAR studies for modeling the antimalarial activity of hybrids 4-anilinoquinoline-triazines derivatives with the wild-type and mutant receptor pf-DHFR. Heliyon 2019;5(8). Available from https://doi.org/10.1016/j.heliyon.2019.e02357.

Harvey AL, Edrada-Ebel R, Quinn RJ. The re-emergence of natural products for drug discovery in the genomics era. Nature Reviews Drug Discovery 2015;14(2):111–29. Available from https://doi.org/10.1038/nrd4510.

Haynes RK. Artemisinin and derivatives: the future for malaria treatment? Current Opinion in Infectious Diseases 2001;14(6):719–26. Available from https://doi.org/10.1097/00001432-200112000-00010.

Haynes RK, Cheu KW, N'Da D, Coghi P, Monti D. Considerations on the mechanism of action of artemisinin antimalarials: part 1 - the 'carbon radical' and 'heme' hypotheses. Infectious Disorders - Drug. Targets 2013;13(4):217–77. Available from https://doi.org/10.2174/1871526513666131129155708.

Hotez PJ, Bottazzi ME, Strych U, Chang LY, Lim YAL, Goodenow MM, et al. Neglected tropical diseases among the association of Southeast Asian Nations (ASEAN): overview and update. PLOS Neglected Tropical Diseases 2015;9(4). Available from https://doi.org/10.1371/journal.pntd.0003575.

Houghton PJ, Howes M-J, Lee CC, Steventon G. Uses and abuses of in vitro tests in ethnopharmacology: visualizing an elephant. Journal of Ethnopharmacology 2007;110(3):391–400. Available from https://doi.org/10.1016/j.jep.2007.01.032.

Huggins DJ, Sherman W, Tidor B. Rational approaches to improving selectivity in drug design. Journal of Medicinal Chemistry 2012;55(4):1424–44. Available from https://doi.org/10.1021/jm2010332.

Jiang M, Chen S, Zhang Z, Xiao Y, Zhu D, Liu L. Structural diversity and bioactivities of marine fungal terpenoids (2020–2024). Marine Drugs 2025;23(8):300. Available from https://doi.org/10.3390/md23080300.

Jomova K, Alomar SY, Valko R, Liska J, Nepovimova E, Kuca K, et al. Flavonoids and their role in oxidative stress, inflammation, and human diseases. Chemico-Biological Interactions 2025;413. Available from https://doi.org/10.1016/j.cbi.2025.111489.

Kar N, Kumari L, Ghosh S. Natural products in the treatment of leishmaniasis. Viral, Parasitic, Bacterial, and Fungal Infections: Antimicrobial, Host Defense, and Therapeutic Strategies. India: Elsevier; 2022. p. 417–28.

Keasling JD. Synthetic biology for synthetic chemistry. ACS Chemical Biology 2008;3(1):64–76. Available from https://doi.org/10.1021/cb7002434.

Kerns EH, Li D. Drug-like Properties: Concepts, Structure Design, and Methods : From ADME to Toxicity Optimization. Second edition Amsterdam: Elsevier/Academic Press; 2008.

King CH. Parasites and poverty: the case of schistosomiasis. Acta Tropica 2010;113(2):95–104. Available from https://doi.org/10.1016/j.actatropica.2009.11.012.

Kitchen DB, Decornez H, Furr JR, Bajorath J. Docking and scoring in virtual screening for drug discovery: methods and applications. Nature Reviews Drug Discovery 2004;3(11):935–49. Available from https://doi.org/10.1038/nrd1549.

Klayman DL. Qinghaosu (artemisinin): n antimalarial drug from China. Science 1985;228(4703):1049–55. Available from https://doi.org/10.1126/science.3887571.

Koehn FE, Carter GT. The evolving role of natural products in drug discovery. Nature Reviews Drug Discovery 2005;4(3):206–20. Available from https://doi.org/10.1038/nrd1657.

Le Bras J, Durand R. The mechanisms of resistance to antimalarial drugs in Plasmodium falciparum. Fundamental & Clinical Pharmacology 2003;17(2):147–53. Available from https://doi.org/10.1046/j.1472-8206.2003.00164.x.

Leeson PD, Springthorpe B. The influence of drug-like concepts on decision-making in medicinal chemistry. Nature Reviews Drug Discovery 2007;6(11):881–90. Available from https://doi.org/10.1038/nrd2445.

Lemmer B, Soloviev M. Drug Discovery and Evaluation: Safety and Pharmacokinetic Assays. Springer; 2013.

Le Roch KG, Zhou Y, Blair PL, Grainger M, Moch JK, Haynes JD, et al. Discovery of gene function by expression profiling of the malaria parasite life cycle. Science 2003;301(5639):1503–8. Available from https://doi.org/10.1126/science.1087025.

Lipinski C, Hopkins A. Navigating chemical space for biology and medicine. Nature 2004;432(7019):855–61. Available from https://doi.org/10.1038/nature03193.

Majhi S, Das D. Chemical derivatization of natural products: semisynthesis and pharmacological aspects- a decade update. Tetrahedron 2021;78. Available from https://doi.org/10.1016/j.tet.2020.131801.

Marchant JS, Harding WW, Chan JD. Structure-activity profiling of alkaloid natural product pharmacophores against a Schistosoma serotonin receptor. International Journal for Parasitology – Drugs and Drug Resistance 2018;8(3):550–8. Available from https://doi.org/10.1016/j.ijpddr.2018.09.001.

Marquis JF, Makhey D, La Voie EJ, Olivier M. Effects of topoisomerases inhibitors protoberberine on Leishmania donovani growth, macrophage function, and infection. Journal of Parasitology 2003;89(5):1048–52. Available from https://doi.org/10.1645/GE-3161.

Menna-Barreto RFS, Goncalves RLS, Costa EM, Silva RSF, Pinto AV, Oliveira MF, et al. The effects on Trypanosoma cruzi of novel synthetic naphthoquinones are mediated by mitochondrial dysfunction. Free Radical Biology and Medicine 2009;47(5):644–53. Available from https://doi.org/10.1016/j.freeradbiomed.2009.06.004.

Mensah KB, Benneh C, Forkuo AD, Ansah C. Cryptolepine, the main alkaloid of the antimalarial cryptolepis sanguinolenta (lindl.) schlechter, induces malformations in zebrafish embryos. Biochemistry Research International 2019;2019. Available from https://doi.org/10.1155/2019/7076986.

Meshnick SR, Thomas A, Ranz A, Xu CM, Pan HZ. Artemisinin (qinghaosu): the role of intracellular hemin in its mechanism of antimalarial action. Molecular and Biochemical Parasitology 1991;49(2):181–9. Available from https://doi.org/10.1016/0166-6851(91)90062-B.

Miotto O, Amato R, Ashley EA, Macinnis B, Almagro-Garcia J, Amaratunga C, et al. Genetic architecture of artemisinin-resistant Plasmodium falciparum. Nature Genetics 2015;47(3):226–34. Available from https://doi.org/10.1038/ng.3189.

Mok S, Stokes BH, Gnädig NF, Ross LS, Yeo T, Amaratunga C, et al. Artemisinin-resistant K13 mutations rewire Plasmodium falciparum's intra-erythrocytic metabolic program to enhance survival. Nature Communications 2021;12(1). Available from https://doi.org/10.1038/s41467-020-20805-w.

Morris GM, Huey R, Lindstrom W, Sanner MF, Belew RK, Goodsell DS, et al. AutoDock4 and autoDockTools4: automated docking with selective receptor flexibility. Journal of Computational Chemistry 2009;30(16):2785–91. Available from https://doi.org/10.1002/jcc.21256.

Müller J, Hemphill A. Drug target identification in protozoan parasites. Expert Opinion on Drug Discovery 2016;11(8):815–24. Available from https://doi.org/10.1080/17460441.2016.1195945.

Muregi FW, Kirira PG, Ishih A. Novel rational drug design strategies with potential to revolutionize malaria chemotherapy. Current Medicinal Chemistry 2011;18(1):113–43. Available from https://doi.org/10.2174/092986711793979742.

Nantasenamat C, Isarankura-Na-Ayudhya C, Naenna T, Prachayasittikul V. A practical overview of quantitative structure-activity relationship. EXCLI Journal 2009;8:74–88.

Newman DJ, Cragg GM. Natural products as sources of new drugs over the nearly four decades from 01/1981 to 09/2019. Journal of Natural Products 2020;83(3):770–803. Available from https://doi.org/10.1021/acs.jnatprod.9b01285.

Nielsen J, Keasling JD. Engineering cellular metabolism. Cell 2016;164(6):1185–97. Available from https://doi.org/10.1016/j.cell.2016.02.004.

Nweze JA, Mbaoji FN, Li YM, Yang LY, Huang SS, Chigor VN, et al. Potentials of marine natural products against malaria, leishmaniasis, and trypanosomiasis parasites: a review of recent articles. Infectious Diseases of Poverty 2021;10(1). Available from https://doi.org/10.1186/s40249-021-00796-6.

Olliaro P, Wells TNC. The global portfolio of new antimalarial medicines under development. Clinical Pharmacology & Therapeutics 2009;85(6):584–95. Available from https://doi.org/10.1038/clpt.2009.51.

O'Neill PM, Barton VE, Ward SA. The molecular mechanism of action of artemisinin—the debate continues. Molecules 2010;15(3):1705–21. Available from https://doi.org/10.3390/molecules15031705.

Orosco D, Mendoza AR, Meléndez CM. Exploring the potential of natural products as antiparasitic agents for neglected tropical diseases. Current Topics in Medicinal Chemistry 2024;24(2):89–108. Available from https://doi.org/10.2174/0115680266256963230921061925.

Paddon CJ, Westfall PJ, Pitera DJ, Benjamin K, Fisher K, McPhee D, et al. High-level semisynthetic production of the potent antimalarial artemisinin. Nature 2013;496(7446):528–32. Available from https://doi.org/10.1038/nature12051.

Pagadala NS, Syed K, Tuszynski J. Software for molecular docking: a review. Biophysical Reviews 2017;9(2):91–102. Available from https://doi.org/10.1007/s12551-016-0247-1.

Patrick GL. An Introduction to Medicinal Chemistry. sixth ed. Oxford University Press; 2017.

Pérez-Victoria FJ, Sánchez-Cañete MP, Seifert K, Croft SL, Sundar S, Castanys S, et al. Mechanisms of experimental resistance of Leishmania to miltefosine: implications for clinical use. Drug Resistance Updates 2006;9(1-2):26–39. Available from https://doi.org/10.1016/j.drup.2006.04.001.

Phillips MA, Burrows JN, Manyando C, van Huijsduijnen RH, Van Voorhis WC, Wells TNC. Malaria disease primers. Nature Reviews 2017;3:17050.

Prichard R, Ménez C, Lespine A. Moxidectin and the avermectins: consanguinity but not identity. International Journal for Parasitology – Drugs and Drug Resistance 2012;2:134–53. Available from https://doi.org/10.1016/j.ijpddr.2012.04.001.

Rashed HAEH, Abu Almaaty AH, Soliman MFM, El-Shenawy NS. The in vitro antischistosomal activity and genotoxicity of the active ingredients of allium sativum (Allicin) and curcuma lon-ga (curcumin). Iranian Journal of Parasitology 2021;16(1):101–10. Available from https://doi.org/10.18502/ijpa.v16i1.5540.

Rautio J, Kumpulainen H, Heimbach T, Oliyai R, Oh D, Järvinen T, et al. Prodrugs: design and clinical applications. Nature Reviews Drug Discovery 2008;7(3):255–70. Available from https://doi.org/10.1038/nrd2468.

Ridley RG. Medical need, scientific opportunity and the drive for antimalarial drugs. Nature 2002;415(6872):686–93. Available from https://doi.org/10.1038/415686a.

Ro DK, Paradise EM, Quellet M, Fisher KJ, Newman KL, Ndungu JM, et al. Production of the antimalarial drug precursor artemisinic acid in engineered yeast. Nature 2006;440(7086):940–3. Available from https://doi.org/10.1038/nature04640.

Robledo SM, Pérez-Silanes S, Fernández-Rubio C, Poveda A, Monzote L, González VM, et al. Neglected zoonotic diseases: advances in the development of cell-penetrating and antimicrobial peptides against leishmaniosis and chagas disease. Pathogens 2023;12(7). Available from https://doi.org/10.3390/pathogens12070939.

Rocamora F, Winzeler EA. Genomic approaches to drug resistance in malaria. Annual Review of Microbiology 2020;74:761–86. Available from https://doi.org/10.1146/annurev-micro-012220-064343.

Rocha LG, Almeida JRGS, Macêdo RO, Barbosa-Filho JM. A review of natural products with antileishmanial activity. Phytomedicine 2005;12(6-7):514–35. Available from https://doi.org/10.1016/j.phymed.2003.10.006.

Santos TB, de Moraes LGC, Pacheco PAF, dos Santos DG, Ribeiro RMdAC, Moreira CdS, et al. Naphthoquinones as a promising class of compounds for facing the challenge of parkinson's disease. Pharmaceuticals 2023;16(11). Available from https://doi.org/10.3390/ph16111577.

Shang X, Dai L, Cao X, Ma Y, Gulnaz I, Miao X, et al. Natural products in antiparasitic drug discovery: advances, opportunities and challenges. Natural Product Reports 2025;42(9):1419–58. Available from https://doi.org/10.1039/d5np00007f.

Shibeshi MA, Kifle ZD, Atnafie SA. Antimalarial drug resistance and novel targets for antimalarial drug discovery. Infection and Drug Resistance 2020;13:4047–60. Available from https://doi.org/10.2147/IDR.S279433.

Soto-Sánchez J. Bioactivity of natural polyphenols as antiparasitic agents and their biochemical targets. Mini-Reviews in Medicinal Chemistry 2022;22(20):2661–77. Available from https://doi.org/10.2174/1389557522666220404090429.

Stokes JM, Yang K, Swanson K, Jin W, Cubillos-Ruiz A, Donghia NM, et al. A Deep learning approach to antibiotic discovery. Cell 2020;180(4):688. Available from https://doi.org/10.1016/j.cell.2020.01.021.

Subramanian A, Narayan R, Corsello SM, Peck DD, Natoli TE, Lu X, et al. A next generation connectivity map: L1000 platform and the first 1,000,000 profiles. Cell 2017;171(6):1437. Available from https://doi.org/10.1016/j.cell.2017.10.049.

Sun J, Xufeng J, Qiu Z, Gao Q, Zhu Z, He J, et al. Artemisiae annuae herba: from anti-malarial legacy to emerging anti-cancer potential. Theranostics 2025;15(15):7346–77. Available from https://doi.org/10.7150/thno.115414.

Sundar S, Singh B. Emerging therapeutic targets for treatment of leishmaniasis. Expert Opinion on Therapeutic Targets 2018;22(6):467–86. Available from https://doi.org/10.1080/14728222.2018.1472241.

Testa B. Prodrugs: bridging pharmacodynamic/pharmacokinetic gaps. Current Opinion in Chemical Biology 2009;13(3):338–44. Available from https://doi.org/10.1016/j.cbpa.2009.04.620.

Tu Y. The discovery of artemisinin (qinghaosu) and gifts from Chinese medicine. Nature Medicine 2011;17(10):1217–20. Available from https://doi.org/10.1038/nm.2471.

Van den Kerkhof M, Sterckx Y, Leprohon P, Maes L, Caljon G. Experimental strategies to explore drug action and resistance in kinetoplastid parasites. Microorganisms 2020;8(6):950. Available from https://doi.org/10.3390/microorganisms8060950.

Vangapandu S, Jain M, Kaur K, Patil P, Patel SR, Jain R. Recent advances in antimalarial drug development. Medicinal Research Reviews 2007;27(1):65–107. Available from https://doi.org/10.1002/med.20062.

Wang J, Zhang CJ, Chia WN, Loh CCY, Li Z, Lee YM, et al. Haem-activated promiscuous targeting of artemisinin in Plasmodium falciparum. Nature Communications 2015;6. Available from https://doi.org/10.1038/ncomms10111.

Wellems TE, Plowe CV. Chloroquine-resistant malaria. The Journal of Infectious Diseases 2001;184(6):770–6. Available from https://doi.org/10.1086/322858.

Westrop GD, Williams RAM, Wang L, Zhang T, Watson DG, Silva AM, et al. Metabolomic analyses of Leishmania reveal multiple species differences and large differences in amino acid metabolism. PLoS ONE 2015;10(9). Available from https://doi.org/10.1371/journal.pone.0136891.

White NJ. Clinical pharmacokinetics and pharmacodynamics of artemisinin and derivatives. Transactions of the Royal Society of Tropical Medicine and Hygiene 1994;88:41–3. Available from https://doi.org/10.1016/0035-9203(94)90471-5.

White NJ. Cardiotoxicity of antimalarial drugs. The Lancet Infectious Diseases 2007;7(8):549–58. Available from https://doi.org/10.1016/S1473-3099(07)70187-1.

White NJ, Pukrittayakamee S, Hien TT, Faiz MA, Mokuolu OA, Dondorp AM. Malaria. Lancet 2014;383(9918):723–35. Available from https://doi.org/10.1016/S0140-6736(13)60024-0.

Wicht KJ, Mok S, Fidock DA. Molecular mechanisms of drug resistance in plasmodium falciparum malaria. Annual Review of Microbiology 2020;74:431–54. Available from https://doi.org/10.1146/annurev-micro-020518-115546.

World Health Organization (WHO). World malaria report 2023. Geneva: World Health Organization; 2023.

Wylie MR, Merrell DS. The antimicrobial potential of the neem tree azadirachta indica. Frontiers in Pharmacology 2022;13. Available from https://doi.org/10.3389/fphar.2022.891535.

Young RJ. Physical properties in drug design. Meanwell N, editor. Tactics in Contemporary Drug Design. Topics in Medicinal Chemistry, vol 9. Berlin, Heidelberg: Springer; 2014.

Zaid H, Raiyn J, Nasser A, Saad B, Rayan A. Physicochemical properties of natural based products versus synthetic chemicals. The Open Nutraceuticals Journal 2010;3(1):194–202. Available from https://doi.org/10.2174/18763960010030100194.

Zhang WW, Matlashewski G. CRISPR-Cas9-mediated genome editing in Leishmania donovani. mBio 2015;6(4). Available from https://doi.org/10.1128/mBio.00861-15.

Zhang H, Zou J, Yan X, Chen J, Cao X, Wu J, et al. Marine-derived macrolides 1990-2020: an overview of cChemical and biological diversity. Marine Drugs 2021;19(4):180. Available from https://doi.org/10.3390/md19040180.

Ziemert N, Alanjary M, Weber T. The evolution of genome mining in microbes-a review. Natural Product Reports 2016;33(8):988–1005. Available from https://doi.org/10.1039/c6np00025h.

CHAPTER 6

Nanotechnology in blood parasite control

Malek Al-Najjar[1], Raja'a Al-Qudah[2], Amin Omar[3], Muna Barakat[2], and Mohammad A A Al-Najjar[3]
[1]Faculty of Medicine, Jordan University of Science and Technology, Irbid, Jordan,
[2]Department of Clinical Pharmacy and Therapeutics, Applied Science Private University, Amman, Jordan,
[3]Department of Pharmaceutical Sciences and Pharmaceutics, Applied Science Private University, Amman, Jordan

6.1 Nanotechnology platforms for parasite targeting: materials, design, and mode of action

Existing modes of antiparasitic therapy exhibit a wide range of limitations, including rapid clearance, poor solubility, and inadequate tissue penetration. However, by utilizing nanotechnology-based drug delivery systems, it becomes possible to bypass these limitations and precisely control material composition, payload integration, surface chemistry, and release behavior tailoring them to the specific biology of the helminth or protozoan infection at hand. In the following subsections, we highlight the classes of nanomaterials used against parasitic infections and explain how they interact with both the host and the parasite through selective delivery. In addition, we discuss their pharmacokinetics, pharmacodynamics, safety considerations, and translational feasibility.

6.2 Material classes and properties: lipid, polymeric, inorganic, and hybrid nanoplatforms

As stated previously, current antiparasitic drugs have several shortcomings, such as poor solubility, rapid clearance, and limited penetration into intracellular or tissue-specific parasite niches. Nanoparticles help negate these shortcomings by engineering the carrier itself, thereby allowing the drug to overcome these inherent limitations (Almeida Furquim de Camargo et al., 2023; Huang et al., 2024). There are four unique classes of nanoparticles, which are lipid, polymeric, inorganic, and hybrid. Each of these classes has distinct physicochemical properties that influence stability, drug loading, release kinetics, and overall biodistribution of the drug (Almeida Furquim de Camargo et al., 2023). Using these nanoparticles effectively for specific protozoal and helminth infections can markedly improve therapeutic efficacy and minimize off-target (Tiwari et al., 2023; Huang et al., 2024). This section will compare each class briefly and highlight its advantages.

Innovative Strategies Against Blood Parasites
DOI: https://doi.org/10.1016/B978-0-443-48509-1.00007-0

First, we have lipid-based nanoparticles such as liposomes, solid lipid nanoparticles (SLNs), and nanostructured lipid carriers (NLCs). These systems are widely used because they are biocompatible, can efficiently encapsulate both hydrophilic and hydrophobic drugs, and maintain good physical stability during circulation (Almeida Furquim de Camargo et al., 2023; Tiwari et al., 2023). They are particularly effective in parasitic infections because they naturally accumulate in macrophages, the primary host cells for Leishmania, and can fuse with cellular membranes to enhance intracellular drug delivery (Almeida Furquim de Camargo et al., 2023). The second major category is polymeric nanoparticles. Polymers such as PLGA, chitosan, and PEGylated copolymers allow controlled degradation and sustained drug release, which are important for chronic intracellular parasitic diseases (Almeida Furquim de Camargo et al., 2023). Chitosan-based nanoparticles also carry an intrinsic positive charge, improving adhesion to and uptake by phagocytic cells, which is an important advantage in leishmaniasis and similar infections. Together, lipid and polymeric platforms represent the core of antiparasitic nanomedicine because they provide stable, adaptable, and biologically compatible systems for targeted drug delivery.

Another class of nanoparticles is the inorganic class, which consisting of gold, silver, iron oxide, silica, and others. They carry a versatile set of advantages, such as magnetic properties, photothermal effects, and ROS generation. These allows them to be used diagnostically or therapeutically by killing parasites directly. However, they also present some limitations as these substances and their effects can be toxic on the host if they aren't monitored correctly. The last class of nanoparticles is the hybrid class. This class combines the benefits of two or more classes of nanoparticles- providing multi-functional behavior, better targeting, and stability. Examples of this class include something like a gold core and a polymer shell allowing for the hybrid to utilize the gold core's photothermal capability (allowing for heating and direct killing of the parasite) and the polymers biocompatible outer layer easing long-term release of drugs and attachment of the nanoparticles (Daraee et al., 2016). Together, the inorganic and hybrid systems allow for further expansion in the capabilities of nanomedicine by adding multifunctional designs, imaging and external activation, that complement the advantages of the lipid and polymeric carriers- further increasing their efficacy.

6.3 Surface engineering and targeting ligands: antibodies, peptides, aptamers, and glycoconjugates

The key to designing effective nanoparticles lies in engineering the right surface rather than focusing only on the core because the surface chemistry determines how nanoparticles are distributed, how they interact with host cells, and how efficiently they are taken up (Monopoli et al., 2012; Almeida Furquim de Camargo et al., 2023). Parasites often hide inside macrophages, erythrocytes, or hepatocytes, which makes it difficult for untargeted drugs to reach them effectively (Almeida Furquim de Camargo et al., 2023; Tiwari et al., 2023). Proper surface engineering improves this by adding ligands such as antibodies, peptides, aptamers, or mannose that help nanoparticles bind infected cells or parasite-associated receptors, thereby increasing drug concentration at relevant sites while reducing off-target toxicity (Singh et al., 2023; Huang et al., 2024). These ligand-based and surface modifications form the foundation of targeted antiparasitic nanomedicine.

As stated previously, several types of ligands can be added to nanoparticles to improve specificity. The first group is antibodies, which are highly specific and can bind parasite antigens or infected-cell markers, although they are larger in size and more difficult to manufacture (Almeida Furquim de Camargo et al., 2023). Peptides are another option; they are smaller, cheaper to produce, and easier to modify than antibodies, giving them better penetration and strong binding to macrophage or endothelial receptors (Almeida Furquim de Camargo et al., 2023; Huang et al., 2024). Aptamers represent a third class: short DNA or RNA sequences with high affinity that are easy to synthesize and well-suited for precise targeting (Mitchell et al., 2021). The final group is glycoconjugates, especially mannose, which target macrophage mannose receptors and are particularly useful for infections such as leishmaniasis that reside in macrophages. Overall, these ligands are essential for improving nanoparticle specificity and accuracy when delivering drugs against parasitic infections.

Once nanoparticles enter the bloodstream, a layer of adsorbed proteins, known as the protein corona, forms around them and changes their biological identity (Monopoli et al., 2012). This can increase opsonization and lead to faster clearance by the immune system (Monopoli et al., 2012; Almeida Furquim de Camargo et al., 2023). To counter this, stealth coatings such as PEG, zwitterionic polymers, or other hydrophilic shells are added to reduce corona formation and keep targeting ligands exposed and functional (Almeida Furquim de Camargo et al., 2023; Huang et al., 2024). When engineering the nanoparticle surface, it is essential to balance stealth to avoid clearance with ligand density to maintain targeting ability, ensuring the particles behave optimally in real biological fluids.

6.4 Stimuli responsive designs: pH, redox, enzymatic, and magnetic/photothermal triggers

Nanoparticles can also be designed to be stimuli-responsive, meaning that they only activate or release their drug when they encounter specific biological conditions inside infected cells or tissues (Mitchell et al., 2021). One example is pH-responsive nanoparticles, which use pH-sensitive lipids or polymers that destabilize and release their payload in acidic environments, such as the phagosomes or parasitophorous vacuoles of parasite-infected macrophages (Almeida Furquim de Camargo et al., 2023).

Another variant is redox-responsive systems, which rely on disulfide linkers that cleave in the high-glutathione (GSH) environment characteristic of infected macrophages, thereby enabling intracellular drug release (Mitchell et al., 2021). The last major type is enzyme-responsive nanoparticles, which incorporate linkers that are cut by parasite or hostderived enzymes, such as proteases or phospholipases, allowing for parasite-specific activation (Huang et al., 2024).

As stated previously, certain nanoparticles, particularly inorganic ones, can respond to external sources such as magnetic fields, heat, or light, allowing for on demand activation (Stiufiuc and Stiufiuc, 2024). Magnetic systems use iron oxide nanoparticles that can be guided externally or heated through alternating magnetic fields, producing localized hyperthermia that damages or kills nearby parasites (Stiufiuc and Stiufiuc, 2024). Photothermal systems, on the other hand, use gold nanoparticles that absorb near-infrared light and convert it into heat for targeted parasite killing (Almeida Furquim de Camargo et al., 2023). Both strategies help minimize systemic toxicity by enabling activation of the therapeutic effect only at the site of infection.

Stimuli-responsive and externally responsive systems offer major advantages in nanotherapy because they improve the precision of drug release and allow activation only in parasite-rich areas (Mitchell et al., 2021). This limits systemic side effects and enables timed release that aligns with parasite life cycle stages (Huang et al., 2024). Overall, these designs increase both the efficacy and safety of nanomedicine compared with conventional carriers.

6.5 Payload integration: small molecules, prodrugs, peptides, and gene cargos (siRNA/CRISPR)

Nanoparticles have the ability to carry a wide range of therapeutic agents, not just small-molecule drugs. They can deliver prodrugs, peptide- and protein-based therapeutics, and gene-based cargos such as siRNA or CRISPR components, all of which benefit from the protection and intracellular access that nanoparticles provide (Almeida Furquim de Camargo et al., 2023; Singh et al., 2023). This significantly expands their utility beyond simple drug delivery, allowing them to act as precise and targeted carriers for multiple classes of therapeutic molecules.

Nanoparticles protect the therapeutic agents loaded onto them, ensuring that they remain stable until reaching the site of action, which increases the potency of peptides, proteins, and small drugs that would otherwise degrade before delivery. This is achieved by loading hydrophobic drugs into the lipid bilayer or hydrophobic polymer core, whereas hydrophilic drugs are incorporated into the aqueous core or polymer matrix (Almeida Furquim de Camargo et al., 2023). Prodrugs can also be chemically attached to the nanoparticle surface using cleavable linkers that detach in specific biochemical environments, such as acidic, redox-rich, or enzyme-rich sites (Mitchell et al., 2021).

Gene cargos, including siRNA and other nucleic acids, bind electrostatically to cationic materials such as chitosan, PEI, or cationic lipids, which protects them from nuclease degradation during circulation (Singh et al., 2023).

Selecting the right loading method directly influences nanoparticle stability, release kinetics, and overall treatment efficacy. Fine-tuning payload integration allows different release profiles, making it a critical step in maximizing nanoparticle performance.

6.6 Release kinetics and control: burst mitigation, sustained delivery, and spatiotemporal dosing

The speed and quantity at which a drug is released from a nanoparticle over time is referred to as release kinetics and is a critical aspect of nanomedicine (Almeida Furquim de Camargo et al., 2023). Controlling these kinetics allows sustained drug levels that avoid toxic spikes and ineffective troughs, thereby improving both efficacy and safety (Tiwari et al., 2023). Nanoparticles enable this level of engineered release control, giving them a significant advantage over conventional formulations (Mitchell et al., 2021).

Nanoparticles can slow or control drug release through several mechanisms, including diffusion through a polymer matrix, degradation-controlled release from systems such as PLGA or chitosan, or modulation of lipid bilayer rigidity (Almeida Furquim de Camargo et al., 2023). These mechanisms, along with additional strategies such as coatings, cross-linking, or multilayer structures, help prevent the burst release often seen in conventional formulations (Tiwari et al., 2023). This enables predictable and sustained dosing that can be tailored to the needs of the infection (Mitchell et al., 2021).

Selecting the appropriate release strategy is essential, because it determines how long the drug remains active, how stable the nanoparticle is, and the overall efficacy of treatment (Mitchell et al., 2021; Almeida Furquim de Camargo et al., 2023). Matching the release profile—whether sustained, controlled, or stimuli-responsive—to the parasite's infection pattern or life cycle significantly improves therapeutic outcomes (Natarajan et al., 2014, Mitchell et al., 2021). For these reasons, release control is a critical component of nanoparticle design in antiparasitic therapy.

6.7 Interaction with parasite and host cells: adhesion, uptake pathways, and intracellular trafficking

Nanoparticles initially interact with host cells through their surface chemistry, charge, coatings, and the composition of the protein corona, which collectively determine whether they bind infected cells, healthy cells, or remain in circulation (Monopoli et al., 2012; Almeida Furquim de Camargo et al., 2023). Parasite-infected cells often express altered receptors, membrane lipids, or activation markers, making them more susceptible to recognition by ligand-modified nanoparticles (Huang et al., 2024). As noted previously, the protein corona can either enhance or mask these interactions, depending on its composition, influencing overall targeting efficiency (Mitchell et al., 2021).

Once nanoparticles attach to the cell surface, they are taken up through several endocytic pathways, including macropinocytosis, caveolae-mediated endocytosis, and clathrin-mediated endocytosis (Mitchell et al., 2021; Almeida Furquim de Camargo et al., 2023). Parasite-infected macrophages readily internalize nanoparticles through these routes, thereby enabling drug delivery directly into intracellular vacuoles where parasites reside (Huang et al., 2024). This uptake behavior is a key advantage of nanoparticle-based antiparasitic therapy (Mitchell et al., 2021).

Following entry into the cell, nanoparticles are routed into endosomes, lysosomes, or parasitophorous vacuoles, allowing them to release their drug directly at the intracellular sites where parasites reside (Mitchell et al., 2021; Almeida Furquim de Camargo et al., 2023). This intracellular routing can also be influenced by surface coatings or ligands, which determine whether nanoparticles escape from endosomes or accumulate within vacuoles (Mitchell et al., 2021; Huang et al., 2024).

6.8 Overcoming biological barriers: hemodynamic shear, protein corona, RES clearance, and biodistribution

For nanoparticles to work efficiently, they must withstand hemodynamic shear and blood flow forces in circulation without destabilizing (Mitchell et al., 2021). This requires appropriate engineering, including hydrophilic surface coatings such as PEG or zwitterionic polymers, optimized sizes in the 50–150 nm range, and stable core–shell architectures to maintain structural integrity under flow (Almeida Furquim de Camargo et al., 2023; Huang et al., 2024).

The mononuclear phagocyte system rapidly clears nanoparticles, a process accelerated by opsonins in the protein corona that label them for immune removal (Monopoli et al., 2012). Nanoparticles can overcome this through stealth coatings, neutral or zwitterionic surfaces, and optimized hydrophilicity, all of which reduce opsonization and prolong circulation (Mitchell et al., 2021; Almeida Furquim de Camargo et al., 2023). Additionally, particles in the 70–120 nm size range and those with spherical geometries exhibit reduced RES uptake (Huang et al., 2024).

Even after withstanding circulation and immune clearance, nanoparticles must still reach parasite-infected tissues, which are often located in poorly perfused or structurally protected areas (Mitchell et al., 2021). Biodistribution can be improved by adjusting nanoparticle size, surface charge, and ligand modifications to promote accumulation in targeted tissues (Almeida Furquim de Camargo et al., 2023). Reaching parasites hidden behind strong physiological barriers, such as those in the liver, spleen, or dermal lesions, requires precise tuning of surface chemistry to enhance penetration and retention (Huang et al., 2024). Optimizing biodistribution is therefore essential to ensure that therapeutic concentrations effectively reach infection sites (Mitchell et al., 2021).

6.9 Pharmacokinetics/pharmacodynamics: Circulation half-life, tissue exposure, and efficacy modeling

By adjusting surface coatings, nanoparticle size, and protein corona composition, nanoparticles can significantly alter the pharmacokinetic profile and circulation half-life of antiparasitic drugs (Mitchell et al., 2021; Almeida Furquim de Camargo et al., 2023). Prolonged circulation increases the duration of drug exposure and enhances the likelihood of reaching infected tissues (Huang et al., 2024). By modifying PK in this way, nanoparticles can also reduce off-target accumulation and systemic toxicity (Mitchell et al., 2021).

Through ligand targeting, controlled release, and optimized surface chemistry, nanoparticles can alter drug distribution by shifting exposure toward infected tissues and away from healthy organs (Mitchell et al., 2021; Almeida Furquim de Camargo et al., 2023). This improves the therapeutic index by increasing drug levels where they are needed and reducing accumulation in sensitive organs prone to toxicity (Mitchell et al., 2021; Huang et al., 2024).

Because nanoparticles create distinct pharmacokinetic and pharmacodynamic profiles, shaped by altered drug exposure, controlled release, and improved tissue accumulation, they can enhance parasite killing while maintaining safety (Mitchell et al., 2021; Almeida Furquim de Camargo et al., 2023). PK/PD modeling is therefore essential for optimizing nanoparticle dose, release rate, and timing in relation to parasite life cycle dynamics, resulting in more predictable and effective therapeutic outcomes (Mitchell et al., 2021; Huang et al., 2024).

6.10 Safety and Hemocompatibility: immunotoxicity, off-target effects, and blood compatibility testing

Although nanomedicine offers many advantages, safety considerations that must be carefully evaluated before clinical translation. Toxic effects may arise from the nanoparticle core, surface coatings, degradation products, or unintended immune activation (Mitchell et al., 2021; Huang et al., 2024). For this reason, hemocompatibility testing is essential, because nanoparticles directly contact blood components during systemic administration (Mitchell et al., 2021).

As stated previously, nanoparticles can trigger immune reactions depending on their size, charge, and surface chemistry, leading to effects such as complement activation, cytokine release, and unintended uptake by immune cells (Mitchell et al., 2021). These immune interactions may contribute to off-target accumulation in organs such as the liver, spleen, or kidneys, which requires careful evaluation during development (Huang et al., 2024). For this reason, surface engineering and optimized biodistribution are essential to minimize immunotoxicity and ensure safe treatment (Mitchell et al., 2021; Almeida Furquim de Camargo et al., 2023).

Another key consideration is how nanoparticles interact with blood, making hemocompatibility testing essential to evaluate their effects on red blood cells, platelets, and plasma proteins (Mitchell et al., 2021). Incompatible nanoparticles can induce hemolysis, platelet activation, coagulation abnormalities, or excessive protein adsorption, all of which pose safety risks (Mitchell et al., 2021). These effects can be minimized through proper surface modification, a neutral or zwitterionic charge, and stable hydrophilic coatings (Huang et al., 2024). Ensuring hemocompatibility is therefore a critical prerequisite for initiating systemic nanotherapy.

6.11 Manufacturing and translation: scalable fabrication, quality attributes, and regulatory considerations

One of the largest hurdles facing the adoption of nanotherapy is the ability to manufacture nanoparticles consistently at scale. During production, disparities in particle size, polydispersity, drug loading, and surface modification can arise, creating significant batch-to-batch variability (Mitchell et al., 2021; Almeida Furquim de Camargo et al., 2023). For nanomedicine to achieve widespread clinical use, precise and reproducible fabrication methods are required to ensure consistent quality and performance (Mitchell et al., 2021; Huang et al., 2024).

To ensure safe clinical use, regulatory agencies such as the FDA and EMA require detailed characterization of nanoparticles before approval (Mitchell et al., 2021). Key quality attributes that must be assessed include particle size and polydispersity, surface charge, drug loading, and release profile, among others (Almeida Furquim de Camargo et al., 2023). These parameters directly influence safety, reproducibility, clinical performance, and regulatory acceptance (Huang et al., 2024). Because of their added complexity, nanoparticles must meet the same regulatory rigor as traditional drugs, often with additional requirements, to ensure the safety and effectiveness of treatment (Mitchell et al., 2021).

Although extremely promising, even well-designed nanoparticles face challenges in full clinical adoption because of issues with scalability, cost, and regulatory hurdles (Mitchell et al., 2021). Clinical translation depends heavily on reproducible manufacturing, validated safety data, and clear therapeutic advantages over existing treatments (Huang et al., 2024). Standardized manufacturing and testing protocols help bridge the gap between laboratory-scale nanoparticle systems and patient-ready formulations

(Almeida Furquim de Camargo et al., 2023). Meeting regulatory requirements is therefore essential for advancing nanoparticle formulations from research prototypes to approved clinical therapies (Mitchell et al., 2021).

6.12 Smart delivery to hematologic niches parasites: RBC, endothelial, and immune cell-directed nanocarriers

Parasitic pathogens that inhabit or transit through hematologic niches, including red blood cells (RBCs), vascular endothelial tissues, macrophages, and circulating immune cell populations, pose enormous therapeutic challenges. Parasites such as *Plasmodium*, *Babesia*, *Trypanosoma*, and *Leishmania* species exploit complex blood microenvironments to invade cells, evade immune detection, adhere to the endothelium, or circulate freely (Akhtar et al., 2023). Nanoparticle-based therapeutics offer a promising alternative to conventional antiparasitic therapy, by enabling targeted delivery, enhanced circulation time, controlled payload release, immune modulation, and improved biodistribution to parasitized hematologic compartments (Alsharedeh et al., 2024). Nanoparticles encounter multiple biological barriers after administration, including the gastrointestinal epithelium, vascular endothelium, and cellular membranes. Their ultrasmall size and high surface area confer strong adhesive interactions that enhance residence time and absorption (Blanco et al., 2015; Cong et al., 2024).

Drawing exclusively from the nanoparticle, biomaterial, BBB-transport, and polymer-engineering concepts, this section of the chapter provides an integrated framework for designing smart nanocarriers for hematologic parasitic infections. This is also supported by examples on using nanocarriers-based antiparasitic drugs that were successfully implemented on specific parasitic infections.

6.13 Pharmacokinetics in blood compartments

Nanoparticle behavior within the bloodstream directly determines their success in targeting hematologic parasites. Treatment against parasites inhabiting erythrocytes, endothelial beds, or phagocytic niches requires nanocarriers that can circulate long enough to encounter target cells, marginate toward vessel walls, penetrate micro-vasculature, and distribute into infected tissues (Hossain et al., 2018; Kumar et al., 2019; do Nascimento et al., 2023; Lee et al., 2023). Therefore, the recent direction of drug delivery research is focusing on the use of polymeric nanocarriers (micelles), nanogels, nanospheres, nanocapsules, dendrimers, and natural cell-inspired nanoparticles that hold significant pharmacokinetic advantages for antiparasitic delivery.

A good example is the treatment of *Naegleria fowleri*, which is the free-living amoeba responsible for primary amoebic meningoencephalitis (PAM). It remains one of the most lethal human pathogens, with mortality exceeding 97% and rapid progression from headache and fever to coma and death within days. Infection occurs when the trophozoite form enters the central nervous system through the nasal cavity, yet treatment success is severely constrained by the blood–brain barrier (BBB), which tightly restricts therapeutic access to neural tissue (Siddiqui and Khan, 2014). Current regimens rely on empirical drug combinations, including amphotericin B, miltefosine, azithromycin, rifampicin, and fluconazole, but their poor penetration and delayed diagnosis limit survival (Güémez and García, 2021). While amphotericin B remains the *in vitro* standard and miltefosine offers BBB permeability, emerging sterol biosynthesis inhibitors and case reports showed that early intervention is vital. Increasingly, research focuses on engineered delivery systems to overcome BBB obstacles (Güémez and García, 2021).

Nanoparticles, such as polymeric carriers, gold and silver particles, and polyaniline-based composites, demonstrate improved drug stability, intracellular uptake, and direct trophozoite killing. Silver nanoparticle conjugates with amphotericin B enhance amoebicidal activity, flavonoid-linked nanoparticles showed to be better than conventional therapy, and modified nanocomposites such as PANI/hBN and PANI/WS2 achieve significant trophozoite reduction with limited host toxicity. Drug-linked nanomaterials such as GA-AgNPs reach up to 99% viability reduction, highlighting their therapeutic promise (Khaleel et al., 2025). Parallel innovations focus on artificial "shuttle peptides" capable of receptor-mediated BBB transport, exemplified by phage-selected sequences such as the dodecapeptide SGVYKVAYDWQH, which show high permeability with low toxicity (Dai et al., 2025). Intranasal delivery is also under investigation as a BBB-bypass route, although formulation barriers and enzyme degradation complicate translation.

6.13.1 Nanocarrier architecture and circulation time

Circulation time depends on carrier size, surface chemistry, hydrophilicity, and structural morphology. This section, the focus will be directed on examples of different types of nanocarriers mentioning their advantages to conduct the medication efficiently (Table 6.1).

Polymeric micelles: wormlike micelles have flexible assemblies and controlled disassembly under stimuli such as pH changes. For antiparasitic use, this means that micelles can circulate stably in the blood before selectively releasing drugs within acidic parasitized compartments, such as macrophage phagolysosomes or inflamed endothelial microenvironments (Blanco et al., 2015; Lee et al., 2023).

Nanogels: are soft, hydrated networks enhance circulation because their deformability minimizes clearance forces. Their responsiveness to environmental cues allows site-specific release at infected vascular foci (Wang et al., 2020; Jafari et al., 2021).

Table 6.1 Comparative overview of polymeric nanocarrier architectures, summarized from (Jafari et al., 2021; Lee et al., 2023).

Nanocarrier type	Typical size range	Core architecture / structure	Suitable cargo types	Main advantages	Key limitations	Common stimuli / design options	Example polymers / notes
Polymeric micelles (including wormlike, mixed, star, flower-like)	~20–200 nm	Self-assembled from amphiphilic copolymers into a **core-corona** structure: hydrophobic core and a hydrophilic shell; can form spherical, wormlike, multicompartment, or unimolecular micelles	Mainly **hydrophobic small molecules** in the core; hydrophilic agents or ligands can be associated with the corona; possible coloading of hydrophilic and hydrophobic drugs in multicompartment or mixed micelles	Very low CMC → high kinetic stability; strong solubilization of poorly soluble drugs; tunable size and shape; good for prolonged circulation; relatively simple self-assembly	Possible **dilution-induced disassembly** in vivo; sensitivity to ionic strength; stability issues may lead to premature drug leakage; sometimes limited loading of large biomacromolecules	pH-, redox-, temperature-, and light-responsive micelles via functional blocks or linkages; morphology changes (sphere ↔ wormlike) can be triggered by pH, solvent, CO_2, etc.	PEG–PCL, PEG–PDPA, PEG-based triblocks (e.g. PEG-b-CPP-b-SA); pH-activated wormlike micelles for endosomal drug release
Polymeric nanovesicles (polymersomes)	Typically ~80–150 nm (can be tuned)	Bilayer vesicles resembling liposomes: hydrophilic inner aqueous core and a hydrophobic membrane plus outer hydrophilic corona; built from amphiphilic block copolymers of higher MW than lipids	Hydrophilic drugs, proteins, nucleic acids in aqueous core; hydrophobic drugs in bilayer; coloading of multiple agents (e.g. DOX·HCl and a hydrophobic dye)	Higher mechanical and chemical stability than liposomes; excellent for codelivery of hydrophilic and hydrophobic drugs; tunable membrane thickness and permeability; a good platform for vaccines and theranostics	Preparation can be more complex; sometimes lower encapsulation efficiency, especially for large proteins; need scalable and reproducible manufacturing	pH-, redox-, and light-responsive membranes; surface can be engineered with targeting ligands, mucoadhesive or ionizable groups; can be designed as viromimetic particles for vaccines	PLGA-based vesicles, PEG–block copolymers, chitosan-based nanovesicles for intranasal SARS-CoV-2 RBD delivery; lipid–polymer hybrids for mRNA/vaccine delivery

(*Continued*)

Table 6.1 (Continued)

Nanocarrier type	Typical size range	Core architecture / structure	Suitable cargo types	Main advantages	Key limitations	Common stimuli / design options	Example polymers / notes
Nanogels	Often ~20–200 nm (soft, swollen)	Crosslinked 3D polymer networks at the nanoscale; can be simple, core–shell, hollow, multilayer, or "hairy" nanogels; high water content	Hydrophilic small molecules; biomacromolecules (proteins, peptides, nucleic acids); some hydrophobic drugs via hydrophobic domains, complexation, or conjugation	Very high loading capacity; soft and deformable (favorable for tissue penetration and even BBB crossing); excellent for multistimuli-responsive release; good biocompatibility when well-designed	Network density and crosslink chemistry can affect cytotoxicity; synthesis can show batch variability; risk of burst release if network is too loosely crosslinked	pH-, temperature-, redox-, H_2O_2-, sugar-, ATP-, and biomolecule-responsive designs; can be engineered as glucose-responsive insulin systems or self-healing networks	Poly(N-isopropylacrylamide), poly(γ-glutamic acid), glycol chitosan/alginate-based nanogels; PCgel (PEG–g–chitosan) hydrogels for localized T-cell delivery to glioblastoma
Nanospheres (polymeric nanoparticles)	~10–200 nm (focus of this article; broader definition up to 1000 nm)	Solid polymer matrices in which the drug is molecularly dispersed or adsorbed on the surface; generally spherical, but rod or star shapes also possible	Broad: hydrophobic or hydrophilic small molecules, sometimes macromolecules; drugs typically dispersed in polymer bulk or on surface	High structural stability; controllable, often sustained release via diffusion and matrix erosion; high surface area allows surface functionalization (e.g., targeting ligands, PEG)	Residual organic solvents from fabrication; possible fragility or aggregation; non biodegradable variants may raise long-term safety concerns	Can incorporate pH- or enzyme-degradable linkers, redox- responsive moieties, or targeting ligands on surface	PLGA nanoparticles for ocular dexamethasone; albumin-based nanospheres; PCL and Eudragit-based systems for ocular or topical delivery

Nanocapsules	Typically ~50–300 nm	Reservoir-type structures: inner core (aqueous or oily) surrounded by a thin polymeric shell; shell may be dense or semipermeable	Hydrophobic or volatile drugs in the oily core; hydrophilic drugs in the aqueous core; suitable for labile compounds that need strong protection	High encapsulation efficiency; strong protection of sensitiveor volatile agents; possibility of controlling burst versus sustained release by tuning shell thickness and permeability	More complex fabrication; achieving uniform shell thickness is challenging; stability of the core-shell interface is critical	Shells can be made pH-, enzyme-, or redox-degradable; surface easily modified for targeting or stealth	Poly (alkylcyanoacrylate) nanocapsules for codelivery of cyclosporin A and doxorubicin; various polyester- or polysaccharide-based capsule shells
Dendrimers	Typically 2–20 nm (generation-dependent)	Highly defined, tree-like branched macromolecules with a central core, repeating internal branches (generations), and dense functional end groups	Small molecules (in internal cavities or on the periphery), imaging agents, nucleic acids via electrostatic interactions, targeting ligands	Precise control over size, shape, and surface chemistry; a high density of functional groups; can carry multiple functions (drug and imaging and targeting) on one scaffold	Synthesis can be multistep and expensive; cationic surfaces can be cytotoxic unless modified; limited "cargo space" compared with larger carriers	pH- and redox-responsive linkers; the surface can be PEGylated or conjugated with targeting ligands, peptides, sugars	PAMAM and other dendrimers used for gene delivery, anticancer drug conjugates, and imaging probes
Nanocomposites (polymer-inorganic hybrids)	Variable; often ~50–200 nm	Hybrid assemblies combining a polymeric matrix or shell with inorganic or organic nanoparticles (e.g., metals, oxides, carbon nanomaterials)	Drugs codelivered with imaging agents (e.g., gold, iron oxide), or combined therapies (chemo plus photothermal or photodynamic)	Integrate multiple functions: imaging, therapy, targeting, and stimuli-responsiveness; can enable theranostic applications (diagnosis and treatment)	Added complexity in synthesis and characterization; inorganic components may introduce long-term toxicity risks; regulatory hurdles	Often designed as light-, magnetic field-, or pH-responsive systems; the polymer segment can be made biodegradable and/or stealth	PEG-b-PCL micelles encapsulating gold for radiosensitization; iron-loaded polymeric particles for anemia treatment and MRI contrast (e.g., dextran, polyglucose-based systems)

Nanospheres and nanocapsules: Nanospheres offer robust structural stability, while nanocapsules provide sustained release, which make them ideal for maintaining therapeutic levels against parasites with long erythrocytic stages, such as *Plasmodium (*Kumar et al., 2019*)*.

Dendrimers: provide exceptional monodispersity and multivalency, allowing precise pharmacokinetic tuning. Their size and uniformity allow predictable accumulation in vascular tissues but require surface modification to avoid rapid clearance (Reineke, 2013).

6.13.2 Margination toward endothelial and immune cell niches

Effective antiparasitic therapy often requires carrier interaction with the vessel wall, especially in diseases where parasites impound in endothelium (e.g., cerebral malaria) or where immune cells serve as reservoirs (*Leishmania* spp. within macrophages) (do Nascimento et al., 2023; Cong et al., 2024). Thus the structural design and size of the nanoparticles should be well understood. Softer nanocarriers (e.g., nanogels) migrate toward vessel walls more effectively, while the elongated micelles demonstrate enhanced lateral drift compared to rigid particles (Blanco et al., 2015).

For hematologic parasites, these margination behaviors directly enhance (I) targeting parasitized RBCs, which often adhere to endothelial surfaces, (II) delivery to infected macrophages, which cluster at inflamed vascular sites, and (III) interruption of endothelial invasion by circulating trypanosomes (Ricci et al., 2017; Singh et al., 2023). The natural cell–inspired nanoparticles (NCINPs) mimic RBCs, leukocytes, or platelets (Li et al., 2025). Therefore RBC-coated nanoparticles circulate the longest; thus they are ideal for *Plasmodium* spp. or *Babesia* spp. targeting (Ricci et al., 2017). The Leukocyte-mimetic nanocarriers are the option against inflamed endothelium; subsequently, they are highly relevant for trypanosome-induced vasculitis. Platelet-coated nanoparticles adhere to activated endothelium, potentially localizing to microvascular regions where parasites accumulate (Zizzari et al., 2020). Lastly, polyaniline (PANI) Nanocomposites; although primarily described as antimicrobial, their membrane-disruptive effects and strong interactions with biological membranes suggest targeted biodistribution potential for bloodstream-residing parasites (Kazemi et al., 2021).

For parasites such as *Trypanosoma brucei* and *Plasmodium falciparum* in cerebral malaria, BBB structure, transport systems, and BBB-crossing nanocarriers strategies are essential (Song et al., 2021). Key transporter-based mechanisms include:

- Shuttle peptides (RVG, transferrin, TAT)
- Nanocarriers exploiting receptor-mediated transcytosis
- Functional polymeric systems capable of pH-dependent BBB penetration

Although originally presented in the context of amoebic infection, these transport insights map directly to hematologic parasites with CNS involvement. To reach hematologic parasites, nanocarriers must evade macrophages and complement activation while preserving the ability to attack the infected tissues. There are multiple strategies for engineering stealth and immune conditioning, which include:

1. **Protein corona engineering**
   Opsonization, which is particle-protein interactions that influence every aspect of blood-based behavior; immune clearance; complement activation; and cellular uptake. It is affected directly by surface chemistry, hydrophobicity (how hydrophilic coatings minimize opsonization), and how responsive polymers adjust PC dynamics under different physiological conditions (Mahmoudi et al., 2016; Nguyen and Lee, 2017). In antiparasitic nanomedicine, PC engineering ensures avoidance of splenic macrophage clearance, prolonged interactions with parasitized RBCs, and moderated immune recognition to prevent premature clearance (Mahmoudi et al., 2016).
   For example, Cell-Inspired Immune Stealth such (i.e., NCINPs) provide built-in immune evasion (Li et al., 2025). Additionally, RBC-Membrane Coated Nanoparticles are ideal for targeting RBC-stage parasites because they contain CD47 "don't eat me" signals to avoid macrophage uptake (Rampado et al., 2020). Leukocyte-membrane coated nanoparticles are suitable for the treatment against inflamed endothelium as they present adhesion ligands for targeted vascular interactions. They mimic immune-cell tropism to reach parasite reservoirs in macrophages or dendritic cells. Platelet-inspired nanocarriers are relevant in malaria-associated microvascular dysfunction because they mimic thrombocytic interactions and adhere to activated endothelium (Zizzari et al., 2020).
2. **Intrinsic immunomodulation: polyaniline nanocomposites**
   PANI nanocomposites have inherent antimicrobial and immunomodulatory activity through a sequence of efficient steps. They have the capability of permeabilization the membrane, followed by modulation of the oxidative stress, leading to alteration of cellular redox systems, and subsequently provide selective cytotoxicity to pathogens. Their cationic nature supports selective association with parasitic membranes rich in anionic lipids (Kazemi et al., 2021).
3. **Payload strategies: small molecules, combinations, and CRISPR/siRNA against parasite targets**

Nanocarrier engineering, especially through exosome-based delivery platforms, has opened new therapeutic possibilities for parasitic infections that colonize or persist within the central nervous system (CNS) (Onohuean et al., 2025). Brain-resident parasites such as *Toxoplasma gondii* and opportunistic coinfections in immunocompromised states (e.g., HIV-associated encephalopathies with latent *T. gondii* cysts) require robust payload strategies. These strategies can penetrate the blood–brain barrier (BBB), reach intracellular reservoirs, and modulate immune and pathogen-derived pathways.

Molecular loading strategies, including small-molecule drug encapsulation, combination payloads, and gene-silencing CRISPR/siRNA systems, all of which can be adapted for nanoparticle-based antiparasitic therapies (Kozela et al., 2025).

6.13.2.1 Small molecule payloads for targeting CNS parasites

Exosomes and other nanocarriers can encapsulate antimicrobial small molecules used against protozoal and fungal pathogens, which offer conceptual parallels for antiparasitic drug delivery (Jafari et al., 2021). Small molecules, whether hydrophobic or hydrophilic, benefit from the natural BBB-crossing ability of exosomes (Blanco et al., 2015). Drug-loaded vesicles bypass efflux pumps and avoid rapid systemic clearance, which is critical for antiparasitics traditionally limited by poor CNS penetration. Amphotericin B and fluconazole-exosome formulations demonstrate substantially improved CNS bioavailability and reduced toxicity (Jafari et al., 2021). Comparable behavior is expected for antiparasitics such as pyrimethamine, sulfadiazine, atovaquone, and azithromycin whose therapeutic indices improve when delivered by nanocarriers.

Exosome membranes can be engineered with ligands such as RVG, transferrin, or mannose, thereby enabling uptake by endothelial cells, neurons, microglia, or infected macrophages (Salvati et al., 2013). This allows small-molecule antiparasitics to reach *T. gondii* cysts in neurons (using SAG1-or CD36-targeting ligands), enter activated microglia or astrocytes where parasites reside, and accumulate in inflamed meninges in cases of cerebral toxoplasmosis. Such ligand-enhanced delivery parallels for HIV neuroinfection and cryptococcal meningitis, which showed selective exosome accumulation in infected brain regions.

6.13.2.2 Combination payload strategies: synergy against parasite survival pathways

Dual or multimodal therapeutic designs, integrating BBB-targeting ligands, pathogen-specific surface markers, and multiple therapeutic payloads (e.g., drug plus siRNA), offer powerful templates for nanoparticle-based approaches to parasitic CNS diseases. Combinatory ligand presentation enhances both brain entry and parasite selectivity. The synergy of multimodal exosome systems in neuroinfection models, where codelivery sharply enhances therapeutic efficacy while minimizing systemic toxicity.

The T7 peptide plus anti-SAG1 aptamer for *T. gondii* demonstrating the feasibility of dual-ligand strategies. Combination-loaded exosomes (i.e., antiviral plus siRNA systems) can be translated directly to antiparasitics. For example:

- Small molecule plus siRNA (e.g., atovaquone with anti-ROP18 siRNA),
- Drug plus immunomodulator (e.g., antiparasitic plus anti-TNF-α miRNA),
- CRISPR plus therapeutic compound to simultaneously suppress parasite replication and modulate host neuroinflammation.

For parasites such as *T. gondii*, CRISPR can target virulence genes (e.g., ROP18, ROP5, SAG1, MIC proteins) or enzymes essential for cyst survival. Ligands such as transferrin or RVG further enhance CNS-specific CRISPR delivery.

6.13.2.3 siRNA payloads for silencing parasite virulence genes

There are several direct examples of siRNA-loaded exosomes targeting HIV genes (tat/rev), HSV genes (ICP0), fungal virulence genes, and, importantly, *T. gondii* genes such as ROP18 and SAG1 that regulate invasion and immune evasion. These platforms showed clear reductions in pathogen replication and cyst load in preclinical models, indicating high translational value for antiparasitic therapy.

6.13.2.4 Aptamer- and lipid assisted targeting of gene silencing cargo

The aptamer-modified exosomes is used to target SAG1 for precise delivery of siRNA and CRISPR components into *T. gondii*–infected neurons and astrocytes. Lipid insertion (e.g., DSPE–PEG aptamer conjugates) enhances membrane anchoring and brain tissue penetration, thereby improving gene-silencing efficiency.

6.13.3 Safety and translation: hemocompatibility, off-target risks, scale-up, and regulatory considerations

The efficiency in using the nanocarriers should also reflect the critical insight into safety considerations that directly inform nanoparticle translation. These considerations should show clear evidences on:

1. **Hemocompatibility**
   Nanocarriers should be designed to minimize hemolysis, complement activation, platelet activation, and endothelial disruption. Hydrophilic polymer coatings and biomimetic covering improve compatibility for hematologic use.
2. **Off-target toxicity**
   Potential risks that should be highlighted include excessive ROS generation by polyaniline composites, off-target receptor interactions by shuttle peptides, and immune overactivation by nonstealth polymers.
3. **Scale-up and manufacturing**
   Scaling up the product should support pharmaceutical grade production, which can be by using scalable fabrication approaches such as nanoprecipitation, ionic gelation, solvent evaporation, and emulsion polymerization.
4. **Regulatory considerations**

Translationally favorable characteristics comprise biocompatible polymers, natural cell-derived membranes, modular synthesis, and predictable PK profiles.

References

Akhtar T, Amanat MU, Wazir N, Naeem MI, Ammar M, Naeem MA, et al. Pathology of parasitic infections. Parasitism and Parasitic Control in Animals: Strategies for the Developing World. CABI Digital Library; 2023. p. 21–39. Available from https://doi.org/10.1079/9781800621893.0002.

Almeida Furquim de Camargo B, Fonseca-Santos B, Gonçalves Carvalho S, Corrêa Carvalho G, Delello Di Filippo L, Sousa Araújo VH, et al. Functionalized lipid-based drug delivery nanosystems for the treatment of human infectious diseases. Critical Reviews in Microbiology 2023;49(2):214–30.

Alsharedeh RH, Rezigue M, Bashatwah RM, Amawi H, Aljabali AA, Obeid MA, et al. Nanomaterials as a potential target for infectious parasitic agents. Current Drug Delivery 2024;21(6):828–51.

Blanco E, Shen H, Ferrari M. Principles of nanoparticle design for overcoming biological barriers. Nature Biotechnology 2015;33:941–51.

Cong X, Zhang Z, Li H, Yang Y-G, Zhang Y, Sun T. Nanocarriers for targeted drug delivery in the vascular system: focus on endothelium. Journal of Nanobiotechnology 2024;22(1):620.

Dai L, Guo X-R, Chen X-R, Ma M-H, Liu Z-H, Lai J, et al. A review of the mechanism, diagnosis, and treatment of Naegleria fowleri infection. Frontiers in Microbiology 2025;16:1686695.

Daraee H, Eatemadi A, Abbasi E, Fekri Aval S, Kouhi M, Akbarzadeh A. Application of gold nanoparticles in biomedical and drug delivery. Artificial Cells, Nanomedicine, and Biotechnology 2016;44(1):410–22.

Güémez A, García E. Primary amoebic meningoencephalitis by naegleria fowleri: pathogenesis and treatments. Biomolecules 2021;11(9):1320. Available from https://doi.org/10.3390/biom11091320.

Hossain F, Ghann W, Kang H, et al. Nanotechnology-based approaches against trypanosomiasis. Nanomedicine 2018;14:1647–63.

Huang Y, Guo X, Wu Y, Chen X, Feng L, Xie N, et al. Nanotechnology's frontier in combatting infectious and inflammatory diseases: prevention and treatment. Signal Transduction and Targeted Therapy 2024;9:34.

Jafari M, Abolmaali SS, Tamaddon AM, Zomorodian K, Shahriarirad B. Nanotechnology approaches for delivery and targeting of amphotericin B in fungal and parasitic diseases. Nanomedicine 2021;16(10):857–77.

Kazemi F, Naghib SM, Zare Y, Rhee KY. Biosensing applications of polyaniline (PANI)-based nanocomposites: a review. Polymer Reviews 2021;61(3):553–97.

Khaleel DS, Mutter TY, Hamid LL, Hassan OM. Morphological transformation of silver nanoparticles to nanofibers via gallic acid conjugation: a synergistic approach against multidrug-resistant pathogens. Chemical Engineering Journal Advances 2025;23:100836. Available from https://doi.org/10.1016/j.ceja.2025.100836.

Kozela E, Smagghe G, Regev-Rudzki N. Message in a vesicle: the role of extracellular vesicle cargo in parasite–host inter-kingdom communication and spread of systemic RNAi in insects. RNA interference in Agriculture: Basic Science to Applications: From Bioinformatics and Laboratory Assays Over Regulatory Issues to Field Uses. Springer; 2025. p. 121–44. Available from https://doi.org/10.1007/978-3-031-81549-2_7.

Kumar R, Gupta A, Sharma A. Nanotechnology-based drug delivery systems for malaria. Journal of Drug Targeting 2019;27:484–500.

Lee SH, Bae J, Kim HY. Nanocarriers for crossing biological barriers: design considerations and recent advances. Advanced Drug Delivery Reviews 2023;192:114–32.

Li Y, Xiong J, Yu H, Wang J, Wu M, Lou X, et al. Natural cell-inspired nanoparticles: preparation, mechanisms, applications, and prospects for clinical translation. Advanced Materials 2025;37(51):e05187. Available from 10.1002/adma.202505187.

Mahmoudi M, Bertrand N, Zope H, Farokhzad OC. Protein corona formation on nanoparticles: implications for nanomedicine. Chemical Reviews 2016;116:11875–910.

Mitchell MJ, Billingsley MM, Haley RM, et al. Engineering precision nanoparticles for drug delivery. Nature Reviews Drug Discovery 2021;20:101–24.

Monopoli MP, Aberg C, Salvati A, Dawson KA. Biomolecular coronas provide the biological identity of nanosized materials. Nature Nanotechnology 2012;7:779–86. Available from https://doi.org/10.1038/nnano.2012.207.

do Nascimento T, Santos-Oliveira R, dos Santos Matos A, Ricci-Júnior E. Nanoparticles for the treatment of visceral leishmaniasis: review. Journal of Nanoparticle Research 2023;10(6):9–21.

Natarajan JV, Nugraha C, Ng XW, Venkatraman S. Sustained-release from nanocarriers: a review. Journal of Controlled Release 2014;193:122–38. Available from https://doi.org/10.1016/j.jconrel.2014.05.029.

Nguyen VH, Lee BJ. Protein corona: a new approach for nanomedicine design. International Journal of Nanomedicine 2017;12:3137–51. Available from https://doi.org/10.2147/IJN.S129300.

Onohuean H, Naik Bukke SP, Thalluri C, Abass KS, Choonara YE. Exosome engineering for targeted therapy of brain-infecting pathogens: molecular tools, delivery platforms, and translational advances. Frontiers in Medical Technology 2025;7. Available from https://doi.org/10.3389/fmedt.2025.1655471.

Rampado R, Crotti S, Caliceti P, Pucciarelli S, Agostini M. Recent advances in understanding the protein corona of nanoparticles and in the formulation of 'stealthy' nanomaterials. Frontiers in Bioengineering and Biotechnology 2020;8:166.

Reineke JJ. Dendrimers for parasite gene delivery. Nanomedicine 2013;8:9–12.

Ricci M, Ferrarini M, Angius F, et al. Red blood cell membrane–coated nanoparticles for targeting plasmodium-infected cells. Nanomedicine 2017;12:2413–25.

Salvati A, Pitek AS, Monopoli MP, et al. Transferrin-functionalized nanoparticles lose targeting capabilities when a biomolecule corona adsorbs on the surface. Nature Communications 2013;4:2719.

Siddiqui R, Khan NA. Primary amoebic meningoencephalitis caused by naegleria fowleri: an old enemy presenting new challenges. PLOS Neglected Tropical Diseases 2014;8(8). Available from https://doi.org/10.1371/journal.pntd.0003017.

Singh K, Tiwari R, Keshari AK, et al. Surface-functionalized nanoparticles for targeting plasmodium-infected erythrocytes. Journal of Controlled Release 2023;361:240–52.

Song J, Lu C, Leszek J, Zhang J. Design and development of nanomaterial-based drug carriers to overcome the blood–brain barrier by using different transport mechanisms. International Journal of Molecular Sciences 2021;22(18):10118.

Stiufiuc GF, Stiufiuc RI. Magnetic Nanoparticles: synthesis, characterization, and their use in biomedical field. Applied Sciences 2024;14(4):1623. Available from https://doi.org/10.3390/app14041623.

Tiwari R, Gupta RP, Singh VK, Kumar A, Rajneesh N, Madhukar P, et al. Nanotechnology-based strategies in parasitic disease management: from prevention to diagnosis and treatment. ACS Omega 2023;8(45):42014–27. Available from https://doi.org/10.1021/acsomega.3c04587.

Wang X, Zhang X, Cheng L, et al. Nanocarrier-mediated drug delivery across biological barriers. Materials Today 2020;32:152–67.

Zizzari AT, Giuliani P, La Barbera A, et al. Platelet-inspired nanoparticles target sites of vascular inflammation in malaria. Biomaterials 2020;226:119548.

CHAPTER 7

Artificial intelligence and machine learning in antiparasitic drug discovery

Shubhradip Singha Roy[1,*], Mahek Sultana[1,*], Diptangshu Modak[1,*], Riddha Saha[1,*], Asmita Samadder[1,2], and Sisir Nandi[3]
[1]Cell and Developmental Biology Special, Department of Zoology, University of Kalyani, Kalyani, West Bengal, India,
[2]Cytogenetics and Molecular Biology Lab., Department of Zoology, University of Kalyani, Kalyani, West Bengal, India,
[3]Global Institute of Pharmaceutical Education and Research, Kashipur, Uttarakhand, India

7.1 Introduction

Artificial intelligence (AI) brings together science and engineering to create smart machines, primarily computer programs. While the idea first came up in the 1950s, the real boom in AI happened in the early 2020s. Significant progress in computing and advancements in machine learning (ML) methods, including deep learning (DL), along with improvements in human resources, have brought us into the heart of the AI revolution. Nowadays, AI has almost touched every part of human life and is ready to change the healthcare sector. Artificial intelligence and machine learning are transforming parasite disease diagnosis and management. They increase disease surveillance, speed up drug discovery, and enhance diagnostics (Parija and Poddar, 2024). The drawbacks of traditional methods, which are costly, time consuming, and vulnerable to new drug resistance, could be overcome by exploring different avenues of thanks to AI and ML. Malaria, leishmaniasis, trypanosomiasis, and microfilariasis are among the parasitic diseases that still afflict people all over the world, especially in environments with inadequate resources and disproportionately affect vulnerable groups. It has made it necessary to investigate novel approaches and restricted the application of traditional methods for disease prevention and healthcare delivery. With the potential for improved diagnostics, precision drug development, predictive modeling, and individualized treatment, AI has emerged as a revolutionary tool with enormous promise in the management of parasitic diseases. By examining enormous volumes of epidemiological data, environmental variables, and population demographics, predictive AI systems have helped to comprehend parasite transmission patterns and epidemics. This has made it possible to take proactive steps to stop the spread of disease by strengthening public health initiatives, resource allocation, and epidemic preparedness tactics (Parija and Poddar, 2024).

---

[*] Equal authorship.

Innovative Strategies Against Blood Parasites
DOI: https://doi.org/10.1016/B978-0-443-48509-1.00009-4

AI has been immensely advantageous to the processing of many images for blood smears, stool samples and tissue biopsies. AI has accurately identified and classified parasitic stages (e.g., eggs, larvae, and adult worms) using ML tools such as CNNs (Convolutional neural network). There has been extensive exploration of the diagnostic value of AI in the differentiation of various intestinal parasites from stool samples, including hookworms, roundworms, and whipworms. Similarly, malaria parasites, blood parasites (African sleeping sickness and leishmaniasis) and schistosomiasis were detected. The development of AIDMAN (AI based object detection system for malaria diagnosis.), an AI based system for detecting malaria parasites in blood smears taken using smartphones, showcases the disruptive capacity of AI in diagnostic parasitology. It achieved 98.62% diagnostic accuracy of cells from blood smears and 97% for examining blood smear images. The clinical validation of AIDMAN demonstrated an accuracy of 98.44%, comparable to skilled microscopists with years of experience. Artificial intelligence (AI) programs can swiftly screen vast libraries of molecules to find potential medications, as opposed to screening millions of chemicals in a lab setting. In order to forecast a compound's safety and effectiveness against specific parasites, machine learning algorithms analyze its chemical structures and properties. This saves a ton of time and money (Serrano et al., 2024).

7.1.1 Blood parasite

Blood parasites are tiny organisms that feed on the blood of their animal hosts, including people, and reproduce there. Both singlecelled protozoa and more complex organisms can be considered parasites. Parasitic infections pose a significant global health burden, particularly in regions with limited medical resources and poor sanitation. These infections often have detrimental effects on the human body, including disruptions to the hematopoietic system, the intricate network responsible for blood cell production. Because they damage red blood cells, activate the immune system, and impact vital organs, they frequently result in serious health issues (Pang et al., 2026). Blood parasites of those are very dangerous and they are dangerous for human health. The following are some of the most well known blood parasites that affect people:

Plasmodium: One of the most common and fatal parasitic diseases, especially in tropical areas, is malaria (*Plasmodium* species). There are five species of Plasmodium that commonly infect humans: P. falciparum, *P. vivax, P. malariae, P. ovale, and P. knowlesi.* From which first four specific for human and fifth one (*P. knowlesi*) is found in macaque monkeys and cause zoonotic disease. But all five *Plasmodium* species causing malaria in humans are transmitted exclusively by anopheline mosquitoes. For example, thalassemia and sickle cell anaemia, each of which affecting RBC. In Central and West Africa people who suffers with Duffy Negative blood type have resistance to *P. vivax*. The spread of this trait in the population is estimated to have begun around 42,000 years ago, and today

P. vivax malaria is rare in these areas. Fever, chills, and other flu like symptoms are caused by the parasite's infection of red blood cells (Zekar and Sharman, 2023).

Today modern world has antimalarial and insecticide treated bed nets, people in some countries remain at risk mainly in Africa. But we are able to decrease the death rate caused by malaria after releasing "combat malaria" programs and use of ITN and other antimalarial drugs. In 2000, the global death caused by malaria is 839,000, but by 2015 these numbers had been reduced to 483,000 (Sato, 2021).

Trypanosoma: It is a genus of single-celled parasites (protozoa). The significant components are *Trypanosoma cruzi and Trypanosoma brucei*. *Trypanosoma cruzi* that causes Chagas disease, is primarily found in Latin America and is spread by the excrement of the triatomine "kissing" bug. This disease has two phases: acute and chronic. Many years after the initial infection, it can result in both an acute illness and a chronic disease that causes serious digestive and cardiac issues, it also causes nerve disorders. It is also transmitted through vertical transmission between mother and child. Other modes of transmission are transfusion of blood products, transplant of an infected organs or consumption of infected food and drinks. It has two phases: acute and chronic. Acute phase lasting for two months. The symptoms are fever, localized edema and unilateral eyelid swelling (Romanas sign). In chronic phase cardiac complications occurs (cardiomegaly, heart failure). Treatment includes antiparasitic medications, nifurtimox and benznidazole, which are most effective in the acute phase. In chronic cases, management focuses on treating complications, with some patients requiring pacemakers, defibrillators, or surgical interventions. The World health organization (WHO) estimates that 6 to 7 million people are currently infected with *T. cruzi*, causing 12,000 deaths annually, with 75 million people at risk of contracting the disease. In endemic regions of the Americas, approximately 28,000 new cases are reported annually (Winters et al., 2025).

Trypanosoma brucei causes African sleeping sickness which is spread by tsetse flies in sub Saharan Africa, can result in fever, headaches, and joint pain in early stages (Winters et al., 2025). When injected by fly, metacyclic form parasites are introduced into the host dermis and then disseminate into the bloodstream as replicative long slender forms. It periodically changes a dense coat of only one kind of Variant surface glycoprotein (VSG), drawing from a genomic repertoire of about 2000 VSG encoding gene. Oral or intravenous drugs like fexinidazole, eflornithine, or nifurtimox are used to treat this disease. In 2015, it caused around 3500 deaths, a sharp drop from 34,000 in 1990. The WHO reported under 1000 new cases in 2018 (Romero-Meza and Mugnier, 2020).

Dengue: A major global health concern, dengue fever is the most common arthropod borne viral disease in the world and is spread by mosquitoes. Intense muscle spasms, joint pain, and a high fever that reflects the severity and duration of symptoms are the hallmarks of this illness, which is also referred to by a number of names, including breakbone or 7 day fever. There are 4 sereotypes of dengue (DENV-1 to DENV-4). The majority of dengue virus cases are asymptomatic, but severe illness and death can happen, particularly in areas where the virus is mostly spread by female Aedes mosquitoes (*Aedes aegypti* and *Aedes albopictus*). Dengue fever can cause serious illness and even death, although the majority of cases are asymptomatic. The virus is spread by *Aedes* mosquitoes, which are prevalent in tropical and subtropical regions of the world and mainly include the female vectors *Aedes aegypti* and *A. albopictus*. Due to increase in world travel dengue fever increased dramatically all over the world over the past few decades. Over 100 million cases and 20 to 25,000 deaths occurs annually all over the world (Schaefer et al., 2024).

Rickettsia: *Rickettsia* is a group of vector-borne organisms that cause acute febrile illness throughout the world. The causative agent can vary depending on the region. *Rickettsia* has mainly four types of arthropod vectors: ticks, flies, lice, and mites. The American dog tick, Rocky mountain wood tick are examples of vectors of spotted fever group. Rickettsia group has four categories: spotted fever group, typhus group, ancestral group, and traditional group. *Rickettsia rickettsii* causes Rocky mounted spotted fever, most severe and most well known of rickettsia infection in North America. Other species are common in other parts of the world, including *Rickettsia africae*, the cause of African tick bite fever in sub Sahara Africa, and *Rickettsia conorii* which causes Mediterranean spotted fever in Europe and North Africa. *Rickettsia* preferentially infects the vascular endothelial cells lining the small and medium vessels throughout the body, causing the systemic symptoms and high mortality seen with these infections. The infection of endothelial cells leads to disseminated inflammation, loss of barrier function, and altered vascular permeability throughout the body. Consequently, those infected develop fever, myalgias, central nervous system symptoms such as headache, confusion, rash, and cardiovascular instability. Mortality can occur in severe cases of infection. Drugs used to treat dengue are doxycycline (Snowden et al., 2023).

Babesiosis (*Babesia* species): A tick borne illness that infects red blood cells and causes symptoms similar to malaria, such as fever, chills, and fatigue. It is most common in the northeastern and midwestern United States (Zimmer et al., 2023). The parasite is also referred to as piroplasm because of its 'pear shaped' that is seen within the infected erythrocyte. In the United States, infection by babesia is rare and only limited to certain geographical regions. *Babesia* species have been subdivided into four categories, known as clades. The nymphal stage of *Ixodes* is the primary vector and typically requires attachment to a host for at least 36 to 72 hours to complete a blood meal. If the tick is carrying the protozoa, the second or third day of attachment is typically when the babesia infection occurs with the transmission of sporozoite forms. These sporozoites attach and enter erythrocytes, where they mature and divide through binary fission to form merozoites. Drugs used to treat this disease are atovaquone, azithromycin.

From 2018 to 2022, babesiosis was the underlying cause of death for an average of 14 United States residents per year (70 deaths over the five year period). When listed among multiple causes contributing to death, the annual average was 20.8 deaths (104 total) (Zimmer et al., 2023).

Filariasis (filarial worms)*:* These are parasitic roundworms transmitted by mosquitoes or black flies. They can live in the lymphatic system, causing severe swelling (elephantiasis), or in the skin and eyes, leading to conditions such as River Blindness (Goldin et al., 2025). *Wuchereria bancrofti, Brugia malayi*, or *Brugia timori* are the most common causes of lymphatic filariasis, which is acknowledged by the World health organization as a major cause of disability globally. Each species has a different set of filariasis symptoms. Usually contracted in childhood, lymphatic filariasis can cause progressive harm to the lymphatic and renal systems while compromising immune function. It can also be asymptomatic for years. The limbs, breasts, vulva, and scrotum may develop chronic lymphedema and elephantiasis as a result of recurrent inflammatory episodes over time. Aden lymphangitis, filarial fever, acute dermatolymphangioadenitis, and tropical pulmonary eosinophilia are examples of acute syndromes. The three symptoms of onchocerciasis, also known as river blindness, are nodular, ocular, and dermatological. Finding microfilariae in blood, skin, or ocular tissues is necessary for diagnosis. Blood smears are frequently used by medical professionals to diagnose lymphatic filariasis. Management includes antiparasitic therapy tailored to the infecting species. Medications include diethylcarbamazine, ivermectin, albendazole, and doxycycline.

Due to widespread drug administration programs, the global incidence of lymphatic filariasis declined from 199 million cases in 2000 to approximately 50 million in 2018. According to the World health organization (WHO), around 36 million people have manifestations of filariasis (Goldin et al., 2025).

7.1.2 Mode of infection

The mode of infection of blood parasites varies between species to species. They are mainly of two types; one is vector borne and another one is direct transmission. Some common parasites transmission methods mentioned below:

Plasmodium: This is the most common mode of transmission, where a living organism acts as vector and transmits the parasite. Plasmodium species mainly cause malaria in human. Anopheles mosquitoes are the main vector for the transmission of the disease. These parasites alternating between sexual stages and asexual stages in *Anopheles* mosquitoes and mammalian tissues respectively. After inoculation into mammalian bloodstream, they finally reached into the liver and interact with heparan sulfate, thereby enabling invasion of hepatocytes. Eruption of the merozoites from infected erythrocytes results in the release of GPIs, which is believed to be prominent virulent factor that contribute to malaria pathogenesis (Cummings and Turco,2009).

Trypanosoma: *Trypanosoma brucei* causes nagana disease in cattle and African sleeping sickness in humans, have been transmitted by blood sucking tsetse flies. These parasites have variations in GPI anchor glycoproteins (VSGs) present on their glycocalyx. As parasites multiply in host bloodstream, the host immune system mounts an immune response specific for certain VSGs (Cummings and Turco, 2009).

Dengue: These diseases have been transmitted by *Aedes aegypti* mosquitoes. After inoculation into mosquito's midgut, dengue virus distributes systemically through the body cavity. The ubiquitin-proteasome, an important pathway, acts significant activity in the regulation of infectious DENV production in vectors. Finally, an infection of the salivary glands and the release of virions into the host's saliva occur throughout the DENV transmission to the host (Islam et al., 2021).

Rickettsia: *Rickettsia* organisms are found all over the world and are carried by a range of hematophagous arthropod vectors, such as fleas, lice, mites, and ticks. Rickettsiae are transmitted through a person's skin. SFG (Spotted fever group) species are spread when an infected tick feeds. Typhus group organisms are spread by injecting infected flea or louse excrement (*R. typhi* and *R. prowazekii*, respectively) onto mucous membranes or bite wounds. *Liponyssoides* sanguineus mites are carriers of *Rickettsia akari*. After being injected into the skin, organisms are taken up by dendritic cells and carried to nearby lymph nodes by lymphatics, where they multiply. After entering the bloodstream, the organisms spread to infect the microcirculation's endothelium (Blanton, 2019).

Babesiosis: Babesia is a protozoan parasite that causes babesiosis. This parasite mainly affects erythrocytes and is spread by ticks. *Babesia* can have an oval or pear shaped appearance and usually infects red blood cells. The red blood cell's ring shape and peripheral location frequently leads to incorrect interpretation of the *plasmodium falciparum* smear. Hemolysis is uncommon in babesiosis, in contrast to *plasmodium*. The damaged red blood cells are captured by the spleen, which may enlarge. The disease typically progresses more severely in patients without a spleen (Zimmer and Simonsen,2023).

Filariasis: *Filaria* is a parasitic infection caused by nematode *Wuchereria bancrofti*. When infected mosquitoes bite humans, it deposits third stage larvae into the skin. The larvae migrate into the lymphatic system and reproduce. Females release microfilariae with nocturnal periodicity, which circulate in the blood. A mosquito ingests the microfilaria during a blood meal. The microfilariae develop into infectious third stage larvae, which are transmitted to another human during feeding (Goldin and Juergens,2025).

7.1.3 Morbidity and mortality

Morbidity and mortality are two metrics that are frequently employed in epidemiological surveillance. These metrics characterize the course and intensity of a specific health event. They are helpful resources for comparing and contrasting health events across various populations and learning about disease risk factors. Morbidity and mortality are not the same, despite their similarities and frequent connections. Being symptomatic or unwell due to a disease or condition is known as morbidity. It is computed by dividing the total number of individuals in a given population by the number of affected individuals. Conversely, mortality is associated with the quantity of deaths brought on by the health event that is being studied. It can be expressed as an absolute number or as a rate. Mortality usually gets represented as a rate per 1000 individuals (Hernandez and Kim, 2022).

Two forms of retrospective data that enable ongoing assessment of the effectiveness of a particular healthcare system or an intervention in place are morbidity and mortality. For instance, it is crucial to use maternal morbidity and mortality to assess the risks associated with pregnancy and childbirth as well as the effectiveness of the medical care they received. In a similar spirit, precise evaluation of these metrics is essential to comprehending and assessing their trajectory and impact. In the end, mortality and morbidity enable epidemiologists to further investigate the potential burdens that a health event may have on a population (Hernandez and Kim, 2022).

Parasitic diseases cause significant morbidity and mortality globally, particularly in tropical and subtropical regions, with malaria being the deadliest parasitic disease, 282 million malaria cases and 610,000 malarial deaths in 80 countries in 2024. In the case of dengue a record 14.1 million cases and over 9500 deaths were reported in 2024. *Trypanosoma cruzi* (Chagas disease) infects 6 to 7 million people globally, causing around 10,000 deaths annually. In case of filariasisas of 2018, 51 million people were infected, a 74% decline since the start of WHO's Global Programme in 2000. Other serious parasitic diseases include those affecting the central nervous system, which are associated with high mortality and can lead to lifelong disabilities. Factors like poor sanitation, lack of clean water, and low socioeconomic status increase the risk of parasitic infections, especially in children, and diseases such as lymphatic filariasis can result in disfiguring conditions.

7.2 Drugs for the treatment

Drugs used to treat parasitic diseases are commonly known as antiparasitic drugs and are designed to act on protozoa, worms, and other parasites. These drugs work by stopping parasites from breaking out, surviving, or reproducing. Choice of the treatment depends on the type of parasite involved (Leder and McGUINNESS, 2023).

7.2.1 Antimalarial drugs

Cerebral malaria has traditionally been treated with several commonly available antimalarial drugs as schizonticides, gametocides or effective against liver and erythrocytic stages based on their mode of action (Mandal et al., 2025). Active marketed tissue schizonticides were reported as pyrimethamine, proguanil, chlorguanil, atovaquone, primaquine, pamaquine, and sulfadoxine (Table 7.1).

There are various drugs that either stop the parasitic heme crystallization process or stop the RBC invasion. These drugs are chloroquine, hydroxychloroquine, amodiaquine, quinine, mefloquine, lumefantrine and halofantrine (Table 7.2).

Table 7.1 Antimalarial tissue schizontocides.

Sl. no	Compound name	Structure	Mode of action	References
1	Pyrimethamine	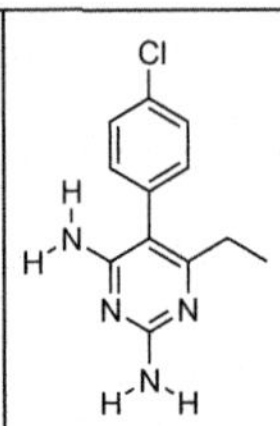	Plasmodium dihydrofolate reductase (DHFR).	Dasgupta and Anderson (2008)
2	Proguanil	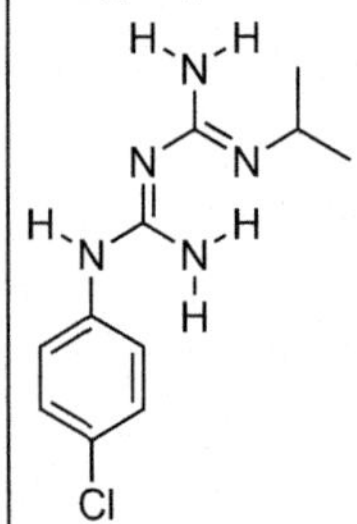		
3	Chlorproguanil	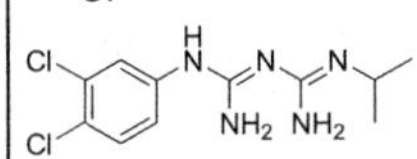	Inhibits dihydrofolate reductase	Tahar et al., 2001; Fidock et al., 2017
4	Atovaquone	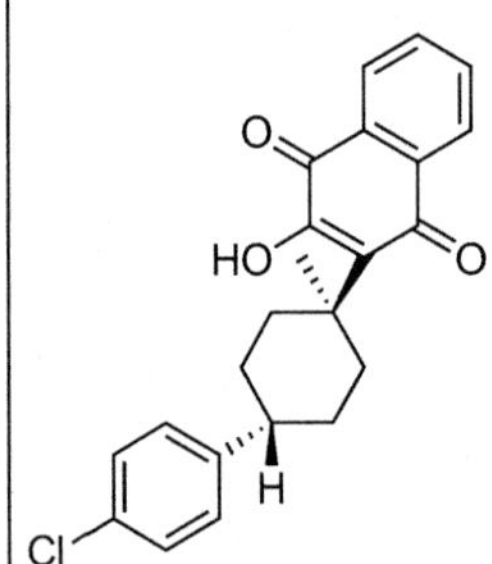	Plasmodium cytochrome bc1 complex	Nixon et al. (2013)
5	Primaquine	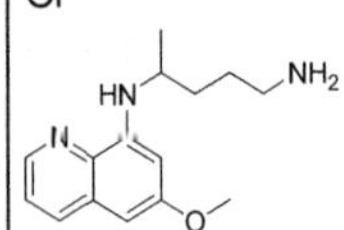	Oxidative pathway	Camarda et al. (2019)
6	Pamaquine	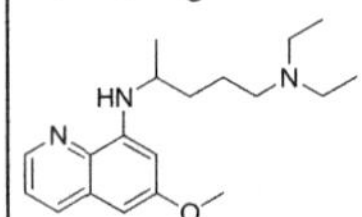	Hypnozoite, gametocytes, mitochondria, ROS pathway.	
7	Sulfadoxine	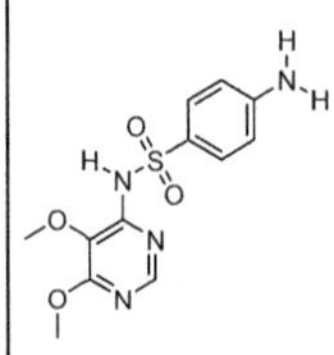	Targets dihydropteroate synthase and dihydrofolate reductase.	Sibley et al., 2001

Table 7.2 Antimalarials that inhibit the erythrocytic phase.

Sl no.	Compound name	Structure	Target	References
8	Chloroquine	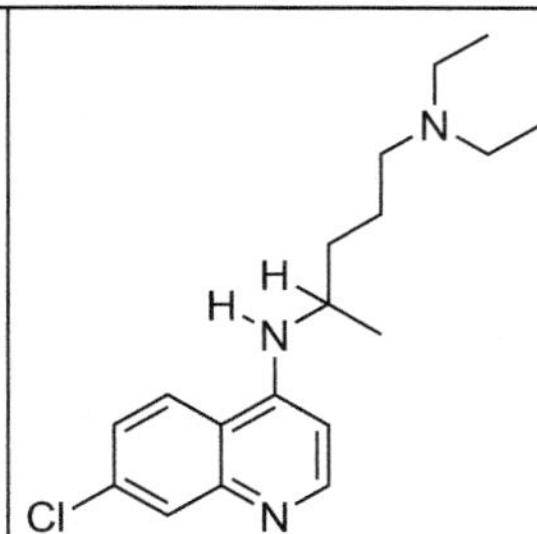	It prevents heme detoxification	Singh et al. (2023)
9	Hydroxychloroquine	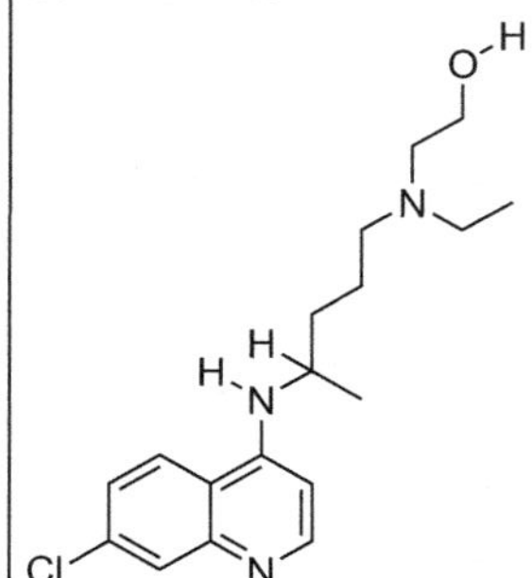	Prevents heme detoxification	Russo et al. (2024)
10	Amodiaquine	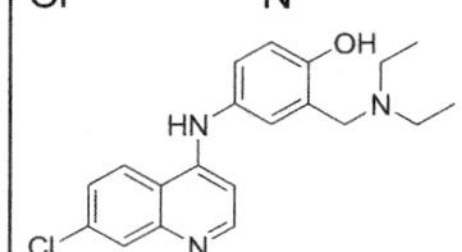	Prevents heme detoxification	Theodoridis and Carvalho (2025)
11	Quinine	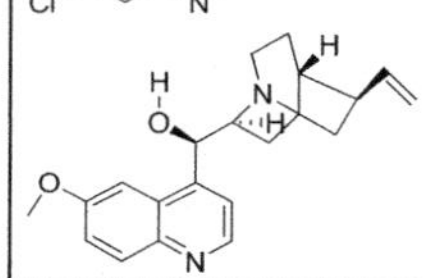	Heme detoxification in parasites.	Abebe and Woldesenbet (2025)

(Continued)

Table 7.2 (Continued)

Sl no.	Compound name	Structure	Target	References
12	Mefloquine	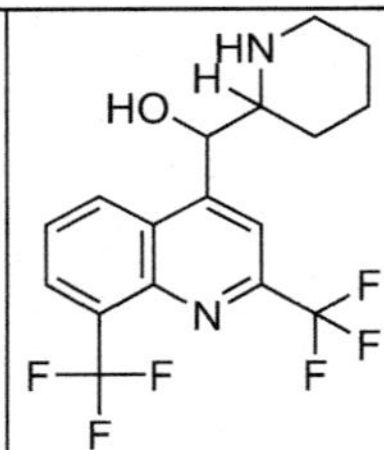	Binds to 80 s ribosome of the parasite and inhibits translation	Wong et al. (2017)
13	Lumefantrine	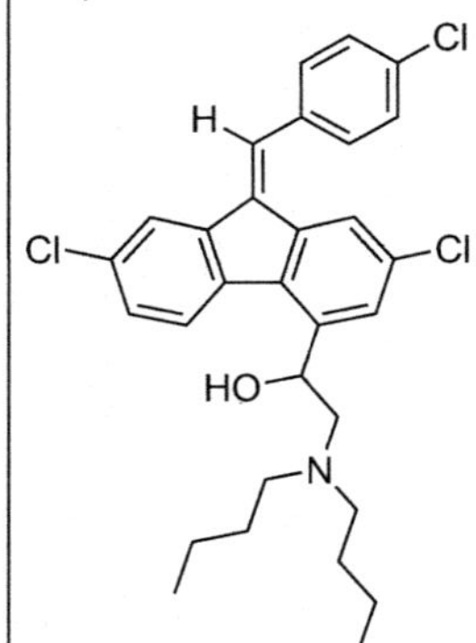	Binds to free heme (ferriprotoporphyrin IX)	Egan (2008)
14	Halofantrine	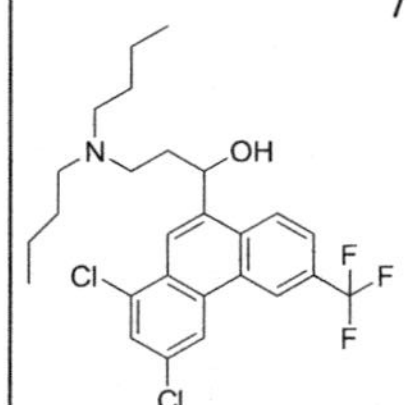	Inhibit protein synthesis. Interfere with the haemoglobin digestion process.	Karbwang and Bangchang (1994)

In the treatment of malaria, the above drugs are widespread, but additionally, these three drugs carry severe side effects and toxicity, particularly cardiotoxicity and ocular toxicity. So drugs such as artemisinin derivatives have been used (Table 7.3).

Table 7.3 Antimalarial artemisin derivatives.

Sl. no	Compound name	Structure	Target	References
15	Artesunate	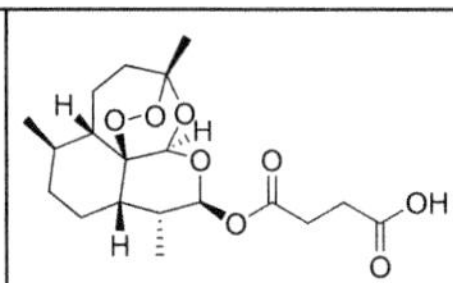	Generate oxidative stress in *plasmodium* parasite.	Sharma and Singh (2019)
16	Artemether	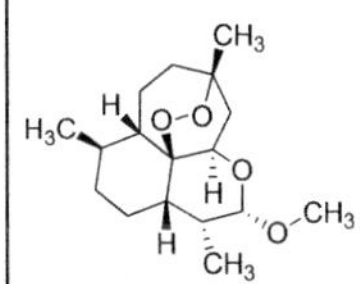	Rapidly kills the asexual erythrocytic stages of the malaria parasite *plasmodium falciparum*	Jelinek (2013)
17	Dihydroarte-misinin,	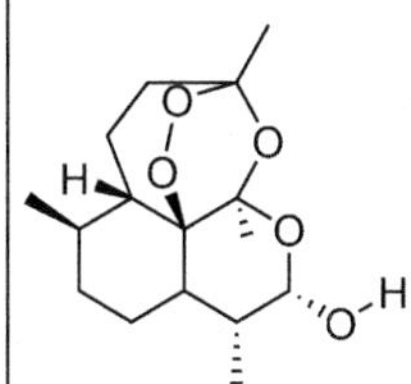	Used especially for severe malaria in combination with other drugs.	Achan et al. (2024)
18	Arteether	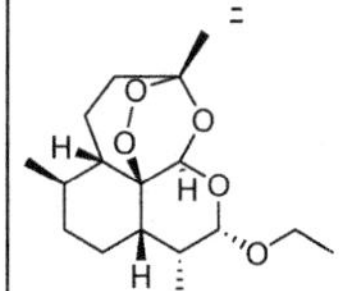	Kills parasites by inhibiting nucleic acid and protein synthesis.	Ayariga et al. (2022)
19	Artemisinin	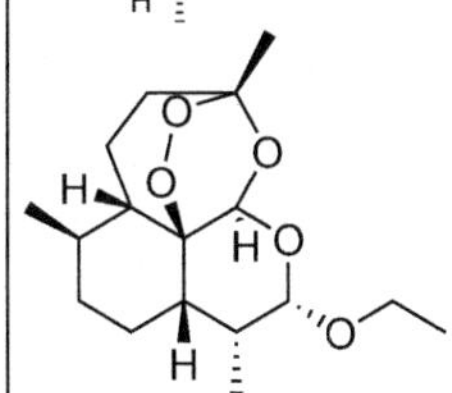	By interacting with hemeiron (Fe^{2+}) to create radicals that kill parasites, artemisinin targets malaria.	Yang et al. (2020)
20	Arterolane	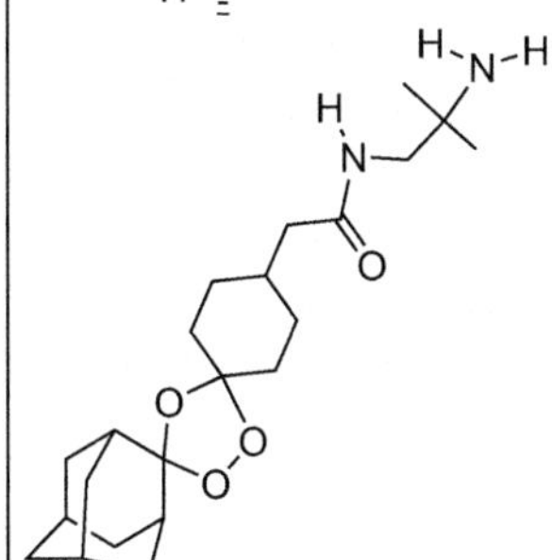	Arterolane works against malaria by damaging PFAT6 and preventing heme detoxification.	Patil et al. (2014)

Artemisinin derivatives (artesunate, artemether, dihydroartemisinin, arteether, artemisinin, and arteolane) are commonly used in combination therapies to prevent malaria. These derivatives are compounds derived from artemisinin, a compound found in the Artemisia annua plant, and are used mainly as antimalarial drugs. Key derivatives include artemether, artesunate, and dihydroartemisinin, which have a rapid onset of action and are highly effective, particularly against multidrug resistant strains of malaria. They are recommended for use in combination with other antimalarials to prevent the development of resistance, and artemisinin derivatives are a cornerstone of Artemisinin based combination therapies (ACTs) (D. Zheng et al., 2024).

In addition to supportive measures like stabilizing the patient at the start of treatment, giving blood transfusions, giving osmotic diuretics, treating conditions like hypoglycemia, acidosis, and hypovolemia, and using immunomodulatory methods (Hall et al., 1991). Establishing standardized supportive management is important to patients with cerebral malaria, even if general supportive care is equally essential. The preferred course of therapy for cerebral malaria is intravenous artesunate injection such as artemether, artesunate is a derivative of artemisinin (Chaudhari et al., 2013).

7.2.2 Antitrypanosomiasis

Treatment for diseases caused by *Trypanosoma* species, particularly American trypanosomiasis (Chagas sickness) and Human African trypanosomiasis (HAT), involves antitrypanosomal drugs (Table 7.4). In tropical areas, these diseases still offer significant health risks, necessitating therapies according to parasite type and disease stage. Pentamidine, suramin, eflornithine, melarsoprol, and nifurtimox are examples of commonly used medications that affect important metabolic processes vital to parasite life, such as energy synthesis, polyamine pathways, and redox balance (Burchmore et al., 2002). Despite the efficacy of these treatments, problems including extreme toxicity, limited availability and growing drug resistance still exist. Recent advancements, however have provided safer and more accessible therapy options, such as oral medications like fexinidazole. recently reviewed drugs to combat trypanosomiasis (Brahma et al., 2025; Saha et al., 2024).

7.2.3 Antidengue

Dengue is a very dangerous mosquito-borne viral infection. The female mosquito (*Aedes aegypti*) carries the dengue virus. The viral infection caused by any of the four dengue viruses (DENV-1, DENV-2, DENV-3, and DENV-4). It kills more than lakhs of people in a year worldwide. There is no specific synthetic drug to kill the dengue virus. It is a big concern for the development of antidengue viral medicines. To date, only the Dengvaxia vaccine has been developed. The vaccine was made by using recombinant DNA, inserting genetic material from the four dengue virus types into a

Table 7.4 Drugs to combat trypanosomiasis.

Sl. no.	Compound name	Structure	Targets	References
21	Pentamidine	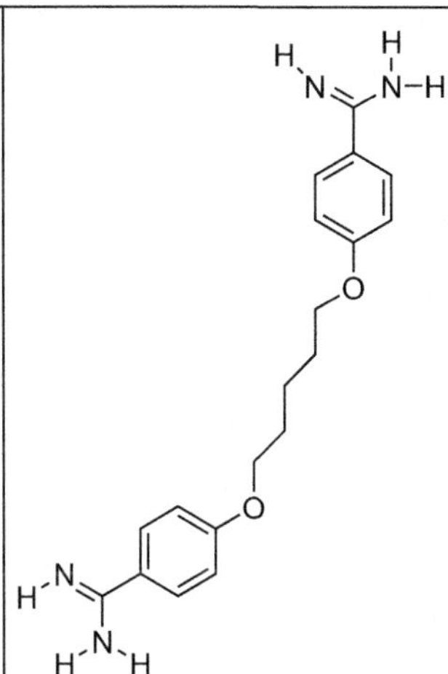	Sleeping sickness	Saha et al. (2024), Brahma et al. (2025)
22	Suramin	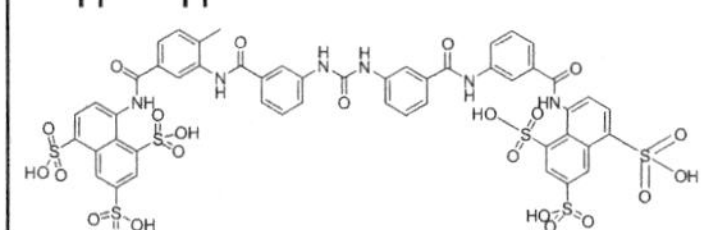	Sleeping sickness	
23	Eflornithine	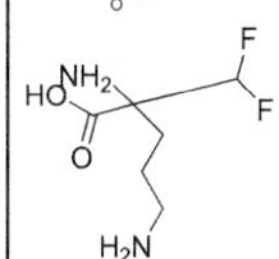	Sleeping sickness	
24	Melarsoprol	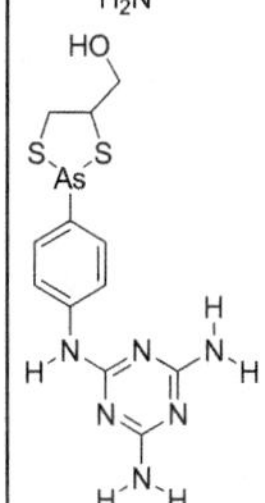	Sleeping sickness	
25	Fexinidazole	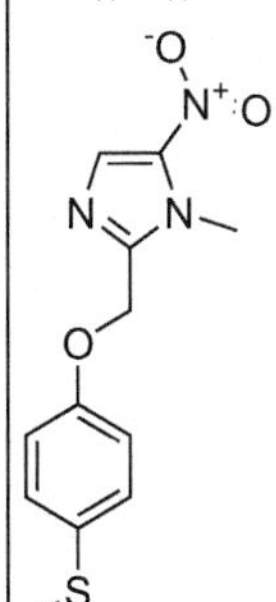	Trypanosome nitroreductase-activated prodrug	

(*Continued*)

Table 7.4 (Continued)

Sl. no.	Compound name	Structure	Targets	References
26	Nifurtimox	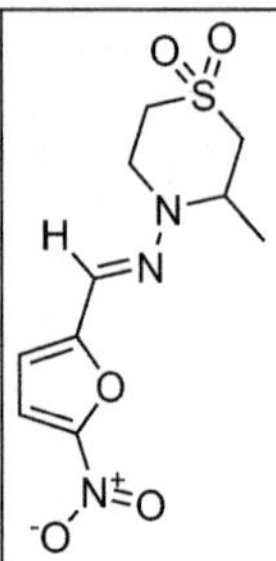	Chagas disease and sleeping sickness	

weakened yellow fever virus. Symptomatic treatment is given to combat dengue. Paracetamol (also called acetaminophen in the United States) is the preferred and safest option for controlling fever and body aches in dengue. It is safe because it does not affect platelet formation or increase the risk of severe bleeding, unlike nonsteroidal antiinflammatory drugs or aspirin. It effectively controls high body temperature and alleviates muscle and joint pain for severe fever, called break bone fever. In this case, adults can take 500 mg of tablets 4 times in 24 hours. The most widely used crystalloid solution is 0.9% or normal saline. It is hypertonic in nature with an osmolarity of 308 mOsm/L, and contains sodium and chloride than normal plasma. it is appropriate for initial fluid revival, but if taken in large amounts can cause hyperchloremic acidosis and lower blood pH value due to high chloride content (Hung, 2012).

Janssen Pharmaceuticals developed a potential compound JNG64281802, which came in fields to clinical trials in the treatment of dengue protease activity. Zanamivir, which was reported as a neuraminidase inhibitor, has been clinically proven for the treatment of dengue. Platelet reduction is a major issue for dengue patients. Therefore, drip is given, and natural medicines such as neem, papaya, kalmegh, turmeric, tejpatta, and goat milk (Fig. 7.1) are given for effective improvement in clinical symptoms and direct inhibitory effect on the dengue virus (Table 7.5) (Starvaggi et al., 2024).

7.2.4 Antimicrofilaria

Antimicrofilarial drugs are essential for treating filarial illnesses caused by parasites such as *Brugia malayi* and *Wuchereria bancrofti*. Lymphatic filariasis, a chronic health problem in many tropical regions, is caused by these parasites. Diethylcarbamazine (DEC), ivermectin, albendazole, doxycycline, and moxidectin (Table 7.6) are the main medications utilized; they all work by either eradicating microfilariae or weakening adult worms. Ivermectin paralyzes and immobilizes circulating microfilariae, DEC efficiently eliminates them, and

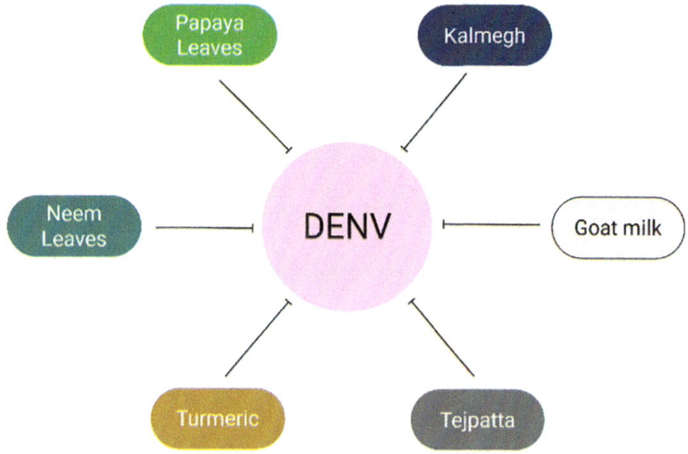

Figure 7.1 Natural medicines against DENV.

Table 7.5 Phyto drugs of DENV and their effective components with potential targets.

Phytocompound name	Effective components	Potential target	References
Papaya leaves	Papain, caricain, chymopapain	NS3	Nath et al. (2024a)
Kalmegh	Andrographolide	—	
Goat milk	Selenium	NS3	
tuemeric	Curcumin	NS2B-NS3 protease	
Neem leaves	Nimbin, nimbidin	Envelope protein	
Tejpatta	Cinnamon, cinnamaldehyde, cinnamyl acetate	Larvae of *Aedes aegypti*	

albendazole disrupts the parasite's vital metabolic functions. These medications have various disadvantages despite their benefits, which highlights the need for better substitutes. The goal of ongoing research is to provide safer and more effective filariasis therapies (Thomas et al., 2016).

7.2.5 Antirickettsia

Antirickettsial drugs are crucial for treating infections brought on by *Rickettsia* species, which cause diseases including spotted fevers and typhus. For the majority of rickettsial illnesses, doxycycline is still the principal treatment that inhibit 30 s rosomal protein synthesis. When doxycycline is not an option, azithromycin, chloramphenicol or tetracycline or rifampin are good substitutes (Fig. 7.2). Early antibiotic medication commencement considerably

Table 7.6 Antimicrofilarial drugs.

Sl. no	Compound name	Structure	Target	References
27	Diethylcarb-amazine (DEC)	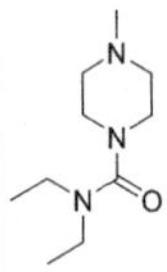	Motility and microfilarial surface membrane.	Maizels and Denham (1992)
28	Ivermectin	B1a: 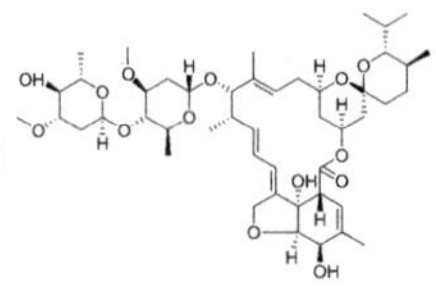 B1b: 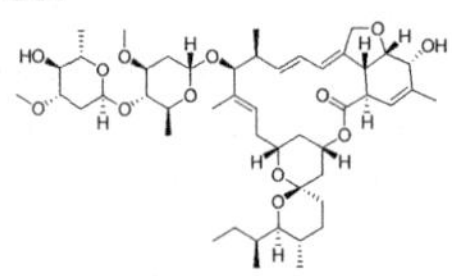	Glutamate gated chloride channels	Moreno et al. (2010)
29	Albendazole	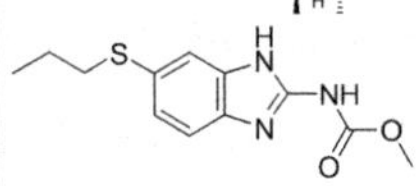	Beta-tubulin polymerization	-
30	Doxycycline	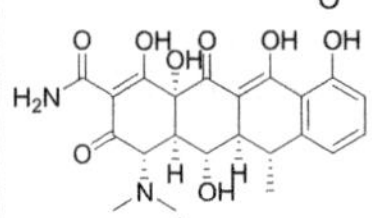	Wolbachia bacteria	Walker et al. (2015)
31	Moxidectin	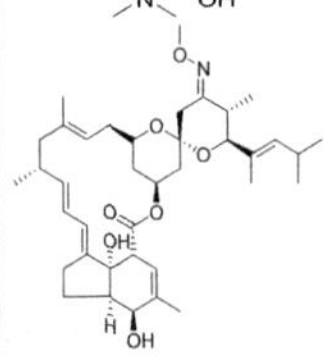	Glutamategated chloride channels	-

improves recovery results and reduces the likelihood of serious sequelae (Gupta et al., 2023). Azithromycin acts by binding to the 50 s ribosomal subunit, specifically the 23 s rRNA, azithromycin limits bacterial growth by impeding polypeptide chain elongation and ribosome assembly, which eventually prevents bacteria from making essential proteins required for life. (Rodgers et al., 2013).After entering Rickettsia cells, tetracycline binds to the 30 s subunit, preventing protein synthesis and aminoacyl tRNA attachment. By preventing their growth, this bacteriostatic action enables the host immune system to eradicate the infection (Holzgrabe, 2005). Rifampicin acts on Rickettsia by inhibiting the bacterial DNA dependent RNA polymerase (RNAP) (Ojetti et al., 2009). Chloramphenicol works by preventing the synthesis of proteins by bacteria. It binds to the 50 s ribosomal subunit and prevents the creation of peptide bonds by inhibiting the action of peptidyl transferase. This stops bacteria from growing by preventing them from producing

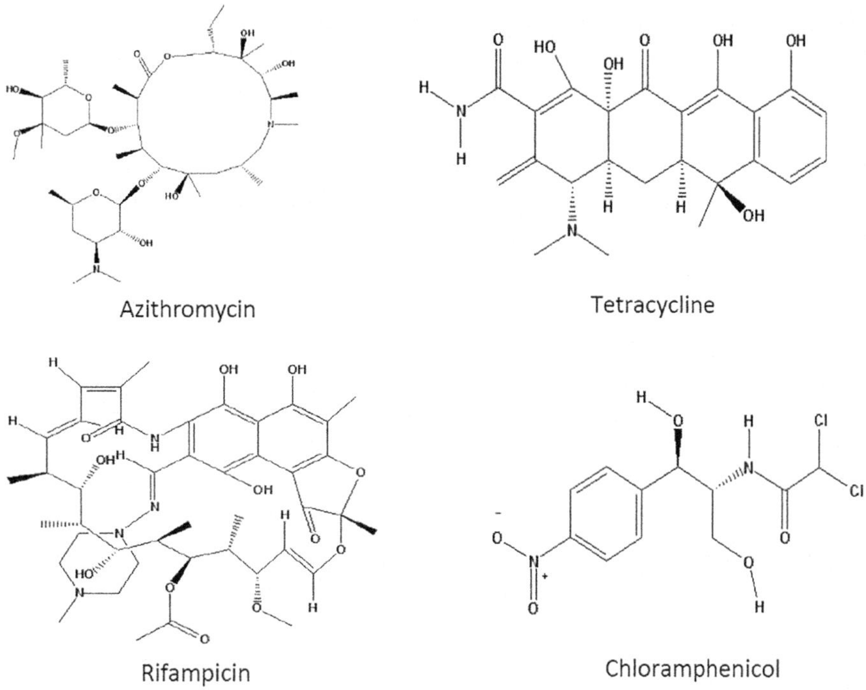

Figure 7.2 Antirickettsial drugs.

essential proteins. Although it usually acts as a bacteriostatic agent, some bacteria may become susceptible to bactericidal effects at greater dosages (Anandabaskar, 2021).

7.3 Artificial intelligence

AI, which can be also referred as machine intelligence, is the ability of computer systems to learn from inputs or past data. The term AI is commonly used when the cognitive behavior associated with human brain during learning and problem solving is mimicked by the machine (Gupta et al., 2021). Nowadays, AI algorithms in the drug designing and discovery process are extensively incorporated by biological and chemical scientists (Harrer et al., 2019). ML contains models and methods including Deep learning (DL) and Artificial neural network (ANN) (Choi et al., 2020). Computational modeling based on AI and ML principles helps in the progress toward identification and validation of chemical compounds, target identification, peptide synthesis, evaluation of drug toxicity and physicochemical properties, drug monitoring, drug effectiveness, and drug repositioning (Zhong et al., 2018). Artificial intelligence is revolutionizing pharmaceutical manufacturing, influencing nearly every stage of the process, from choosing suitable excipients and predicting synthesis routes to optimizing production, designing new drugs, managing supply chains, and even performing predictive maintenance. Its integration in the pharmaceutical sector has the potential to significantly cut down both the time and the costs involved in drug discovery and development. In drug discovery, AI speeds up crucial steps such as hit identification, lead optimization, and preclinical testing by quickly pinpointing promising compounds and accurately forecasting their biological effects. Traditionally, the drug discovery phase takes around 14 to 16 years, but AI powered systems can shorten this by 1 to 2 years by predicting drug efficacy, toxicity, and ideal molecular structures more precisely. Since drug discovery typically represents about 35% of the total 1000 billion dollars spent on developing a new drug (Paul, et al., 2021). AI can substantially lower expenses by reducing the number of compounds that need to be tested and improving early stage trial success rates. Furthermore, AI can enhance the efficiency of clinical trials by improving study design, optimizing patient selection and recruitment and enabling continuous patient monitoring. These applications ultimately help reduce both the duration and the overall cost of clinical trials. AI helps shorten clinical trial timelines by automating how data is gathered and analyzed, making it easier to track patient progress in real time. With faster and more efficient monitoring, the overall duration of trials can be reduced by about 15 to 30% (Serrano et al., 2024). AI based technologies are increasingly being used to discover new antiparasitic drugs. For instance, researchers identified LabMol-167 as a promising PK7 inhibitor with strong in vitro antiplasmodial activity by using AI assisted virtual screening combined with shape-based and machine learning models. LabMol-167 showed minimal toxicity in mammalian cells while effectively inhibiting *Plasmodium falciparum* at nanomolar concentrations (Lima et al., 2021) Similarly, another AI driven approach called DeepMalaria, which uses a Graph Convolutional Neural Network (GCN) framework, was developed to identify new potential antimalarial compounds (Fig. 7.3) (Keshavarzi et al., 2024).

7.3.1 Convolutional pool neural network

A Convolutional neural network (CNN) is a special case of an ANN where it preserves the spatial relationship between pixels in an image. Rather than using single pixels as input, a CNN feeds patches of an image to specific nodes in the next layer of nodes. A CNN preserves the spatial context from which a feature was extracted. These patches of nodes learn to extract specific features and are known as convolutional filters. The feature maps formed extracting specific features from images are used as input for the next layer, which uses new filters to create another new feature map. The extracted features become abstract but highly useful for prediction (Choi et al., 2020; Hinton and Salakhutdinov, 2006; LeCun et al., 2015). Convolutions are widely used in image processing and are often used to blur or sharpen images or in edge detection (Choi et al., 2020). CNN are built from different kind of layers including convolutional layers, pooling layers. After the convolutional layer, pooling layer is

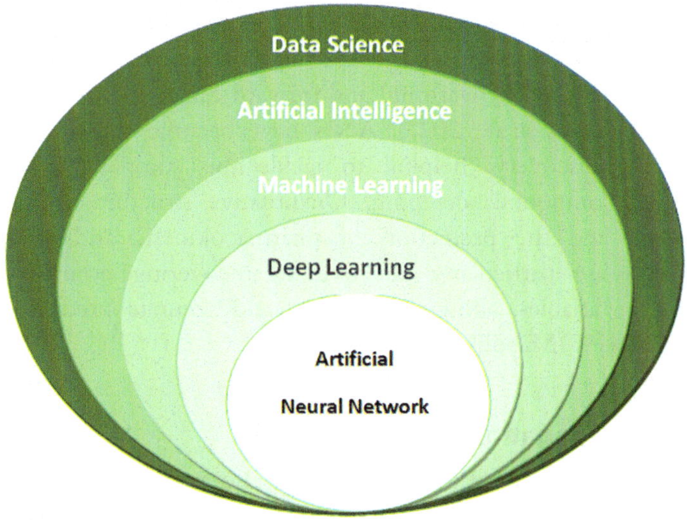

Figure 7.3 Hierarchy of data science techniques.

crucial for reducing computational complexity by performing downsampling while maintaining essential features (Zafar et al., 2024). CNNs work by identifying local features through filters that process groups of nearby data points. When multiple CNN layers are stacked, they can capture both local and global features from the input. CNNs are typically used for single modal data, such as images, where the same convolutional filter is applied across all inputs. Although larger datasets require more computations, the number of model parameters remains relatively stable, making CNNs efficient for training. They are also known for their robustness to noise in input data. Because CNNs are well suited to handling atomistic or spatial structures, they are often paired with voxel-based or image like data representations. For example, DEEPScreen uses 2D molecular images, while models such as RoseNet, AK score, and DeepDrug3D predict Drug target interactions (DTIs) by converting proteins and ligands into 3D voxel forms. While CNNs are not naturally optimized for sequential data formats like SMILES strings or amino acid sequences, they are sometimes applied in place of Recurrent neural networks (RNNs). Models such as DeepConv DTI and Transformer CNN use CNNs to process sequential input data and develop Quantitative structure–activity relationship (QSAR) models (Kim et al., 2021).

7.3.2 Artificial neural network

An ANN is a machine learning algorithm which is mainly inspired by the biological neural network. Each ANN contains nodes which are analogous to cell bodies and communicate with other nodes through connections that are analogous to axons and dendrites. It resembles the way synapses between neurons are strengthened when theose neurons have correlated outputs in a biological neural network (Hebb, 1950; Choi et al., 2020). ANN can learn knowledge and reason about the results from the learned knowledge by: training mode (learning) and forward calculation mode (reasoning) (Di Piazza et al., 2021; Zhu et al., 2021). ANN have become valuable tools in systems biology and drug discovery, helping to tackle the complexity of mathematical modeling, virtual compound screening, Quantitative structure activity relationship (QSAR) analysis, and the prediction of pharmacokinetic and pharmacodynamic behaviors. ANNs are particularly effective at uncovering nonlinear relationships between multiple variables, allowing for early and accurate predictions during the drug discovery process (Mandlik et al., 2016).

7.3.3 Counter propagation neural network

Counter propagation neural networks (CPNNs), also known as Counter-propagation artificial neural networks (CPANNs), represent a class of multilayer feedforward networks that integrate both supervised and unsupervised learning strategies. Structurally, a CPNN consists of three layers an input layer, a competitive (Kohonen) layer, and an output (Grossberg) layer, organized according to the instar outstar model. The connections between the input and competitive layers form the instar structure, whereas the connections between the competitive and output layers constitute the outstar structure. This architecture enables the network to perform efficient input output data mapping based on principles of fuzzy competitive learning (Sakhre et al., 2015). In CPANNs, the weight matrix can be conceptualized as a three dimensional structure divided into two functional layers. Each column of weights corresponds to a single neuron, with the Kohonen layer encoding the independent variables (e.g., molecular descriptors) and the Grossberg layer encoding the dependent variables (e.g., toxicity endpoints). CPANNs are typically trained in two stages. During the first stage, the input vectors are clustered according to Euclidean distance, allowing the network to self organize and improve performance through a topologically constrained learning process. The competitive learning mechanism determines a "winning neuron" by comparing the independent variable vector of an input object against all neurons in the Kohonen layer; the neuron with the minimum Euclidean distance is selected as the central neuron. Once the winning neuron is identified, weight adjustments are applied to both the central neuron and its neighbors. These corrections depend on the learning rate, the neighbourhood function, and the difference between the neuron's current weights and the corresponding components of the input vector. The second training stage employs supervised learning within the outstar connections, enabling the network to map clustered inputs to their appropriate output categories (Bajželj and Drgan, 2020). A Self organizing map or SOM is a type of unsupervised neural network which uses a competitive learning algorithm to make complex, high dimensional data easier to visualize by converting it into a low dimension.In the construction of a SOM,usually only descriptors are taken into consideration. An extension of SOM is the CPANN where additionally the output values (biological activities) are included into modeling (Nandi et al., 2007a).

CPANNs are employed to model the nonlinear relationships between molecular structure and drug-induced hepatotoxicity. Owing to their hybrid learning framework and ability to integrate high dimensional molecular descriptors with complex biological responses, CPANNs have been successfully applied to various QSAR (Quantitative structure-activity relationship) tasks and provide a robust modeling strategy for toxicity prediction (Bajželj and Drgan, 2020).

7.4 Machine learning

Over the past years, Artificial intelligence (AI) has gained popularity within and outside of the scientific community. AI focuses on automated intellectual tasks which are normally performed by humans, and ML is a specific method of achieving this. ML focuses on developing algorithms that best represent a set of data. ML differs from classical programming as ML generates an algorithm based on the relation between the dataset and output provided whereas classical programming gives output based on dataset and the operating algorithm provided. There are many ML types such as supervised, unsupervised, semi supervised, and reinforcement learning (Choi et al., 2020). Discovering new and effective drugs is a lengthy and complex process, often considered the most difficult stage of drug development. However Machine learning (ML) has emerged as a powerful solution due to its ability to analyze data, identify hidden patterns, and make informed predictions. ML based techniques are now being applied across various phases of drug discovery, from designing and screening new drugs to repurposing existing ones and optimizing chemical synthesis. In addition, significant research efforts are focused on creating ML driven models, software tools, and databases to overcome the limitations and uncertainties of traditional drug development approaches (Qi et al., 2024). Drug discovery, the process of finding and developing new medicines, is traditionally slow and complex, relying heavily on experimental methods like trial and error testing and high-throughput screening. Today, Artificial intelligence (AI) techniques such as Machine learning (ML) and Natural language processing (NLP) are transforming this field by enabling faster and more precise analysis of vast datasets. Recent studies have shown that Deep learning (DL) models can accurately predict the effectiveness of drug compounds, while other AI tools can assess the potential toxicity of new candidates. These advancements demonstrate AI's ability to enhance both the speed and success of drug discovery (Blanco-González et al., 2023).

7.4.1 Machine learning process

The machine learning process has many steps involving data collection and preparation, feature engineering, choosing the right machine algorithm, model training and evaluation, lastly model deployment and maintenance. ML comprises mainly three types – supervised, unsupervised, and reinforcement learning.

- **Supervised learning:** Supervised learning involves training computational models on labeled datasets so they can predict outcomes or classify new samples with known accuracy. In pharmacology, this approach is widely applied in areas such as Drug-target interaction (DTI) prediction, virtual screening, bioactivity estimation, and toxicity assessment. Algorithms like Support vector machines (SVMs) and Random forests remain highly favored because of their robustness, interpretability, and strong performance across diverse pharmacological datasets (Singh et al., 2023). Supervised learning (SL) is a core machine learning framework in which models are trained to associate input data with corresponding output labels. During training, the algorithm learns from datasets where each input is paired with its correct outcome, enabling the model to capture underlying relationships or patterns. Once trained, the model can generalize these learned mappings to accurately predict outputs for new, previously unseen data. Supervised learning supports two major types of tasks: classification, where the goal is to assign inputs to predefined categories (such as identifying an email as spam or not), and regression, which involves predicting continuous numerical values (such as estimating property prices). SL is widely applied across fields including image recognition, natural language question answering, sentiment analysis, and speech recognition, as well as numerous domain specific analytical and predictive tasks. The most widely used learning algorithms are support vector machines, linear regression, logistic regression, linear discriminant analysis, decision trees, k nearest neighbors algorithm, eural networks (e.g., multilayer perceptron), and others (Mohri et al., 2012). SVMs are supervised learning algorithms used for classification and regression. They learn from labeled examples by constructing a decision boundary that separates data into categories. A key advantage of SVMs is their ability to perform nonlinear classification through the kernel trick, which implicitly projects data into high-dimensional feature spaces. Because of their generalization ability, SVMs are widely applied in text and hypertext categorization, image classification, and handwritten character recognition (Cortes and Vapnik, 1995).
- **Unsupervised learning:** Unsupervised learning focuses on uncovering hidden structures, relationships, or patterns within unlabeled data. In pharmacological research, clustering methods, including k-means, hierarchical clustering, and density based approaches, are frequently used to group drugs, compounds, or patient populations based on shared molecular, biochemical, or clinical characteristics.

Additionally, dimensionality reduction techniques such as Principal component analysis (PCA) are essential for simplifying high dimensional datasets, facilitating visualization, and improving downstream analytical tasks (Singh et al., 2023). Unsupervised learning refers to machine learning methods that identify patterns or structures in data without relying on labeled examples. With the advancement of deep learning, many large scale unsupervised tasks now employ general neural architectures optimized through gradient-based training to reveal meaningful representations directly from raw data. Unsupervised learning has a wide range of applications, including image generation, video synthesis, speech production, and creative text generation, making it a foundational tool for modern generative modeling (Li et al., 2020).

- **Reinforcement learning:** Reinforcement learning (RL), although comparatively less explored in pharmacology, offers support for adaptive and personalized therapeutic strategies. In RL, an agent learns to make optimal sequential decisions by interacting with an environment and receiving feedback in the form of rewards or penalties. Studies have applied RL frameworks to dosage optimization, treatment adaptation over time, and designing dynamic therapeutic regimens, highlighting its potential for precision medicine (Singh et al., 2023). RL differs from supervised and unsupervised approaches by training an agent through continual interaction with its environment. The agent learns to maximize cumulative rewards by balancing exploration, where it tests new actions to gather information, and exploitation, where it uses existing knowledge to select the most rewarding actions. Modern RL encompasses a variety of advanced forms, including deep RL, fuzzy RL, multi-objective RL, safe RL, and RL methods integrated with natural language processing. These variants enable RL to be applied across complex decision making and adaptive learning tasks (Kaelbling et al., 1996).

7.4.2 Machine learning application

The field of machine learning is concerned with the development and application of computer algorithms which improve with experience. ML is highly applicable in the field of genetics and genomics such as in identifying transcription start sites, splice sites, exons, and in predicting gene function and expression (Libbrecht and Noble, 2015). ML is extensively used in the medical field for surgery, disease prediction, drug discovery, medical image analysis, psychiatry, and seizure detection. ML is also applied in cybersecurity, traffic prediction, disease outbreak prediction, natural language processing, and sentiment analysis, as well as in sustainable agriculture. Since the 1990s, computational techniques such as homology modeling, molecular docking, Quantitative structure-activity relationship (QSAR) modeling, and Molecular dynamics (MD) simulation have played a central role in elucidating drug activity mechanisms.

Among these approaches, QSAR represents an empirical model framework that employs regression and classification analyzes on large structure property datasets to identify statistically significant relationships between chemical structures and their corresponding biological activities.

A key advantage of QSAR is its ability to predict the biological and toxicological properties of novel compounds solely from their chemical structures, thereby overcoming more time consuming procedures such as molecular docking. This capability greatly enhances the efficiency of both model development and downstream virtual screening workflows (Mao et al., 2021). The mathematical relationships between chemical structures and pharmacological action have been transformed into QSAR utilizing computed structural properties to ensure accurate predictions and useful insights into chemical component activity. Computational algorithm uses statistical and machine learning methods to predict the activity of various chemicals using QSARs for better understand the biochemical mechanisms of the compounds (Nandi and Bagchi, 2007b; Nandi et al., 2022). QSAR models rely fundamentally on molecular descriptors, which are numerical representations capturing chemical, structural, or physicochemical features of molecules. These descriptors are typically categorized into one-dimensional (1D), two-dimensional (2D), and three-dimensional (3D) classes, corresponding to properties such as molecular weight, topological indices, molecular shape, and electrostatic potential distributions.

Over the past decade, QSAR has seen expanded application in drug design and toxicity prediction. When integrated with modern AI methods, its predictive power enables large scale virtual screening of chemical libraries containing billions of compounds, as well as de novo molecular design and lead optimization for specific therapeutic targets. Advances in machine learning, including neural networks, generative modeling, and reinforcement learning, are transforming how candidate molecules are selected, modified, and evaluated. Moreover, the incorporation of omics datasets, real world clinical evidence, and multi-parametric optimization strategies is further advancing the development of personalized and targeted therapeutic interventions (Koirala et al., 2025).

7.4.3 Random forest algorithm

A decision tree is a supervised learning technique primarily used for classification tasks. It starts with a root node, which represents the first feature chosen to split the dataset effectively. Each split creates branches; some lead to further decision nodes, where the additional features divide the data again, while others end in a terminal node or leaf node, which gives the final prediction. The repeated process of splitting into two binary partitions is known as recursive partitioning. A random forest builds on this concept by using multiple decision trees together, making it an ensemble method. Instead of constructing every tree with all available features, it randomly selects a subset of features for each tree (Choi et al., 2020; Shimizu et al., 2015). The random forest algorithm is therefore more accurate than a single decision tree based model (Sarker, 2021). Predicting Drug–target interactions (DTIs) is one of the most complex challenges in the drug discovery process. To address this, machine learning methods have become essential for achieving faster and more accurate results. In this study, the Random Forest algorithm was applied to predict DTIs. As an ensemble learning method, it is relatively simple, efficient, and faster than many other comparable algorithms. Experimental analyzes based on accuracy and average ranking across multiple datasets demonstrated that random forest achieved strong predictive performance and outperformed several other algorithms in terms of accuracy (Mehta et al., 2020).

7.4.4 Multiple linear regression

Regression is a statistical method that involves predicting numeric data, such as test scores, laboratory values, or prices of an item. Linear regression is considered as the simplest machine learning algorithm. Linear regression is an analysis technique used to solve a regression problem by a straight line, which is used to describe a dataset (Choi et al., 2020; Shimizu et al., 2015). Multiple linear regression predicts a single dependent variable (such as a student's math score) using multiple predictor or independent variables (that student's study hours and previous test scores). It helps to understand the influence of multiple independent variables on the outcome of one dependent variable (Freedman, 2009; Prasad, 2024). This statistical method helps to predict drug's toxicity or its potency based on its chemical structure and physicochemical properties. Multiple linear regression is a statistical technique used to identify which among several explanatory variables best predict a specific response variable. Like simple linear regression, it assumes that the response variable follows a normal distribution with constant variance and that the error terms are random and independent. This method is often applied in clinical research, for example, to predict changes in a disease-related biomarker when several treatments are given simultaneously. It also provides a framework for determining the most significant predictors and building models that can be used for future predictions (Hill, 2006).

7.5 Artificial intelligence and Machine learning in antiparasitic drug discovery

Artificial intelligence (AI) and Machine learning (ML) have become essential tools in modern day drug discovery, enabling researchers to analyze large scale biological data and accelerate the identification of potential therapeutic agents. In the context of parasitic diseases such as malaria, dengue, African sleeping sickness, American sleeping sickness, trypanosomiasis, leishmaniasis, schistosomiasis etc., which continue to impose a heavy global health burden, these computational approaches provide new strategies in aiding the limitations of traditional drug discovery, such as high cost effectiveness, lengthy timelines, and frequent failures during clinical trials. By introducing AI and ML, researchers point out the gaps and predict the safety and efficacy of drugs.

7.5.1 Artificial intelligence in predicting parasitic disease outbreaks

Predictive AI based models have been applied to forecast parasitic infection outbreaks. For instance, a Convolutional neural network (CNN) was trained on data from 2013 to 2017 for three vector borne diseases—chikungunya, malaria, and dengue. The resulting model achieved an accuracy of 88% in predicting disease outbreaks. In addition, multiple predictive algorithms have been designed specifically for malaria outbreak forecasting. Shabanpour et al. employed a geospatial AI framework that combined ML techniques with Geographic information system (GIS) tools to map cutaneous leishmaniasis (caused by *Leishmania* sp.). Their analysis identified the northern and central regions of Isfahan as high risk areas for the disease (Parija and Poddar, 2024).

7.5.2 Parasitic drug discovery using artificial intelligence

With the help of AI algorithms, AI driven computational methods analyze a vast amount of data, including genomic, proteomic, and structural information, to unfold the mechanisms behind parasitic diseases and identify potential therapeutic targets.

AI can point out critical proteins or enzymes that are essential for pathogen survival and replication inside the body of the host. It enables researchers to:

- Identify novel drug targets.
- Predict the efficacy and safety of potential drug candidates.
- Optimize the design of new therapies.
- Repurpose existing drugs within a shorter timeframe.

AI is transforming drug discovery by rapidly identifying targets and optimizing drug candidates involving screening of vast chemical library (Parija and Poddar, 2024).

7.5.2.1 AI based virtual screening methods

Virtual screening, a computational method to predict the binding affinity of compounds to target proteins, has been significantly improved by AI algorithms. AI driven models accelerate drug candidate's identification by analyzing molecular structures, predicting binding affinities, and filtering ineffective compounds. This reduces the number of compounds required for experimental testing (Ezenwaka and Nwalozie, 2023).

Robotics, introduced in drug discovery during the 1990s, made automated compound screening a standard practice to speed up the process. A 2011 study showed **phenotypic screening** led to more first-in-class medicines than target based methods. Today, High throughput screening (HTS) systems and assay miniaturization allow millions of compounds to be screened rapidly, making phenotypic HTS vital for discovering new mechanisms of action, especially in antiinfectives where validated targets are limited (Rao et al., 2023). LabMol-167 has been identified as a promising PK7 inhibitor, demonstrating in vitro antiplasmodial activity. To discover this compound, researchers applied AI assisted virtual screening combined with shape based and machine learning models. Remarkably, LabMol-167 inhibited *Plasmodium falciparum* at nanomolar concentrations while showing low cytotoxicity in mammalian cells. (Parija and Poddar, 2024).

For schistosomiasis, phenotypic screening data from multiple developmental stages of *Schistosoma mansoni* were normalized using two "rule books" and applied to develop eight Bayesian machine learning models of antischistosomal activity. These models screened chemical libraries, identified potential active compounds, and generated high quality binary datasets for further machine learning applications, with performance compared across six additional algorithms (Zorn et al., 2021)

Computer-aided drug design (CADD), or molecular modeling, helps in reducing drug discovery limitations by cutting down cost and time using in silico simulations. One of the key steps in CADD is Virtual screening (VS) that work through the large compound libraries and analyzes it and identify molecules with potential biological activity against specific target. Virtual screening has three approaches to follow – Structure based (SBVS), Ligand based (LBVS), and Fragment based (FBVS). Each of these approaches follows a distinct way of identifying potential drug candidates (Oliveira et al., 2023).

7.5.2.2 Predictive modeling for drug-target interaction

AI powered predictive modeling helps in decoding complex drug target interactions by analyzing molecular data to predict compound protein binding accuracy. By using ML methods such as support vector machines, random forests, and deep neural networks, these models assess molecular descriptors, physicochemical, and structural features. They can forecast binding affinities, detect off target effects, and evaluate adverse reaction risks, making drug development faster and more efficient (Ezenwaka and Nwalozie, 2023).

7.5.3 Application of machine learning in analysing parasite genomic data

The analysis of parasitic genomic data requires processing large genetic datasets, and AI/ML tools have become essential for managing this complexity. One major use is genome annotation, where AI identifies genes, regulatory elements, and functional regions. Techniques such as hidden Markov models and deep learning help accurately in predicting gene structures and functions. ML also detects conserved motifs, regulatory sequences, and noncoding RNAs, revealing key genetic factors linked to parasite life cycles, virulence, and drug resistance. Overall, AI integration makes genomic analysis faster and more insightful. (Ezenwaka and Nwalozie,2023).

7.5.4 Specific antiparasitic drug predicted using Artificial intelligence/ machine learning

Sl. no.	Compound name	Structure	References
1.	DC - 9237	-	Keshavarzi Arshadi et al. (2020)
2.	LabMol-167	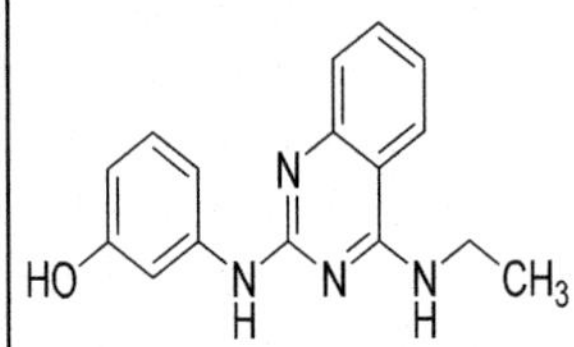	Lima et al. (2021)
3.	KDU691	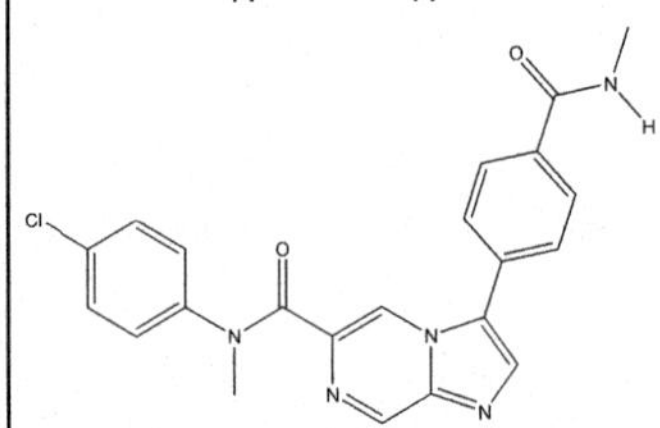	Oduselu et al. (2025)
4.	Fumagillin	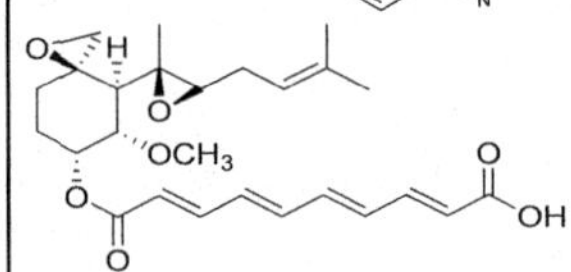	Guruceaga et al. (2020)
5.	Nifuroxazide	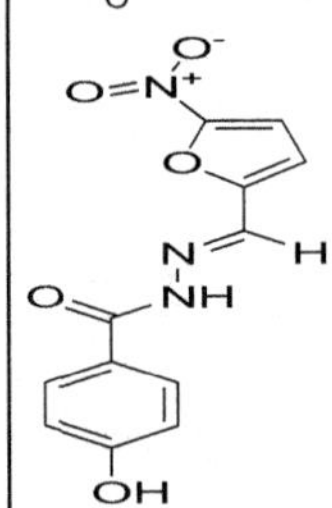	Roquini et al. (2023)
6.	Capecitabine	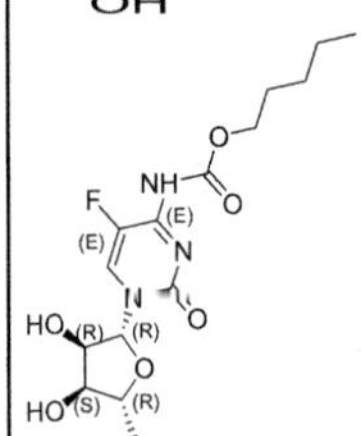	Lye et al. (2024)
7.	CBL0137	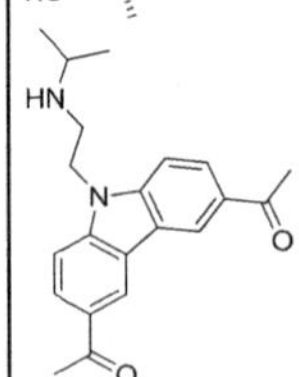	Sanz-Rodríguez et al. (2022)
8.	Silymarin	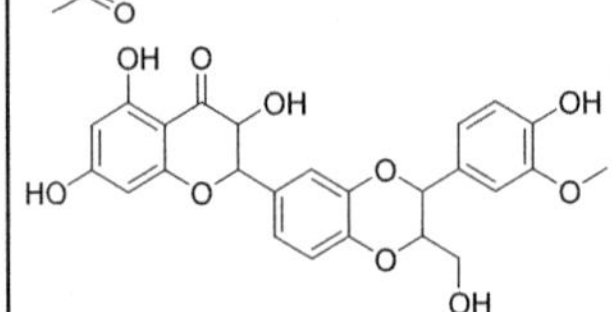	Low et al. (2021)

- **DC-9237**: This compound has been identified as a potent antimalarial drug. It is a macrocyclic chemical compound that was found through an artificial intelligence-driven drug discovery process (Deep Malaria). The compound is found to be successful in inhibiting all asexual blood stages of the *Plasmodium falciparum* parasite. A library of ~2400 macrocyclic compounds against the multidrug resistant *Plasmodium falciparum* strain Dd2 was screened using a SYBR-Green I fluorescence assay. Among the compounds, DC-9237 showed strong inhibition (95% inhibition in the initial 1 μM fixed point screen) and it was tested further to analyze its potency (EC_{50}). The measured EC_{50} was 0.49 μM± 44 nM. No publicly available in vivo data for DC-9237 have been reported; all validations are limited to in-vitro blood stage assays(Keshavarzi Arshadi et al., 2020).
- **LabMol**-167: This compound was found to be a potential PK7 inhibitor which also has in vitro antiplasmodial activity. It emerged from a shape-based and machine-learning virtual screening campaign targeting PfPK7(and potential other kinases) as antimalarial hits. This compound is low cytotoxic for mammalian cells and has shown in vitro inhibitory function for blood stages of *Plasmodium falciparum* at nanomolar concentration. EC_{50} ~ 0.17 μM for 3D7 (sensitive) strain and EC_{50} ~ 0.34 μM for Dd2 (multidrug-resistant). LabMol-167 showed strong activity against the sexual/mosquito-stage parasite form: in assays using *Plasmodium berghei* ookinete conversion, the compound inhibited conversion with EC_{50} ~833 Nm at 10 μM dose showed 97% inhibition (Lima et al., 2021).
- **KDU691**: A high throughput screen involving 1.7 million compounds led to the identification of a novel imidazopyrazine/imidazopyridazine series with strong antimalarial properties. The lead molecule, KDU691, showed potent inhibition of *Plasmodium falciparum* asexual blood stage parasites and was confirmed to act through selective inhibition of Plasmodium falciparum phosphatidylinositol 4 kinase beta (PfPI4KB), which is very crucial for survival of the parasite. Besides killing the parasite in blood stage, it also targets *P. yoelii* liver stage schizonts, *P. cynomolgi* hypnozoites and *P. falciparum* oocysts. Although the compound showed huge effectiveness against multiple life stages of the parasite in vitro, it failed in inhibition of hypnozoite forms in an in vivo *P. cynomolgi* model. In mouse models (*P. berghei*), the compound KDU691 showed a prophylactic effect: a single 7.5 mg/kg dose cleared liver stage parasites, and 50 mg/kg twice daily achieved about 80% cure in blood stage infection. However KDU691 is a potent multistage inhibitor but has some limitations in achieving complete in vivo cure (Ong et al., 2023).
- **Fumagillin**: Fumagillin, a potent antiparasitic agent, has potently blocked in vitro growth of *Plasmodium falciparum* and *Leishmania donovani* which cause Malaria and **Visceral Leishmaniasis** respectively. Another study (Arico Muendel et al.) shows that some of the derivatives of this compound inhibit the in vitro growth of *Entamoeba histolytica* (causes amoebiasis), *p. falciparum* and *Trypanosoma brucei* (causes

African sleeping sickness). This compound works by binding to an enzyme MetAP2, inhibiting the growth of these parasites in vivo and in vitro(Guruceaga et al., 2020). In biochemical assays, the recombinant EhMetAP2 with an inhibitory constant of ~ 60 ± 33 nM, which is comparable to its IC_{50} (~ 49–94 Nm) against *E. histolytica* trophozoites(Watanabe et al., 2023).

- **Nifuroxazide**: Nifuroxazide (NFZ), an oral nitrofuran antibiotic, is found to be effective on the helminth *Schistosoma mansoni,* that causes the disease schistosomiasis. Significant antiparasitic activity with 50% effective concentration (EC_{50}) and 90% effective concentration (EC_{90}) values of 8.2 to 10.8 and 13.7 to 19.3 μM, respectively is seen in the in vitro study. NFZ has shown its efficacy by causing severe damage to the outer tegument of the adult schistosomes, which was more pronounced in male than in female helminths; the male helminths manifested substantial tegumental damage all over the body and gradually losing their natural shape. In patent infections (established, egg producing) it was strongly effective (egg count reduced by ~80%) than in prepatent infections (early infection). In silico target fishing methods suggest that NFZ may target serine/threonine kinases, which are important parasite enzymes. This drug also possesses antischistosomal activity especially egg burden reduction with patent *S. mansoni* infection (Roquini et al., 2023)
- **Capecitabine**: This compound was identified as a potent inhibitor of mitochondrial DNA primase (LdmtPR/1) of *Leishmania donovani* by in silico method and in vitro drug repurposing approaches. The inhibitors were first recognized using structure based virtual screening and computational predictions (molecular modeling and docking)(Lye et al., 2024). The LdmtPR/1 gene was cloned, the protein was overexpressed and purified, and a primase activity assay was established. In this biochemical assay, capecitabine inhibited primase activity, with an IC_{50} of ~15.27 Nm. In parasite assays (in vitro), capecitabine has shown activity against *L. donovani* promastigotes (IC_{50} for the inhibition was ~12.40 μM)(Nath et al., 2024b).
- **Duartin**: Duartin was identified by an intracellular Rickettsia high throughput fluorescence screening combined with a machine learning prioritization pipeline. In the primary intracellular assay (using Rickettsia candidates with a fluorescence reporter), duartin was among the most active compounds: IC_{90}=0.81 μg. mL^{-1} (~ 2.4 μM). The compound was reported as highly specific and noncytotoxic at active concentrations. Duartin showed potent inhibitory function of intracellular *Rickettsia* growth in vitro and was highlighted as a selective, efficacious antirickettsial hit suitable for follow up medicinal chemistry and mechanistic studies (Lemenze et al., 2022).
- **CBL0137**: CBL0137 is a drug studied in trypanosomes, the parasites that cause African sleeping sickness. This compound inhibits nucleus mitosis, nuclear DNA replication, polypeptide synthesis. It specifically targets two DNA binding proteins: RPA1 and RPA2 (Sanz-Rodríguez et al., 2022). CBL0137 (a carbazole "curaxin" scaffold) potently inhibits growth of bloodstream T. brucei in cell based assays; it was identified in a phenotypic

screen as a lead antitrypanosomal compound. Oral dosing of the CBL0137 cured 100% of mice infected with the parasite in the original lead discovery study, with no observed toxicity at the efficacious dose, qualifying CBL0137 as a bona fine lead for HAT drug development (Thomas et al., 2016). Functional assays stated inhibition of nuclear DNA synthesis (reduced EdU incorporation), implicating disruption of DNA replication as a principal mode of action (Sanz-Rodríguez et al., 2022).

- **Silymarin**: Silymarin (a flavonolignan mixture from *Silybum marianum*) has demonstrated in vitro antiviral activity against dengue virus. Silymarin is well tolerated in Vivo cells in vitro reported CC_{50} ~749.7 μg. Ml^{-1}; so high concentrations were required for host cell toxicity. In cell-based assays silymarin showed virucidal activity against dengue virus-3 (DENV-3) and demonstrated antiviral effects across all four DENV serotypes in vitro. At the highest nontoxic concentrations silymarin reduced extracellular infectivity substantially (~95% inhibition of DENV-3 infectivity in one study). Time of addition and attachment/entry assays indicated silymarin acted primarily by interfering with viral attachment/entry and by inactivating extracellular virions rather than acting intracellularly on replication in that dataset. Molecular docking analysis indicated that silymarin could interact directly with dengue envelope (E) protein, showing a binding affinity of around -8.5 kcal/mol. This compound was also predicted to form hydrogen bonds with specific amino acids on the E protein, especially GLN120, TRP229, ASN89, and THR223 (Low et al., 2021).

7.6 Conclusion

For the design synthesis and experimental validation of a single molecule, it takes a lot of time, labor, effort, and animal sacrifices. To minimize time, labor, money, animal sacrifices, AI and ML have been taking a great role for high throughput screening of new molecules and existing molecules to repurpose against any diseases. In the present review, we have been using the ML and AI as an in silco tool to screen potent antiparasitic compounds and through the studies it was found that DC-9237, LabMol-167, KDU691, fumagillin, nifuroxazide, capecitabine, CBL0137, and silymarin have been screened to combat different blood parasitic diseases. AI and ML is a giant tool for high throughput screening of potent existing compounds but still the compounds against microfilaria are under investigation and has to be explored by using AI and ML.

References

Abebe W, Woldesenbet D. A review on molecular markers of Plasmodium falciparum. Journal of Parasitic Diseases: Official Organ of the Indian Society for Parasitology 2025;49(4):821–33. Available from https://doi.org/10.1007/s12639-025-01840-0.

Achan J, Barry A, Leroy D, Kamara G, Duparc S, Kaszubska W, Gandhi P, Buffet B, Tshilab P, Ogutu B, Taylor T, Krishna S, Richardson N, Ramachandruni H, Rietveld H. Defining the next generation of severe malaria treatment: a target product profile. Malaria Journal 2024;23(1):174. Available from https://doi.org/10.1186/s12936-024-04986-z.

Anandabaskar N. Protein Synthesis Inhibitors. Introduction to Basics of Pharmacology and Toxicology. Springer Nature Singapore; 2021. p. 835–68.

Ayariga JA, Huffman AM, Napier A, Robertson BK, Abugri DA. In silico elucidation of dihydroquinine mechanism of action against *Toxoplasma gondii*. bioRxiv 2022. Available from https://doi.org/10.1101/2021.12.30.474617.

Bajželj B, Drgan V. Hepatotoxicity modeling using counter-propagation artificial neural networks: handling an imbalanced classification problem. Molecules (Basel, Switzerland) 2020;25(3):481. Available from https://doi.org/10.3390/molecules25030481.

Blanco-González A, Cabezón A, Seco-González A, Conde-Torres D, Antelo-Riveiro P, Piñeiro Á, Garcia-Fandino R. The role of AI in drug discovery: challenges, opportunities, and strategies. Pharmaceuticals (Basel, Switzerland) 2023;16(6):891. Available from https://doi.org/10.3390/ph16060891.

Blanton LS. The rickettsioses: a practical update. Infectious Disease Clinics of North America 2019;33(1):213–29. Available from https://doi.org/10.1016/j.idc.2018.10.010.

Brahma S, Moitra S, Bagchi SR, Samadder A, Nandi S. To explore potential inhibitors against various enzymatic targets of human African trypanosomiasis. Combinatorial Chemistry & High Throughput Screening 2025;28(9):1553–93. Available from https://doi.org/10.2174/0113862073293708240416113543.

Burchmore RJS, Ogbunude POJ, Enanga B, Barrett MP. Chemotherapy of human African trypanosomiasis. Current Pharmaceutical Design 2002;8(4):256–67. Available from https://doi.org/10.2174/1381612023396159.

Camarda G, Jirawatcharadech P, Priestley RS, Saif A, March S, Wong MHL, Leung S, Miller AB, Baker DA, Alano P, Paine MJI, Bhatia SN, O'Neill PM, Ward SA, Biagini GA. Antimalarial activity of primaquine operates via a two-step biochemical relay. Nature Communications 2019;10(1):3226. Available from https://doi.org/10.1038/s41467-019-11239-0.

Chaudhari H, Mehta JB, Chaudhari K, Farrow J. Treatment of cerebral malaria and acute respiratory distress syndrome (ARDS) with parenteral artesunate. Tennessee Medicine: Journal of the Tennessee Medical Association 2013;106(5):41–3.

Choi RY, Coyner AS, Kalpathy-Cramer J, Chiang MF, Campbell JP. Introduction to machine learning, neural networks, and deep learning. Translational Vision Science & Technology 2020;9(2):14. Available from https://doi.org/10.1167/tvst.9.2.14.

Cortes C, Vapnik VN. Support-vector networks. Machine Learning 1995;20(3):273–97. Available from https://doi.org/10.1007/BF00994018.

Cummings R, Turco S. Parasitic infections. In: Varki A, editor. Essentials of glycobiology. 2nd ed.Cold Spring Harbor (NY):: Cold Spring Harbor Laboratory Press; 2009.

Dasgupta T, Anderson KS. Probing the role of parasite-specific, distant structural regions on communication and catalysis in the bifunctional thymidylate synthase-dihydrofolate reductase from Plasmodium falciparum. Biochemistry 2008;47(5):1336–45. Available from https://doi.org/10.1021/bi701624u. PMCID: PMC2658879.

Fidock DA, Blasco B, Leroy D. Antimalarial drug resistance: linking Plasmodium falciparum parasite biology to the clinic. Nature Medicine 2017;23(8):917–28. Available from 10.1038/nm.4381.

Egan TJ. Recent advances in understanding the mechanism of hemozoin (malaria pigment) formation. Journal of Inorganic Biochemistry 2008;102(5–6):1288–99. Available from https://doi.org/10.1016/j.jinorgbio.2007.12.004.

Ezenwaka CO, Nwalozie R. Artificial intelligence (AI) and machine learning (MI) in parasitological laboratory. South Asian Journal of Parasitology 2023;6(3):113–24.

Freedman DA. Statistical models: theory and practice. Cambridge University Press; 2009. p. 26.

Goldin J, Juergens AL. Filariasis. StatPearls. StatPearls Publishing; 2025.

Gupta N, Boodman C, Jouego CG, Van Den Broucke S. Doxycycline vs azithromycin in patients with scrub typhus: a systematic review of literature and meta-analysis. BMC Infectious Diseases 2023;23(1):884. Available from https://doi.org/10.1186/s12879-023-08893-7.

Gupta R, Srivastava D, Sahu M, Tiwari S, Ambasta RK, Kumar P. Artificial intelligence to deep learning: machine intelligence approach for drug discovery. Molecular Diversity 2021;25(3):1315–60. Available from https://doi.org/10.1007/s110310217-3.

Guruceaga X, Perez-Cuesta U, Abad-Diaz de Cerio A, Gonzalez O, Alonso RM, Hernando FL, Ramirez-Garcia A, Rementeria A. Fumagillin, a mycotoxin of *Aspergillus fumigatus*: biosynthesis, biological activities, detection, and applications. Toxins 2020;12(1):7. Available from https://doi.org/10.3390/toxins12010007.

Hall A, Kwiatkowski D, Molyneux M, Taylor T, Klein N, Curtis N, Smit M, Greenwood BM, Poser C, Roman G, Kirkham FJ, Newton CRJC, Winstanley PA, Pasvol G, Peshu N, Warrell DA, Marsh K, Birley HL, Mabey DW, Singer M. Cerebral malaria. Lancet 1991;337(8752):1281–4. Available from https://doi.org/10.1016/0140-6736(91)92949-3.

Harrer S, Shah P, Antony B, Hu J. Artificial intelligence for clinical trial design. Trends in Pharmacological Sciences 2019;40(8):577–91. Available from https://doi.org/10.1016/j.tips.2019.05.005.

Hebb DO. Animal and Physiological Psychology. Annual Review of Psychology 1950;1(1):173–88. Available from 10.1146/annurev.ps.01.020150.001133.

Hernandez JBR, Kim PY. Epidemiology morbidity and mortality. StatPearls. StatPearls; 2022. Available from https://www.ncbi.nlm.nih.gov/books/NBK547668/.

Hill SA. Statistics. Foundations of Anesthesia. Elsevier; 2006. p. 207–17. Available from 10.1016/b978-0-323-03707-5.50024-3.

Hinton GE, Salakhutdinov RR. Reducing the dimensionality of data with neural networks. Science (New York, N.Y.) 2006;313(5786):504–7. Available from https://doi.org/10.1126/science.1127647.

Holzgrabe U. New paths to highly effective tetracyclines. Pharmazie in Unserer Zeit 2005;34(4):258–9. Available from https://doi.org/10.1002/pauz.200590066.

Hung NT. Fluid management for dengue in children. Paediatrics and International Child Health 2012;32(Suppl 1):39–42. Available from https://doi.org/10.1179/2046904712Z.00000000051.

Islam MT, Quispe C, Herrera-Bravo J, Sarkar C, Sharma R, Garg N, Fredes LI, Martorell M, Alshehri MM, Sharifi-Rad J, Daştan SD, Calina D, Alsafi R, Alghamdi S, Batiha GE, Cruz-Martins N. Production, transmission, pathogenesis, and control of dengue virus: a literature-based undivided perspective. BioMed Research International 2021;2021:4224816. Available from https://doi.org/10.1155/2021/4224816.

Jelinek T. Artemisinin based combination therapy in travel medicine. Travel Medicine and Infectious Disease 2013;11(1):23–8. Available from https://doi.org/10.1016/j.tmaid.2013.01.005.

Yang J, He Y, Li Y, Zhang X, Wong YK, hen S S, Zhong T, Zhang J, Liu Q, Wang J. Advances in the research on the targets of anti-malaria actions of artemisinin. Pharmacol Ther 2020;216:107697. Available from 10.1016/j.pharmthera.2020.107697.

Mohri M, Rostamizadeh A, Talwalkar A. Foundations of Machine Learning. The MIT Press; 2012. http://www.jstor.org/stable/j.ctt5hhcw1.

Kaelbling LP, Littman ML, Moore AW. Reinforcement learning: a survey. Journal of Artificial Intelligence Research 1996;4:237–85. Available from https://doi.org/10.1613/jair.301.S2CID1708582. arXiv:cs/9605103.

Karbwang J, Bangchang KN. Clinical Pharmacokinetics of Halofantrine. Clinical Pharmacokinetics 1994;27(2):104–19. Available from 10.2165/00003088-199427020-00003.

Keshavarzi Arshadi A, Salem M, Collins J, Yuan JS, Chakrabarti D. DeepMalaria: artificial intelligence driven discovery of potent antiplasmodials. Frontiers in Pharmacology 2020;10:1526. Available from https://doi.org/10.3389/fphar.2019.01526.

Kim J, Park S, Min D, Kim W. Comprehensive survey of recent drug discovery using deep learning. International Journal of Molecular Sciences 2021;22(18):9983. Available from https://doi.org/10.3390/ijms22189983.

Koirala M, Yan L, Mohamed Z, DiPaola M. AI-integrated QSAR modeling for enhanced drug discovery: from classical approaches to deep learning and structural insight. International Journal of Molecular Sciences 2025;26(19):9384. Available from https://doi.org/10.3390/ijms26199384.

LeCun Y, Bengio Y, Hinton G. Deep learning. Nature 2015;521(7553):436–44. Available from https://doi.org/10.1038/nature14539.

Leder K, McGUINNESS SL. Antiparasitic agents. ClinMicroNow. Wiley; 2023. p. 1–27. Available from https://doi.org/10.1002/9781683670438.mcm0153.

Lemenze A, Mittal N, Perryman AL, Daher SS, Ekins S, Occi J, Ahn YM, Wang X, Russo R, Patel JS, Daugherty RM, Wood DO, Connell N, Freundlich JS. *Rickettsia* Aglow: A fluorescence assay and machine learning model to identify inhibitors of intracellular infection. ACS Infectious Diseases 2022;8(7):1280–90. Available from https://doi.org/10.1021/acsinfecdis.2c00014.

Li Z, Wallace E, Shen S, Lin K, Keutzer K, Klein D, Gonzalez J. Train big, then compress: rethinking model size for efficient training and inference of transformers. Proceedings of the 37th International Conference on Machine Learning, in Proceedings of Machine Learning Research 2020;119:5958–68.

Libbrecht MW, Noble WS. Machine learning applications in genetics and genomics. Nature Reviews. Genetics 2015;16(6):321–32. Available from https://doi.org/10.1038/nrg3920.

Lima MNN, Borba JVB, Cassiano GC, Mottin M, Mendonça SS, Silva AC, Tomaz KCP, Calit J, Bargieri DY, Costa FTM, Andrade CH. Artificial intelligence applied to the rapid identification of new antimalarial candidates with dual-stage activity. ChemMedChem 2021;16(7):1093–103. Available from https://doi.org/10.1002/cmdc.202000685.

Low ZX, OuYong BM, Hassandarvish P, et al. Antiviral activity of silymarin and baicalein against dengue virus. Scientific Reports 2021;11:21221. Available from https://doi.org/10.1038/s41598-021-98949-y.

Lye L-F, Lin C-F, Ou Y-C, Chen C-M. Recent advances in antileishmanial drugs: New leishmaniasis medicine through repurposing approach. Tungs' Medical Journal 2024;18(Suppl 1):S1–5. Available from https://doi.org/10.4103/ETMJ.ETMJ-D-24-00017.

Maizels RM, Denham DA. Diethylcarbamazine (DEC): immunopharmacological interactions of an antifilarial drug. Parasitology 1992;105(Suppl):S49–60. Available from https://doi.org/10.1017/s0031182000075351.

Mandal S, Chattoraj N, Nandi S, Samadder A. To explore molecular targets and combination antimalarial chemotherapeutics as tissue and erythrocytic schizonticides. Journal of Parasitic Diseases: Official Organ of the Indian Society for Parasitology 2025. Available from https://doi.org/10.1007/s12639-025-01882-4.

Mandlik V, Bejugam P, Singh S. Application of Artificial Neural Networks in Modern Drug Discovery. Artificial Neural Network for Drug Design, Delivery and Disposition. Elsevier; 2016. p. 123–39. Available from 10.1016/b978-0-12-801559-9.00006-5.

Mao J, Akhtar J, Zhang X, Sun L, Guan S, Li X, Chen G, Liu J, Jeon HN, Kim MS, No KT, Wang G. Comprehensive strategies of machine-learning-based quantitative structure-activity relationship models. iScience 2021;24(9):103052. Available from https://doi.org/10.1016/j.isci.2021.103052.

Nandi S, Vracko M, Bagchi MC. Anticancer activity of selected phenolic compounds: QSAR studies using ridge regression and neural networks. Chem Biol Drug Des 2007;70(5):424–36. Available from 10.1111/j.1747-0285.2007.00575.x.

Walker M, Specht S, Churcher TS, Hoerauf A, Taylor MJ, Basáñez MG. Therapeutic Efficacy and Macrofilaricidal Activity of Doxycycline for the Treatment of River Blindness. Clinical Infectious Diseases 2014;60(8):1199–207. Available from 10.1093/cid/ciu1152.

Mehta S, Sharma S, Anand S, Sharma S, Goel A. Random forest algorithm for enhanced prediction of drug target interactions. International Journal of Innovative Technology and Exploring Engineering 2020;9:2008–12. Available from https://doi.org/10.35940/ijitee.D1722.029420.

Moreno Y, Nabhan JF, Solomon J, Mackenzie CD, Geary TG. Ivermectin disrupts the function of the excretory-secretory apparatus in microfilariae of Brugia malayi. Proceedings of the National Academy of Sciences of the United States of America 2010;107(46):20120–5. Available from https://doi.org/10.1073/pnas.1011983107.

Nandi S, Bagchi MC. QSAR Analysis of BABQ compounds via calculated molecular descriptors. Medicinal Chemistry Research 2007;15(7-8):393–406. Available from 10.1007/s00044-006-0010-4.

Nandi S, Kumar M, Kumari R, Saxena A. Exploring the inhibitory mechanisms of indazole compounds against SAH/MTAN-mediated quorum sensing utilizing QSAR and docking. Drug target insights 2022;16:54–68. Available from https://doi.org/10.33393/dti.2022.2512.

Nath M, Bhowmik D, Saha S, Nandi R, Kumar D. Identification of potential inhibitor against Leishmania donovani mitochondrial DNA primase through in-silico and in vitro drug repurposing approaches. Sci Rep 2024;14(1):3246. Available from 10.1038/s41598-024-53316-5.

Nath S, Malakar P, Biswas B, Das S, Sabnam N, Nandi S, Samadder A. Exploring the targets of dengue virus and designs of potential inhibitors. Combinatorial Chemistry & High Throughput Screening 2024;27(17):2485–524. Available from https://doi.org/10.2174/0113862073247689231030153054.

Nixon GL, Moss DM, Shone AE, Lalloo DG, Fisher N, O'Neill PM, Ward SA, Biagini GA. Antimalarial pharmacology and therapeutics of atovaquone. The Journal of Antimicrobial Chemotherapy 2013;68(5):977–85. Available from https://doi.org/10.1093/jac/dks504.

Oduselu GO, Elebiju OF, Ogunnupebi TA, Akash S, Ajani OO, Adebiyi E. Employing hexahydroquinolines as *Pf*CDPK4 inhibitors to combat malaria transmission: an advanced computational approach. Advances and Applications in Bioinformatics and Chemistry 2025;17:83–105. Available from https://doi.org/10.2147/AABC.S476404.

Ojetti V, Lauritano EC, Barbaro F, Migneco A, Ainora ME, Fontana L, Gabrielli M, Gasbarrini A. Rifaximin pharmacology and clinical implications. Expert Opinion on Drug Metabolism & Toxicology 2009;5(6):675–82. Available from https://doi.org/10.1517/17425250902973695.

Oliveira TAd, Silva MPd, Maia EHB, Silva AMd, Taranto AG. Virtual ccreeningaAlgorithms in drug discovery: a review focused on machine and deep learning methods. Drugs Drug Candidates 2023;2:311–34. Available from https://doi.org/10.3390/ddc2020017.

Ong HW, Adderley J, Tobin AB, Drewry DH, Doerig C. Parasite and host kinases as targets for antimalarials. Expert Opinion on Therapeutic Targets 2023;27(2):151–69. Available from https://doi.org/10.1080/14728222.2023.2185511.

Pang B, Raoufi A, Taghinejad Z, Fakhraei M, Esfahani ML, Heydari P, Sargazi Aval O, Soleimani Samarkhazan H. Parasites in the bloodstream: unraveling hematological chaos and clinical implications. Parasitology International 2026;111:103172. Available from https://doi.org/10.1016/j.parint.2025.103172.

Parija SC, Poddar A. Artificial intelligence in parasitic disease control: a paradigm shift in healthcare. Tropical Parasitology 2024;14(1):2–7. Available from https://doi.org/10.4103/tp.tp_66_2.

Patil C, Katare S, Baig M, Doifode S. Fixed dose combination of arterolane and piperaquine: a newer prospect in antimalarial therapy. Annals of Medical and Health Sciences Research 2014;4(4):466–71. Available from https://doi.org/10.4103/2141-9248.139270.

Paul D, Sanap G, Shenoy S, Kalyane D, Kalia K, Tekade RK. Artificial intelligence in drug discovery and development. Drug Discovery Today 2021;26(1):80–93. Available from https://doi.org/10.1016/j.drudis.2020.10.010.

Prasad S. Regression. Advanced statistical methods. Singapore: Springer; 2024. p. 1–45. Available from https://doi.org/10.1007/978-981-99-7257-9_1.

Qi X, Zhao Y, Qi Z, Hou S, Chen J. Machine learning empowering drug discovery: applications, opportunities and challenges. Molecules (Basel, Switzerland) 2024;29(4):903. Available from https://doi.org/10.3390/molecules29040903.

Rodgers W, Frazier AD, Champney WS. Solithromycin inhibition of protein synthesis and ribosome biogenesis in staphylococcus aureus, streptococcus pneumoniae, and haemophilus influenzae. Antimicrobial Agents and Chemotherapy 2013;57(4):1632–7. Available from https://doi.org/10.1128/AAC.02316-12.

Romero-Meza G, Mugnier MR. Trypanosoma brucei. Trends in Parasitology 2020;36(6):571–2. Available from https://doi.org/10.1016/j.pt.2019.10.007.

Roquini V, Mengarda AC, Cajas RA, Martins-da-Silva MF, Godoy-Silva J, Santos GA, Espírito-Santo MCC, Pavani TFA, Melo VA, Salvadori MC, Teixeira FS, Rando DGG, de Moraes J. The Existing drug nifuroxazide as an antischistosomal agent: In vitro, In vivo, and In silico studies of macromolecular targets. Microbiology Spectrum 2023;11:e01393–23. Available from https://doi.org/10.1128/spectrum.01393-23.

Russo A, Patanè GT, Putaggio S, Lombardo GE, Ficarra S, Barreca D, Giunta E, Tellone E, Laganà G. Mechanisms underlying the effects of chloroquine on red blood cells metabolism. International Journal of Molecular Sciences 2024;25(12):6424. Available from https://doi.org/10.3390/ijms25126424.

Saha A, Pushpa, Bagchi SR, Samadder A, Nandi S. To explore potential natural inhibitors of cysteine proteases to combat human African Trypanosomiasis and chagas disease. Current Medicinal Chemistry 2024;31. Available from https://doi.org/10.2174/0109298673311070240807104229.

Sakhre V, Jain S, Sapkal VS, Agarwal DP. Fuzzy counter propagation neural network control for a class of nonlinear dynamical systems. Computational Intelligence and Neuroscience 2015;2015:719620. Available from https://doi.org/10.1155/2015/719620.

Sanz-Rodríguez CE, Hoffman B, Guyett PJ, Purmal A, Singh B, Pollastri MP, Mensa-Wilmot K. Physiologic targets and modes of action for CBL0137, a lead for human African trypanosomiasis drug development. Molecular Pharmacology 2022;102(1):1–16. Available from https://doi.org/10.1124/molpharm.121.000430.

Sarker IH. Machine learning: algorithms, real-world applications and research directions. SN Computer Science 2021;2(3):160. Available from https://doi.org/10.1007/s42979-021-00592-x.

Sato S. Plasmodium-a brief introduction to the parasites causing human malaria and their basic biology. Journal of Physiological Anthropology 2021;40(1):1. Available from https://doi.org/10.1186/s40101-020-00251-9. W.

Schaefer TJ, Panda PK, Wolford RW. Dengue fever. StatPearls [Internet]. Treasure Island (FL): StatPearls Publishing; 2024. Available from https://www.ncbi.nlm.nih.gov/books/NBK430732/.

Serrano DR, Luciano FC, Anaya BJ, Ongoren B, Kara A, Molina G, Ramirez BI, Sánchez-Guirales SA, Simon JA, Tomietto G, Rapti C, Ruiz HK, Rawat S, Kumar D, Lalatsa A. Artificial intelligence (AI) applications in drug discovery and drug delivery: revolutionizing personalized medicine. Pharmaceutics 2024;16(10):1328. Available from https://doi.org/10.3390/pharmaceutics16101328.

Sharma V, Singh S. Mechanistic and structural insights into oxidative stress in malaria and antimalarial drug metabolism. Oxidative Stress in Microbial Diseases. Singapore: Springer; 2019. p. 531–8.

Shimizu Y, Yoshimoto J, Toki S, Takamura M, Yoshimura S, Okamoto Y, Yamawaki S, Doya K. Toward probabilistic diagnosis and understanding of depression based on functional MRI data analysis with logistic group LASSO. PLoS One 2015;10(5):e0123524. Available from https://doi.org/10.1371/journal.pone.0123524.

Starvaggi J, Previti S, Zappalà M, Ettari R. The Inhibition of NS2B/NS3 Protease: A New Therapeutic Opportunity to Treat Dengue and Zika Virus Infection. International Journal of Molecular Sciences 2024;25(8):4376. Available from 10.3390/ijms25084376.

Singh S, Kumar R, Payra S, Kumar Singh S. Artificial intelligence and machine learning in pharmacological research: bridging the gap between data and drug discovery. Cureus 2023;15. Available from https://doi.org/10.7759/cureus.44359.

Sibley CH, Hyde JE, Sims PF, Plowe CV, Kublin JG, Mberu EK, Cowman AF, Winstanley PA, Watkins WM, Nzila AM. Pyrimethamine-sulfadoxine resistance in Plasmodium falciparum: what next? Trends Parasitol 2001;17(12):582–8. Available from 10.1016/s1471-4922(01)02085-2.

Snowden J, Ladd M, King KC. Rickettsial infection. StatPearls. StatPearls Publishing; 2023. Available from https://www.ncbi.nlm.nih.gov/books/NBK431127/.

Theodoridis L, Carvalho TG. Antimalarial drug resistance and drug discovery: learning from the past to innovate the future. Int J Parasitol Drugs Drug Resist 2025;28:100602. Available from 10.1016/j.ijpddr.2025.100602.

Wong W, Bai XC, Sleebs BE, Triglia T, Brown A, Thompson JK, Jackson KE, Hanssen E, Marapana DS, Fernandez IS, Ralph SA, Cowman AF, Scheres SHW, Baum J. Mefloquine targets the Plasmodium falciparum 80S ribosome to inhibit protein synthesis. Nat Microbiol 2017;2:17031. Available from 10.1038/nmicrobiol.2017.31.

Thomas SM, Purmal A, Pollastri M, Mensa-Wilmot K. Discovery of a carbazole-derived lead drug for human African trypanosomiasis. Scientific Reports 2016;6:32083. Available from https://doi.org/10.1038/srep32083.

Tahar R, de Pécoulas PE, Basco LK, Chiadmi Md, Mazabraud A, et al. Kinetic properties of dihydrofolate reductase from wild-type and mutant Plasmodium vivax expressed in Escherichia coli. Molecular and Biochemical Parasitology 2001;113(2):241–9. Available from 10.1016/s0166-6851(01)00230-4.

Watanabe N, Saito-Nakano Y, Kurisawa N, Otomo K, Suenaga K, Nakano K, Nozaki T. Fumagillin inhibits growth of the enteric protozoan parasite *Entamoeba histolytica* by covalently binding to and

selectively inhibiting methionine aminopeptidase. Antimicrobial Agents and Chemotherapy 2023;67(11):e0056023. Available from https://doi.org/10.1128/aac.00560-23.
Di Piazza A, Di Piazza MC, La Tona G, Luna M, et al. An artificial neural network-based forecasting model of energy-related time series for electrical grid management. Mathematics and Computers in Simulation 2021;184:294–305. Available from 10.1016/j.matcom.2020.05.010.
Winters R, Nguyen T, Waseem M. Chagas disease. StatPearls. StatPearls Publishing; 2025.
Zekar L, Sharman T. Plasmodium falciparum malaria. StatPearls. Treasure Island (FL): StatPearls Publishing; 2023. Available from https://www.ncbi.nlm.nih.gov/books/NBK555962/.
Zhong F, Xing J, Li X, Liu X, Fu Z, Xiong Z, Lu D, Wu X, Zhao J, Tan X, Li F, Luo X, Li Z, Chen K, Zheng M, Jiang H. Artificial intelligence in drug design. Science China Life Sciences 2018;61(10):1191–204. Available from 10.1007/s11427-018-9342-2.
Zimmer AJ, Simonsen KA. Babesiosis. StatPearls. StatPearls Publishing; 2023. Available from https://www.ncbi.nlm.nih.gov/books/NBK441864/.
Zheng D, Liu T, Yu S, Liu Z, Wang J, Wang Y. Antimalarial Mechanisms and Resistance Status of Artemisinin and Its Derivatives. Tropical Medicine and Infectious Disease 2024;9(9):223. Available from 10.3390/tropicalmed9090223.
Zorn KM, Sun S, McConnon CL, Ma K, Chen EK, Foil DH, Lane TR, Liu LJ, El-Sakkary N, Skinner DE, Ekins S, Caffrey CR. A machine learning strategy for drug discovery identifies antischistosomal small molecules. ACS Infectious Diseases 2021;7(2):406–20. Available from https://doi.org/10.1021/acsinfecdis.0c00754.

Further Reading

Di Piazza A, Di Piazza MC, La Tona G, Luna M. An artificial neural network-based forecasting model of energy-related time series for electrical grid management. Mathematics and Computers in Simulation 2021;184:294–305. Available from 10.1016/j.matcom.2020.05.010.
Mohri M, Rostamizadeh A, Talwalkar A. Foundations of Machine Learning. The MIT Press; 2012. http://www.jstor.org/stable/j.ctt5hhcw1.
Rao SPS, Manjunatha UH, Mikolajczak S, Ashigbie PG, Diagana TT. Drug discovery for parasitic diseases: powered by technology, enabled by pharmacology, informed by clinical science. Trends Parasitol 2023;39(4):260–71. Available from 10.1016/j.pt.2023.01.010.
Zhu N, Wang K, Zhang SL, Zhao B, Yang JN, Wang SW. Application of artificial neural networks to predict multiple quality of dry-cured ham based on protein degradation. Food Chem 2021;344:128586. Available from 10.1016/j.foodchem.2020.128586.

CHAPTER 8

In silico tools and computational biology in natural product research

Debdiya Majumdar[1,*], Ahana Ghosh[1,*], Soni Shaw[1,*], Sisir Nandi[2], and Asmita Samadder[1,3]
[1]Cell and Developmental Biology Special, Department of Zoology, University of Kalyani, Kalyani, West Bengal, India,
[2]Global Institute of Pharmaceutical Education and Research, Kashipur, Uttarakhand, India,
[3]Cytogenetics and Molecular Biology Lab., Department of Zoology, University of Kalyani, Kalyani, West Bengal, India

8.1 Introduction

Natural products (NPs) are compounds or substances which are obtained from nature or from natural sources. Natural sources consist of living organisms found in nature. Living organisms are plants, natural animals, microorganisms and also marine sources. NPs derived from diverse biological sources have historically served as an important foundation for food, medicine, and health care. A substantial proportion of modern pharmaceuticals are derived directly or indirectly from NPs, particularly from plant and microbial sources (Najmi et al., 2022).

Several plants derived from medicines and products have been discovered. So, there are several crucial medicines which are mainly obtained from the plants. Reserpine is obtained from *Rauwolfia serpentina* (commonly known as Indian snakeroot) which is an antihypertensive drug (Strawbridge et al., 2023). Morphine is obtained from *Papaver somniferum* (commonly known as *Opium poppy*) which is used as a powerful analgesic and also remains present in some opioid pain medications (Benyhe, 2011). Quinine is obtained from the *Cinchona* tree which is used as an antimalarial drug (Achan et al., 2011). Vincristine is obtained from *Catharanthus roseus* (formerly *Vinca roseus*; commonly known as the Madagascar periwinkle plant) which is used in cancer treatment (Awosika et al., 2023). *Ocimum sanctum* (commonly known as holy basil, tulsi) has been traditionally used for the symptomatic management of respiratory ailments such as cough and cold (Sareen et al., 2024). Compounds derived from *Piper nigrum* and *Cinnamomum cassia* have been reported to exhibit immunomodulatory and antiinflammatory properties (Meghwal and Goswami, 2013; Thomas and Kuruvilla, 2012). The bark of the willow tree containing salicin, has pain relieving properties (Schrör, 2008). Colchicine is obtained from *Colchicum autumnale* (commonly called autumn crocus flowering plant) which is used in the treatment of gout (Hartung, 1954). Taxol is

[*] Equal authorship.

Innovative Strategies Against Blood Parasites
DOI: https://doi.org/10.1016/B978-0-443-48509-1.00006-9

obtained from the bark of *Taxus brevifolia* which is used to treat breast cancer (Cragg, 1998).

Certain therapeutically important biomolecules have historically been obtained from animal sources. For example, insulin was originally isolated from animal pancreases before the development of recombinant DNA technology (Atkinson et al., 2020). Heparin, an anticoagulant, has traditionally been extracted from the intestinal mucosa and lung tissue of mammals (Oduah et al., 2016). Thyroxine is a naturally occurring thyroid hormone produced by vertebrates, including sheep, and has been studied extensively using animal models to understand its physiological transport and regulation; clinically, it is used in the treatment of hypothyroidism rather than hypertension (Zibara et al., 2021). There are medicines which are of microbial origin. Penicillin is used in the broadspectrum of antibacterial which is obtained from the fungi (*Penicillium chrysogenum* and *Penicillium rubens*) (Kück and Dahlmann, 2021). Streptomycin is obtained from the soil bacterium (*Streptomyces griseus*) which is an aminoglycoside, used in the treatment of tuberculosis Waksman et al., 1946). *Piptoporus betulinus* is a type of fungus, found in the birches, that has antiseptic and disinfectant properties (Swanton 1914). *Agaricus campestris* (commonly called the field mushroom) has been widely used in the traditional treatment for diabetes (Gray and Flatt, 1998). Phylum *Basidiomycota* and *Ascomycota* (wood-rotting fungi) are a major component for pharmacologically active substances (Zjawiony, 2004).

The marine environment is also a novel source of NPs. Some of the medicines are also obtained from marine sources. Ziconotide is a type of peptide which is mainly to relieve pain, first found in the venom of a fish hunting marine snail (Williams et al., 2008). Plitidepsin is a type of peptide having antitumor activity, was first discovered in a Mediterranean marine tunicate (*Aplidium albicans*) (Alonso-Álvarez et al., 2017). Ecteinascidin743 is a type of alkaloid which has antitumor activity, and was isolated from *Ecteinascidia turbinata* (Erba et al., 2001).

NPs can also be divided into two parts. These are primary metabolites and secondary metabolites. Primary metabolites are substances which remain involved in the survival of the organisms. But in contrast the secondary metabolites are not involved in the growth of the organisms but some of them have very useful medicinal properties (for e.g., morphine) (Wink, 2015).

These NPs can be derivatized to produce synthetic drugs and those could be synthesized in the laboratory because nowadays several complicated diseases have been generated and also there are several complications found within the biological system because of the use of several prescribed drugs.

A lot of time is taken for the synthesis of new synthetic drugs. First, the compound is synthesized by a series of reactions, then it is tested in vitro, after that in the in vivo condition by animal sacrifices and then it is gone through the human trial (phase I, phase II, phase III, phase IV). For these reasons, it is a very long process of drug discovery which may take up to 14 to16 years . The synthetic drugs are designed to treat specific diseases or specific reactions but its "side effects" become a risk against its primary effect. But in the case of NPs they tend to have several useful actions on the biological as well as the physiological system and the most important thing is that these actions have rarely adversely affected our body (Kazemipoor et al., 2012). The major reasons to use of NPs rather than the synthetic ones are:

- □ A synthetic drug can have harmful or toxic effects depending upon its chemical components its dosage.
- □ Synthetic drugs are sometimes chemically unnatural.
- □ The synthetic drugs sometimes have addictive potential.
- □ For the reduction of time and labor there are several techniques introduced for the treatment of several diseases with the help of NP use.

Now there are some synthetic drugs which have beneficial values and also have harmful effects and these beneficial effects can also be found in some NPs as followed in Table 8.1.

In drug discovery, we must have to know about the major two constituents that are the main backbone for the drug discovery and also the involvement of computers in them. These are computers in chemistry and computers in biology.

The three major components of experiments are in vitro (means "in the glass," referring to experiments conducted in a controlled and artificial environment such as a test tube or petri dish), in vivo (means "within the living," referring to studies performed within a whole, living organism, such as a human, animal or plant) and in silico (means the use of the computers to improve the drug discovery, helping in the stimulation of responses in disease manifestation in cell and also in case of tissue and organ) studies (Colquitt et al., 2011).

To identify the potentially harmful effect during the early developmental process, researcher groups use the in silico process that helps in toxicity prediction. Then with the help of virtual ligand screening and molecular modeling and docking based virtual screening processes, help to observe and predict the binding modes and interaction pattern of the drugs. So that the novel and promising compounds can be identified.

8.1.1 Use of natural products in in silico method

The European commission launched the European center for the validation of alternative methods (ECVAM) in 1991 to focus on finding alternative methods to reduce experiments on living beings; in silico and in vitro methods are among them. In silico study is very much simple and effective. So that it represents an alternative to the chemical analysis of NPs. Most importantly, organic compounds having both of the biological and pharmaceutical activities can be evaluated with the help of computational analysis (Sow et al., 2022).

Table 8.1 Beneficial effects of natural drugs over synthetic drugs. Synthetic drugs which have beneficial values and also have harmful effects, and these beneficial effects can also be found in some natural products.

Drug type	Example	Harmful effects	Comparison with the natural product having the same effect
Anti inflammatory	Paracetamol, aspirin	Can cause ulcer, liver and kidney damage (mainly due to the long-term use in high doses)	Turmeric (Curcumin) have an antiinflammatory property .but its effects take a longer time and also very fewer side effects when used for a long period (Chaachouay 2024).
Opioids	Heroin, morphine	Have very much high potential for addiction and ; also the overdose may lead to respiratory depression	Opium is a naturalproduct, containing many other medicinal components from which many drugs and opioids can be derived and very much less potent than their synthetic forms.
Anxiolytics	Benzodiaze-pines	Problems in the central nervous system, cognitive impairment.	Valerian root (Bent et al., 2006.) . is used in case of stress removal and also mild insomnia with fewer side effects .

No permission required.

8.2 Methods of natural products discovery

The discovery of NPs spans multiple stages, from the identification of bioactive sources to structural characterization and eventual clinical development. Historically, this process has often been slow because of limited data availability and reliance on empirical trial and error approaches. However advances in biological data generation, computational chemistry, and information science have significantly improved the efficiency of NP based drug discovery. In particular, artificial intelligence and computational approaches enable rapid analysis of large datasets, support predictive modeling, and facilitate the prioritization of promising lead compounds (Gangwal and Lavecchia, 2025).

8.2.1 Experimental method

From historical knowledge, the therapeutic use of plant products has notably helped in the isolation of a pure chemical entity and its incorporation into the modern system of medicine. Ethnopharmacological practices of the plant formed as one of the major sources of lead compounds for initial drug discovery and development. Ignited by the discovery of penicillin and streptomycin, the golden age of antibiotics began and researchers discovered microbial secondary metabolites as an important source of new antibacterial compounds. Today, NPs remain the main source of new therapeutic agents. The genus *Streptomyces* has especially been chemically exploited for decades in the search for new drugs. Traditional methods for discovering NPs mostly relied on bioactivity assays and product isolation and purification technologies (Najmi et al., 2022; Ziemert et al., 2016). In another approach, those plants are selected as potentially active candidates that are ingested by animals for self-medication purposes and to restore physiological balance, e.g. in order to alleviate microbial or parasitic infections, to enhance reproduction rates, to moderate thermoregulation, and to increase alertness. This concept is also referred to as zoopharmacognosy. For example, compounds with antimalarial and antiprotozoal activity could be isolated from plant species that were ingested by chimpanzees and baboons in the wild in unusual feeding behavior, in order to possibly control intestinal parasite infections (Atanasov et al., 2015).

8.2.1.1 Bioactivity guided fractionation

One of the most widely used methods of drug discovery is bioactivity guided fractionation (Fig. 8.1), in which, instead of looking for a specific type of chemical, researchers break down plant crude extracts into smaller fractions and test each of them for their useful biological activity. Fractions that demonstrate good potential are studied further in more detail. The most active extracts are separated into smaller subfractions with solvents arranged from decreasing polarity such as butanol, chloroform, and hexane. These subfractions further undergo additional separation and refinement using column chromatography or high performance liquid chromatography (HPLC). The purified compounds are further tested for their biological activity, and their structures are identified and clarified with methods such as nuclear magnetic resonance (NMR) and mass spectrometry, LC MS, etc. A variety of plant derived NPs has been discovered using this method for example anticancer agents, camptothecin, and paclitaxel from *Camptotheca acuminata* and *Taxus brevifolia*, respectively (Najmi et al., 2022).

8.2.1.2 Chromatographic techniques

Qualitative and quantitative analysis of NP is another crucial step in NP discovery. Several chromatographic techniques, such as thin layer chromatography (TLC), high performance thin layer chromatography (HPTLC), high performance liquid

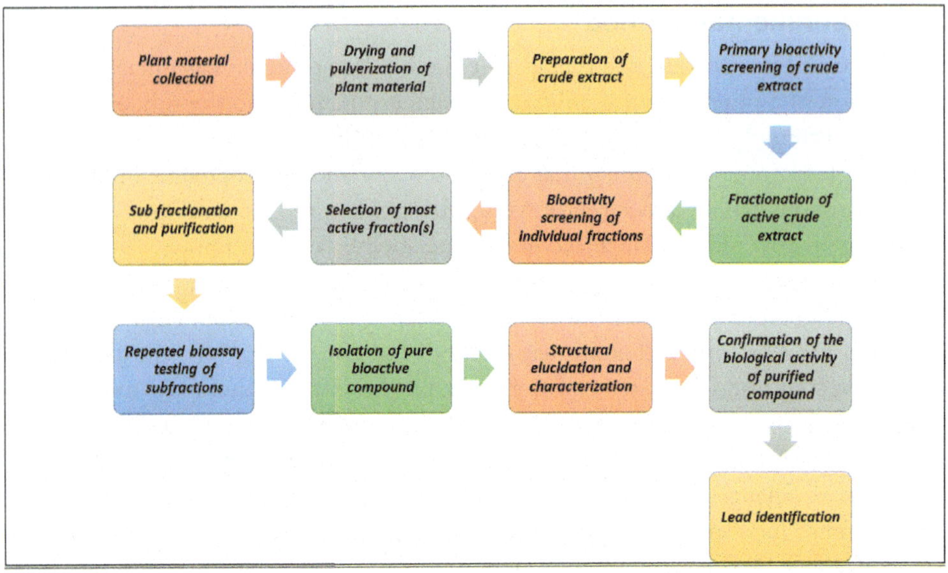

Figure 8.1 Bioactivity guided fractionation workflow for natural product discovery. Plant crude extracts are sequentially fractionated and screened for biological activity. Active fractions are progressively purified using chromatographic techniques, followed by the structural elucidation of bioactive compounds using spectroscopic methods. *No permission required.*

chromatography (HPLC), and capillary electrophoresis (CE) are extremely useful procedures to separate and quantify the desired compounds from crude extract. These methods provide preliminary fingerprinting and are simple and fast as it analyzes multiple samples in a single run. Gas chromatography technique (GC) is a method designed to analyze herbal medicine possessing volatile compounds such as terpenes, monoterpenes, sesquiterpenes, and their oxygenated derivatives which account for the unique fragrance of essential oils, a key source of NPs that has pharmacological activities as per Fig. 8.2 (Najmi et al., 2022)(Ibekwe 2015)

8.2.1.3 *Spectroscopic techniques*

Nuclear magnetic resonance (NMR) and mass spectrometry (MS) are primary tools that are used for structural elucidation. Both provide complementary data as NMR provides structural arrangement and has the ability to can distinguish between isobaric compounds and positional isomers. Furthermore MS provides details about molecular weight and functional group data such as nitro and sulfate groups. Due to their complementary capabilities, the combined technique is used in various fields such as in NP discovery, metabolomics, and drug metabolite identification, one of the most powerful methods for separating and elucidating the structures of NPs in mixtures is by

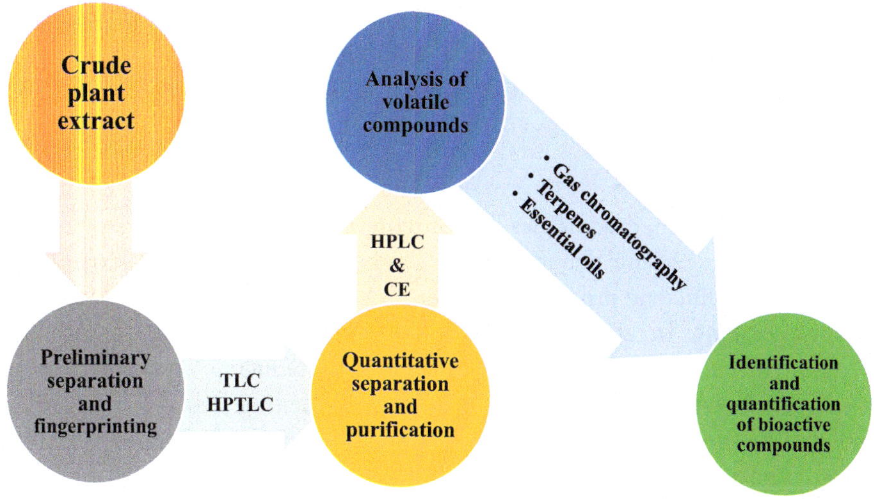

Figure 8.2 Chromatographic techniques used for qualitative and quantitative analysis of natural products. Flowchart representing the process of chromatographic techniques. *No permission required.*

coupling of HPLC with NMR (LC NMR), it generated spectral data that can be used for dereplication and *de novo* structure determination (Gashaw et al., 2025).

8.2.1.4 High throughput screening

High throughput screening (HTS) is a fundamental approach in this framework that involves screening and assaying of a large number of biological modulators and effectors against selected targets. It accelerates drug discovery by screening large compound libraries per day. HTS methods are also used to characterize metabolic, pharmacokinetic, and toxicological data about new drugs. This method reduces the costs and time of drug development. It consists of several steps, such as target identification, reagent preparation, compound management, assay development, and high throughput library screening (Szymański et al., 2012). Despite its advantages, major challenge were reported such as regulations on international access to natural bioresources, biological extracts are typically too complex to be compatible with HTS for specific molecular targets, and the costly efforts to reduce chemical complexity make this approach less attractive. To overcome these challenges, advances in genomics and computational tools are increasingly being integrated with traditional screening (Gaudêncio et al., 2023). But these methods are time consuming and often result in rediscovering of known chemical entities and hence lead to low return on investment.

With advancement and revolutionary (Ayon, 2023) technological advancements in automation and robotics have enabled automated streamlined workflow to weigh, transfer, grow, extract, fractionate, and screen NPs for bioactivity, which, when combined with bioprospecting, high throughput mass spectrometry, rapid chromatography, high performance column chemistry, and genomics, has tremendous potential in discovering bioactive molecules from natural sources.

8.2.2 In silico methods

In silico based analysis methodologies do not require the isolation of chemicals, allowing the determination of health benefits before synthesis or purification. Modern desktop computers have sufficient processing power to run simulations of low to moderate complexity, making in silico research methods more accessible. In silico based approaches have transformed NP drug discovery by reducing cost and time and by improving its efficiency. Techniques such as virtual screening, molecular dynamics, and binding free energy predictions help to identify effective NP hits for experimental validation. The early prediction of absorption, distribution, metabolism, elimination, and toxicity (ADMET) profiles prevents latestage failures, supporting appropriate drug design. With the growth of NP databases, AI technologies such as machine learning and deep learning now play a central role in biosynthetic gene cluster detection, predicting the biological function of a gene, predictive modeling, and in designing of NP analogs. Together, these computational methods are accelerating NP based drug discovery and shaping future strategies for developing clinically relevant drugs (Simoben et al., 2023).

8.2.2.1 Virtual screening

Virtual screening is often the initial step in the computational analysis of NPs to identify potential hits; this method is enhanced by machine learning (ML) which is used to predict chemical properties based on the structural characteristics of different compounds. This means that AI models can determine how a compound might behave based on its molecular shape and composition. However open access NP resources often have incomplete data, especially stereochemistry. To address this, nonredundant NP structures have been compiled in the compounds Collection of open natural products (COCONUT) for efficient virtual screening and molecular analysis (Sorokina and Steinbeck, 2020). Using virtual screening techniques such as similarity searching, researchers can efficiently explore the chemical space represented by NPs and predict their interactions with biological targets. Recent applications show the practical use of these approaches. For example Juárez Mercado et al. identified SARSCoV2 protease inhibitors using ligand based virtual screening based on similarity searching of many small-molecule databases, including the NPs database COCONUT (Zeng et al., 2024). HTS done by computational techniques or in silico techniques consists of several stimulation tools called virtual screening. In silico screening consists of ligand based and structure based methods (Nandi et al., 2018).

8.2.2.1.1 Ligand based screening

Ligand based screening consists of QSAR (Quantitative structure activity relationship) and pharmacophore, whereas structurebased in silico screening consists of molecular docking methods (Nandi and Bagchi, 2010).

QSAR means Quantitative structure activity relationship that can explain the quantitative relationship between biological activity and structural parameters of a chemical compound. QSAR is a quantitative model that can predict biological activity, affinity, toxicity, and expose the property property relationship. Ligand-based pharmacophore is for the assessment of many features of structurally diverse compounds, and these structurally diverse compounds have a common mode of binding. Common pharmacophore features are hydrogen bond acceptors, hydrogen bond donors, hydrophobicity, positive ionization and negative ionization (Kumar et al., 2023).

8.2.2.1.2 Structure based screening

Structure based docking is a simulation for the assessment of biochemical mechanisms of chemical compounds inside the target cavity, when a ligand or drug approaches toward the receptor, both the conformational changes occur and the drug can bind inside the receptor cavity to produce a drug receptor complex responsible for biological activities.

Drugs have affinity to bind with the receptor cavity and produce a drug receptor complex. This affinity is expressed in terms of binding energy or docking score; that is called docking between the ligand and receptor.

A drug may bind and produce a drug receptor complex but may not produce intrinsic biological activity. This means the drug has affinity, but it may or may not produce the real biological activity. To explore the affinity of the ligand towards the receptor site and molecular mechanism, in silico docking has been used as a prime simulation tool (Dey et al., 2021)

8.2.2.2 Molecular docking

Following virtual screening, molecular docking has become an essential step in silico drug development. In molecular docking we can predict whether a drug or ligand can reach the target cavity or bind the receptors because biological activity will only be produced when a drug can bind the target cavity or active site of the target and produce a drug receptor complex. That is why molecular docking is an HTS simulation technique in structure based drug design. Thus this technique involves predicting the interaction between a small molecule and a protein at the atomic level molecular docking of compounds in various databases helps to virtually screen large numbers of small molecules in an effort to identify potential hits. There are several computational tools and algorithms available for molecular docking techniques, according to Agu et al. some of the most commonly used docking programs include AutoDock Vina,

Discovery Studio, Surflex, AutoDock GOLD, Glide, MCDock, MOEDock, FlexX, DOCK, LeDock, rDock, ICM, Cdcker, LigandFit, FRED, and UCSF Dock. Among these programs, AutoDock Vina, Glide, and AutoDock GOLD have been considered as top ranking choices with the best scores. After finding a hit, this technique also helps to improve its structure and design new analogs with better binding and selectivity (Agu et al., 2023; Asiamah et al., 2023).

8.2.2.3 Genome mining

Currently, In silico approaches are focusing on DNA sequences to predict the chemical structures of NPs produced by a groups of genes that function together known as biosynthetic gene clusters (BGCs), which are encoded in the genome of the producing organisms. To our benefit more than 2500 BGCs and their products have been already defined through experimental data. This led the foundation for computational genomic analysis, also known as genome mining, to potentially identify a great deal of biosynthetic pathways for unexplored molecules (Mullowney et al., 2023). Tools such as antiSMASH, PRISM, and the MIBiG database help to predict BGCs and their potential chemical products.

8.3 Pharmacoinformatics

Pharmacoinformatics refers to the application of computational and information based methods to integrate chemical and biological data for drug discovery and development. In the context of natural product research, pharmacoinformatics is particularly important because it provides systematic approaches to analyze structurally complex molecules alongside heterogeneous biological datasets. Two interdependent components of pharmacoinformatics, cheminformatics and bioinformatics, collectively support data driven, efficient, and rational natural product based drug discovery.

8.3.1 Cheminformatics

Cheminformatics is an interdisciplinary discipline that applies computational techniques, statistical methods, and information science to solve chemical problems, particularly those encountered during drug discovery. Within natural product research, cheminformatics plays a central role because of the structural diversity, high stereochemical complexity, and nonclassical chemical features commonly exhibited by natural compounds (Chen and Kirchmair, 2020).

A major contribution of cheminformatics is the organization, curation and large scale analysis of chemical data. NPs often occupy distinct regions of chemical space compared with synthetic small molecules, necessitating tailored computational workflows. Cheminformatics tools enable the systematic evaluation of molecular diversity, physicochemical properties, and biological activity, thereby facilitating the prioritization of compounds with favorable drug like profiles at early discovery stages (Medina-Franco et al., 2020).

Established cheminformatics approaches remain foundational in natural product based drug discovery. Molecular docking is widely employed to explore potential ligand target binding modes and to generate hypotheses regarding molecular interactions. Virtual screening techniques extend this capability by enabling the rapid evaluation of large chemical libraries, including natural product databases, using ligand based and structure based strategies. In parallel, quantitative structure activity relationship (QSAR) modeling supports lead optimization by identifying statistical relationships between molecular descriptors and biological activity, allowing the estimation of trends in potency, selectivity, and ADME related properties (Chen and Kirchmair, 2020). Curated chemical databases underpin many of these workflows. Resources such as ChEMBL and specialized natural product databases provide access to annotated chemical structures, physicochemical parameters, and bioactivity data. These datasets support dereplication, chemical space analysis, and virtual screening, while cheminformatics software frameworks facilitate descriptor calculation, model construction, and data integration (Medina-Franco et al., 2020).

Recent advances in machine learning and deep learning have substantially expanded the scope of cheminformatics. Predictive models are increasingly applied to molecular property estimation, ADMET profiling, and activity classification. Graph based molecular representations, particularly graph neural networks, have proven effective in capturing complex molecular relationships. Conditional generative models further enable *de novo* molecule generation guided by predefined biological or physicochemical objectives, supporting rational molecular design (Abate et al., 2023).

Deep learning approaches are also being explored for specialiszd tasks such as drug drug interaction prediction and oral bioavailability estimation. Hybrid models that integrate chemical descriptors with biological and network level features have demonstrated improved predictive performance, although their robustness remains dependent on data quality, chemical domain coverage, and appropriate validation strategies (Lin et al., 2023; Ng and Lu, 2023).

Despite these advances, cheminformatics based predictions require careful interpretation. Docking scores and machine learning outputs provide relative or probabilistic assessments rather than definitive measures of binding affinity or clinical efficacy. Consequently, experimental validation remains essential, particularly for NPs whose structural complexity may challenge existing models. When applied appropriately, however cheminformatics substantially reduces the number of compounds progressed to experimental evaluation, improving overall discovery efficiency (Chen and Kirchmair, 2020).

8.3.2 Bioinformatics

Bioinformatics encompasses computational and statistical approaches for the analysis and interpretation of large scale biological data, including genomic, transcriptomic, proteomic, and metabolomic datasets. Its importance in natural product research lies in its ability to elucidate the genetic and biochemical basis of secondary metabolite biosynthesis and biological activity. One of the most prominent applications of bioinformatics in natural product discovery is the identification of biosynthetic gene clusters (BGCs). Advances in genome sequencing and annotation have enabled systematic exploration of microbial, plant, and marine genomes for genes encoding natural product biosynthesis. Computational tools such as antiSMASH, together with curated repositories including MIBiG, support the prediction, annotation, and comparative analysis (with the help of PRISM) of BGCs, facilitating the prioritization of organisms with high biosynthetic potential (Kaur and Singh, 2023).

Transcriptomic and metabolomic analyzes provide complementary insights into natural product biosynthesis. Gene expression profiling reveals regulatory mechanisms controlling pathway activation under different environmental or physiological conditions, while metabolomics links genetic information to observed chemical outputs. The integration of these datasets through bioinformatics frameworks supports the reconstruction of biosynthetic pathways and informs pathway engineering strategies (Carbonell et al., 2016).

Beyond biosynthesis, bioinformatics contributes to target identification and mechanistic studies. Comparative genomics, proteomics, and network based analyzes enable the identification of potential molecular targets and pathways modulated by NPs. Such systems level approaches are particularly relevant for antiparasitic and multi target therapies, where biological effects often arise from the modulation of interconnected pathways rather than single targets (Kaur and Singh, 2023).

Artificial intelligence and machine learning techniques are increasingly integrated into bioinformatics workflows. These methods enable automated genome mining, pattern recognition across complex datasets, and improved prediction of biological activity and toxicity. Recent developments emphasize the use of explainable models to enhance interpretability and facilitate the regulatory acceptance of computational prediction (Zhang et al., 2025).

8.3.3 Integration of cheminformatics and bioinformatics in natural product research

The integration of cheminformatics and bioinformatics provides a unified framework for connecting chemical structures with biosynthetic origin and biological function. By linking genome derived information with chemical space analysis, integrated workflows enable the tracing of NPs from gene clusters to molecular structures and onward to pharmacological activity (Chen and Kirchmair, 2020; Lagunin et al., 2014). In practice, such integration supports genome mining to identify biosynthetically capable organisms, virtual screening and target prediction to prioritize associated compounds, and optimization of drug like properties prior to experimental validation. When applied to antiparasitic drug discovery, integrated chemoinformatics bioinformatics approaches leverage multi omics data to decode complex biosynthetic pathways, identify relevant molecular targets, and prioritize candidate compounds for further investigation (Romano and Tatonetti, 2019).

Machine learning methods further enhance integrative workflows by enabling the simultaneous analysis of chemical descriptors, biological annotations and experimental data. Applications of these approaches have demonstrated effective prioritization of natural product derived scaffolds with antiparasitic potential, reducing dependence on exhaustive experimental screening while maintaining biological relevance (Moshawih et al., 2022).

Despite significant progress, several challenges limit the widespread and seamless application of pharmacoinformatics in natural product research. Data heterogeneity, inconsistent annotation standards, and limited interoperability between chemical and biological databases complicate integrative analyzes. In addition, the limited interpretability of many predictive models presents challenges for mechanistic understanding and regulatory acceptance (Zeng et al., 2024).

Future developments are expected to focus on improved data harmonization, the development of robust and explainable machine learning models, and closer integration of computational predictions with biologically relevant experimental systems. Advances in synthetic biology, high throughput screening, and multi omics technologies are likely to further strengthen the impact of integrated pharmacoinformatics. Collectively, these approaches position cheminformatics and bioinformatics as central drivers of efficient, rational, and scalable natural product based drug discovery.

8.4 Case studies in computational natural product discovery

Computational approaches have gradually moved from being supplemental tools in natural product (NP) research to form a core part of modern discovery pipelines. This shift has not happened suddenly; rather, researchers have come to recognize that the structural idiosyncrasies of many natural compounds, long regarded as their greatest biological asset, also make them unusually difficult to screen through conventional laboratory methods. The following case studies highlight how in silico approaches are being applied in practice. They offer a sense of the opportunities these methods create, as well as the occasional points where theory and biological reality do not entirely align.

8.4.1 Pharmacophore based screening of natural products

Pharmacophore modeling tends to become particularly useful when one is trying to make sense of NP collections that do not share an obvious structural theme yet seem to act on related targets. This is precisely the case in studies examining membrane transporters such as OAT3 and URAT1, where flavonoids, saponin like molecules, and other plant metabolites, despite their markedly different scaffolds, were found to express a similar constellation of donor, acceptor, and hydrophobic features (Ancuceanu et al., 2025). Rather than relying on structural similarity, the pharmacophore acted as a kind of conceptual sieve, filtering out compounds that lacked the necessary interaction geometry. A parallel strategy has been used to understand NP interactions with CYP3A4 and CYP1A1. These enzymes are notoriously flexible and sometimes unpredictable in wet lab assays, which makes their ligand preferences difficult to infer strictly from structural data. Pharmacophore alignment helped narrow down which functional groups were most compatible with the dynamic CYP binding region, providing a more stable rationale for prioritizing candidates (Ancuceanu et al., 2025).

The value of this approach becomes even clearer at scale. In a large virtual screen involving nearly 23,000 NPs, only a very small fraction, 18 compounds, emerged as likely anticancer leads, and several of these shared little to no superficial similarity with conventional anticancer scaffolds (Ancuceanu et al., 2025). Their coherence was visible only at the level of pharmacophoric patterning, illustrating why motif based screening is essential in NP focused work.

8.4.2 QSAR-based modeling in natural product analysis

QSAR modeling plays a complementary role, particularly when datasets are modest but chemically diverse enough to reveal systematic structure activity relationships. Fang and colleagues, working with 21 flavonoids, produced a 2D QSAR model that linked Caco 2 permeability to key physicochemical descriptors (Fang et al., 2017). Even in such a small system, the model captured distinctions in polarity, flexibility, and ring substitution that experimental assays alone struggle to disentangle.

Another instructive example comes from Van Zanden's classic MRP1 inhibition study, which investigated 29 flavonoids. The analysis showed that increasing hydroxyl or methoxy groups tended to improve inhibitory activity, whereas a larger B C ring dihedral angle worked against it (Van Zanden et al., 2005). These kinds of geometric influences often hide in plain sight when examining raw structures; QSAR offers a systematic way to reveal them.

QSAR models may not always deliver perfect predictive performance, but they remain invaluable as reasoning tools. They provide a principled basis for deciding which natural analogs should be isolated or modified next, reducing the trial and error burden that traditionally characterizes natural products work.

8.4.3 Structure based methods: molecular docking of natural compounds

Structure based approaches, particularly molecular docking, now sit at the center of many NP discovery programs. Docking has gradually evolved from a rigid geometric exercise into a more nuanced framework for evaluating binding feasibility, exploring interaction networks, and generating mechanistic hypotheses.

8.4.3.1 Methodological developments in docking for natural products

A number of reviews have charted the progression of docking methodologies and their relevance to NPs. (Ferreira et al. (2015)) highlighted improvements in scoring functions, sampling algorithms, and receptor flexibility modeling that collectively make docking more reliable for compounds with bulky ring systems or multiple stereocenters, features common in natural metabolites. Meng et al. (2011) stressed that docking accuracy is often limited not by scoring functions alone but by subtler issues such as how the binding site is defined and how protonation states are handled (Ferreira et al., 2015; Meng et al., 2011).

More recent work has continued to refine the computational landscape. Koh et al. (2021) demonstrated that machine learning scoring functions frequently outperform classical scoring in environments dominated by ambiguous hydrophobic contacts, precisely the kind of interactions that many NP scaffolds rely on. Simoben and co-authors (2023) further noted that ensemble docking, solvent aware scoring, and consensus based filtering can markedly improve hit reliability in NP screening campaigns. Meanwhile, Zoste et al. (2023) introduced high throughput, workflow integrated docking systems specifically tuned for natural product libraries, enabling smoother transitions between database filtering and binding pose evaluation (Koh et al., 2021; Simoben et al., 2023; Zoste et al., 2023).

8.4.3.2 Applications of docking in NP discovery

These methodological advances have enabled a broad range of NP focused docking applications. For example, Majumder and Bhattacharya (2025) evaluated tomato derived phytochemicals for potential activity against the tumor suppressor PTEN, an important enzyme frequently mutated in endometrial cancer. Docking made it possible to reduce a chemically unwieldy set of metabolites to a handful of plausible binders (Majumder and Bhattacharya, 2025). Food derived peptides have also been studied extensively through docking. Romo-Hernández et al., (2025) found that several peptides from *Phaseolus vulgaris*, for example, EGLELLLLLLAG and FEELN, exhibited predicted binding affinities for DPP IV that surpassed those of Sitagliptin. In related work, ACE inhibitory peptides from *Miichthys miiuy* and amylase binding peptides from *Ocimum basilicum* were flagged as promising modulators of metabolic pathways. These results would have been far harder to anticipate without docking based triage (Romo-Hernández et al., 2025). Docking has also played a central role in identifying more specialized NP hits.

Among these are:

A benzofuran derivative was predicted to inhibit STAT3, a transcription factor implicated in various hematologic conditions (Fang et al., 2017). In this case, STAT3 becomes hyperactivated in several hematological conditions and it is activated by phosphorylation at tyrosine residues (Tyr705). STAT3 then becomes dimerized and translocated to the nucleus, where it induces gene transcription. Here, some benzofuran derivatives act as inhibitors that disrupt this process. Firstly these bind to the SH2 domain that is essential for the phosphorylation and also for the dimerization of STAT3. So that the phosphorylation and the dimerization process becomes inhibited. Because of the absence of a stable dimer the activated STAT3 cannot bind to the promoters of the target genes such as cMyc, cyclin D1 which remains involved in cell proliferation and survival. As a result of which the cell cycle becomes arrested, and the cell undergoes apoptosis (Kumar et al., 2024; Wang et al., 2020).

Organic anion transporters (OATs) such as OAT1 (SLC22A6), and OAT3 (SLC22A8) are located on the basolateral membrane of kidney proximal tubules cells. They facilitate the uptake of organic anions from the blood into renal cells for excretion. By using molecular docking, researchers predict how NPs bind with these transporters. By using MOE site finder, 22 compounds isolated from *Cassiae semen* were tested to predict specific binding pockets, and London Dg was used as a scoring function. These docking studies reveal that hydrogen bonding and ππ interactions determine selectivity and binding strength and this docking result were supported by in vitro outcomes for example, dicaffeoylquinic acid bind to OAT3 active site where as caffeic, ferulic and gallic acids act as inhibitors of OATs (Ancuceanu et al., 2025).

A cysteine alkaloid capable of disrupting the menin MLL interaction, which is of significant interest in leukemia research (Fang et al., 2017). The MLL fusion proteins (e.g., MLL AF9, MLL AF4) having leukemogenic activity that depends on the ability to interact with the menin protein and leads to express the target genes such as HOXA9, MEIS1. The inhibitor is designed in such a way that it fits in the MLL binding pocket on the menin protein. This inhibitor has a group which is highly reactive in nature and forms a covalent bond with the sulfhydryl group of the cystine residue (Cys329) in menin. Because of the formation of this stable covalent bond, this inhibitor becomes blocked in that binding pocket. So the MLL protein fragments cannot interact with menin. As the interaction becomes blocked, the target genes become downregulated (Zhang et al., 2021; Manka et al., 2012).

These examples underscore docking's role not just as a preliminary filter but as a hypothesis generating tool that can guide subsequent biochemical and pharmacological evaluation.

8.4.3.3 *The emergence of AI-generated protein structures*

Perhaps one of the more transformative developments in recent years has been the advent of AlphaFold and AlphaFold Multimer, which offer high-confidence structural predictions for proteins that previously lacked experimentally resolved structures (Jumper et al., 2021; Evans et al., 2023). For natural product research, where many therapeutic targets remain structurally inaccessible, this breakthrough has broadened the universe of proteins amenable to docking studies. Although uncertainties still persist, especially around flexible loops and induced fit phenomena, the availability of predicted models has already accelerated several NP screening projects.

8.4.4 Integrated ligand and structure-based pipelines

Increasingly, researchers rely not on a single computational approach but on integrated pipelines that draw on the strengths of multiple methods. A typical sequence might start with QSAR based filtering, followed by pharmacophore validation, and finally docking to assess steric and energetic feasibility. Molecular dynamics (MD) simulations are often inserted at the end to determine whether a predicted ligand protein pose is stable once thermal motion and solvent effects are taken into account.

These layered workflows help to correct biases inherent in any one technique. An example often cited is the evaluation of compounds against CYP3A4, where static docking originally suggested that glycyrrhizin would outperform myricetin as a binder. MD simulations later reversed this ranking, revealing that myricetin formed a more persistent and energetically favorable interaction in a dynamic environment (Ancuceanu et al., 2025). Situations such as this are not at all unusual for NPs, whose conformational flexibility and stereochemical richness can sometimes confound rigid docking methods.

Taken together, integrated computational pipelines provide a more balanced and reliable framework for natural product screening. They minimize false positives, help clarify structure activity relationships, and ultimately reduce the experimental burden. As these tools evolve further, particularly with the incorporation of machine learning and AI guided structure prediction, they are poised to play an even larger role in shaping the future landscape of NP based drug discovery.

8.5 Conclusion

In silico ligand and structure based drug design approaches have become increasingly important in modern drug discovery, particularly in the context of NPs. The in silico ligand and structure based drug design reduces cost, time, and labor required to synthesize and screen large libraries and increases the rate of success for designing of new leads. These computational strategies allow researchers to prioritize promising molecules before committing to resource intensive experimental studies. NPs serve as valuable templates for virtual compound generation because of their inherent biological relevance and chemical diversity. A large number of virtual compounds considering the natural compounds as template as discussed will be generated by combinatorial library synthesis. This approach enables the exploration of structurally diverse analogs while maintaining key functional features associated with biological activity.

To efficiently evaluate these virtual compounds, predictive modeling techniques are essential. Prediction of activities of these types of compounds can be carried out by QSAR models. Such models help establish relationships between molecular descriptors and biological responses, guiding rational lead optimization. Then pharmacophore modeling can be carried out for designing new active leads and predicting the mode of binding of these leads. Pharmacophore analysis further refines candidate selection by identifying the spatial and chemical features required for effective target interaction. Beyond activity prediction, the assessment of drug likeness is a critical step in lead selection.

Finally, by incorporating absorption, distribution, metabolism, and excretion (ADME) predictions, we can identify lead candidates that are more likely to exhibit satisfactory pharmacokinetic and pharmacodynamic profiles of the compounds. Early evaluation of these properties helps minimize late stage failures and improves translational potential. By integrating these computational strategies, natural product based drug discovery becomes more systematic and efficient. Promising lead compounds with potential activities arising out of these studies could be proposed for synthesis and testing to combat the specific targets. Overall, the combined application of QSAR, pharmacophore modeling, structure based screening, and ADME prediction provides a rational framework for accelerating the identification of safe and effective therapeutic candidates derived from natural sources.

References

Abate C, Decherchi S, Cavalli A. Graph neural networks for conditional de novo drug design. WIREs Computational Molecular Science 2023;13(4). Available from https://doi.org/10.1002/wcms.1651.

Achan J, Talisuna AO, Erhart A, Yeka A, Tibenderana JK, Baliraine FN, et al. Quinine, an old antimalarial drug in a modern world: role in the treatment of malaria. Malaria Journal 2011;10. Available from https://doi.org/10.1186/1475-2875-10-144.

Agu PC, Afiukwa CA, Orji OU, Ezeh EM, Ofoke IH, Ogbu CO, Ugwuja EI, Aja PM. Molecular docking as a tool for the discovery of molecular targets of nutraceuticals in diseases management. Scientific Reports 2023;13(1). Available from https://doi.org/10.1038/s41598-023-40160-2.

Alonso-Álvarez S, Pardal E, Sánchez-Nieto D, Navarro M, Caballero MD, Mateos MV. A. Martín, Plitidepsin: design, development, and potential place in therapy. Drug Design, Development and Therapy 2017;11:253–64. Available from https://doi.org/10.2147/DDDT.S94165.

Ancuceanu R, Lascu BE, Drăgănescu D, Dinu M. In silico ADME methods used in the evaluation of natural products. Pharmaceutics 2025;17(8). Available from https://doi.org/10.3390/pharmaceutics17081002.

Asiamah I, Obiri SA, Tamekloe W, Armah FA, Borquaye LS. Applications of molecular docking in natural products-based drug discovery. Scientific african 2023;20. Available from https://doi.org/10.1016/j.sciaf.2023.e01593.

Atanasov AG, Waltenberger B, Pferschy-Wenzig EM, Linder T, Wawrosch C, Uhrin P, et al. Discovery and resupply of pharmacologically active plant-derived natural products: a review. Biotechnology Advances 2015;33(8):1582–614. Available from https://doi.org/10.1016/j.biotechadv.2015.08.001.

Atkinson MA, Campbell-Thompson M, Kusmartseva I, Kaestner KH. Organisation of the human pancreas in health and in diabetes. Diabetologia 2020;63(10):1966–73. Available from https://doi.org/10.1007/s00125-020-05203-7.

Awosika AO, Below J, Das JM. Vincristine. StatPearls publishing; 2023.

Ayon NJ. High-throughput screening of natural product and synthetic molecule libraries for antibacterial drug discovery. Metabolites 2023;13(5):625. Available from https://doi.org/10.3390/metabo13050625.

Bent S, Padula A, Moore D, Patterson M, Mehling W, et al. Valerian for Sleep: A Systematic Review and Meta-Analysis. The American Journal of Medicine 2006;119(12):1005–12. Available from https://doi.org/10.1016/j.amjmed.2006.02.026.

Benyhe S. Morphine: new aspects in the study of an ancient compound. Life Sciences 2011;89(25–26):823–5. Available from https://doi.org/10.1016/j.lfs.2011.08.012.

Carbonell P, Currin A, Jervis AJ, Rattray NJW, Swainston N, Yan C, et al. Bioinformatics for the synthetic biology of natural products: integrating across the design-build-test cycle. Natural Product Reports 2016;33(8):925–32. Available from https://doi.org/10.1039/c6np00018e.

Chaachouay N, Zidane L. Plant-Derived Natural Products: A Source for Drug Discovery and Development. Drugs and Drug Candidates 2024;3(1):184–207. Available from 10.3390/ddc3010011.

Chen Y, Kirchmair J. Cheminformatics in natural product-based drug discovery. Molecular Informatics 2020;39(12). Available from https://doi.org/10.1002/minf.202000171.

Colquitt RB, Colquhoun DA, Thiele RH, et al. In silico modelling of physiologic systems. Best Practice & Research Clinical Anaesthesiology 2011;25(4):499–510. Available from 10.1016/j.bpa.2011.08.006.

Cragg GM. Paclitaxel (Taxol®): A success story with valuable lessons for natural product drug discovery and development. Medicinal Research Reviews 1998;18(5):315–31. Available from hhttps://doi.org/10.1002/(SICI)1098-1128(199809)18:5<315::AID-MED3>3.0.CO;2-W.

Dey R, Nandi S, Samadder A, et al. "Pelargonidin mediated selective activation of p53 and parp proteins in preventing food additive induced genotoxicity: an in vivo coupled in silico molecular docking study" European Journal of Pharmaceutical Sciences 2021;156:105586. Available from https://doi.org/10.1016/j.ejps.2020.105586.

Erba E, Bergamaschi D, Bassano L, Damia G, Ronzoni S, Faircloth GT, et al. Ecteinascidin-743 (ET-743), a natural marine compound, with a unique mechanism of action. European Journal of Cancer 2001;37(1):97–105. Available from https://doi.org/10.1016/s0959-8049(00)00357-9.

Evans R, et al. Protein complex prediction with alphaFold-multimer. Nature 2023;614:1–9. Available from https://doi.org/10.1038/s41586-023-05905-z.

Fang J, Liu C, Wang Q, Lin P, Cheng F. In silico polypharmacology of natural products. Briefings in Bioinformatics 2017;19(6):1153–71. Available from https://doi.org/10.1093/bib/bbx045.

Ferreira LG, Dos Santos RN, Oliva G, Andricopulo AD. Molecular docking and structure-based drug design strategies. Molecules 2015;20(7):13384–421. Available from https://doi.org/10.3390/molecules200713384.

Gangwal A, Lavecchia A. Artificial intelligence in natural product drug discovery: current applications and future perspectives. Journal of Medicinal Chemistry 2025;68(4):3948–69. Available from https://doi.org/10.1021/acs.jmedchem.4c01257.

Gashaw AD, Desta MA, Yaya EE. A comprehensive review-current development in spectroscopic and chromatographic techniques for natural product analysis. Results in Chemistry 2025;16. Available from https://doi.org/10.1016/j.rechem.2025.102341.

Gaudêncio SP, Bayram E, Lukić Bilela L, Cueto M, Díaz-Marrero AR, Haznedaroglu BZ, et al. Advanced methods for natural products discovery: bioactivity screening, dereplication, metabolomics profiling, genomic sequencing, databases and informatic tools, and structure elucidation. Marine drugs 2023;21(5):308. Available from https://doi.org/10.3390/md21050308.

Gray A, Flatt P. Insulin-releasing and insulin-like activity of Agaricus campestris (mushroom). Journal of Endocrinology 1998;157(2):259–66. Available from https://doi.org/10.1677/joe.0.1570259.

Hartung EF. History of the use of colchicum and related medicaments in gout. Annals of the Rheumatic Diseases 1954;13(3):190–200. Available from https://doi.org/10.1136/ard.13.3.190.

Ibekwe N, Ameh S, et al. Hyphenated Techniques in Liquid Chromatography as Current Trends in Natural Products Analysis. International Research Journal of Pure and Applied Chemistry 2015;7(3):132–49. Available from https://doi.org/10.9734/irjpac/2015/14458.

Jumper J, Evans R, Pritzel A, Green T, Figurnov M, Ronneberger O, et al. Highly accurate protein structure prediction with AlphaFold. Nature 2021;596(7873):583–9. Available from https://doi.org/10.1038/s41586-021-03819-2.

Kaur H, Singh L. Bioinformatics approaches in natural product research. International Journal of Advanced Research in Medicinal Chemistry 2023;5(2):1–5.

Kazemipoor M, Radzi CWJWM, Cordell GA, Yaze I, et al. Safety, Efficacy and Metabolism of Traditional Medicinal Plants in the Management of Obesity: A Review. International Journal of Chemical Engineering and Applications 2012:288–92. Available from https://doi.org/10.7763/ijcea.2012.v3.201.

Koh I, Kang N, Lee I. Machine-learning-based scoring for structure-based drug discovery. Computers in Biology and Medicine 2021;136:104688. Available from https://doi.org/10.1016/j.compbiomed.2021.104688.

Kück U, Dahlmann TA. The confusion in renaming species: penicillium chrysogenum and penicillium rubens. Microbiology Resource Announcements 2021;10(48). Available from https://doi.org/10.1128/MRA.00464-21.

Kumar S, Jayan J, Manoharan A, Benny F, Abdelgawad MA, Ghoneim MM, et al. Discerning of isatin-based monoamine oxidase (MAO) inhibitors for neurodegenerative disorders by exploiting 2D, 3D-QSAR modelling and molecular dynamics simulation. Journal of Biomolecular Structure and Dynamics 2023;42(5):2328–40. Available from 10.1080/07391102.2023.2214216.

Kumar S, Arwind DA, Kumar B H, Pandey S, Nayak R, Vithalkar MP, et al. Inhibition of STAT3: a promising approach to enhancing the efficacy of chemotherapy in medulloblastoma. Translational Oncology 2024;46. Available from https://doi.org/10.1016/j.tranon.2024.102023.

Lagunin AA, Goel RK, Gawande DY, Pahwa P, Gloriozova TA, Dmitriev AV, et al. Chemo- and bioinformatics resources for in silico drug discovery from medicinal plants beyond their traditional use. Natural Product Reports 2014;31(11):1585–611. Available from https://doi.org/10.1039/c4np00068d.

Lin X, Dai L, Zhou Y, Yu ZG, Zhang W, Shi JY, et al. Comprehensive evaluation of deep and graph learning on drug–drug interactions prediction. Briefings in Bioinformatics 2023;24(4). Available from https://doi.org/10.1093/bib/bbad235.

Majumder A, Bhattacharya M. Computational biology tools in herbal medicine: a review. Journal of Medicinal Plants Studies 2025;13(3):185–97. Available from https://doi.org/10.22271/plants.2025.v13.i3c.1859.

Manka JT, Daniels RN, Dawson ES, Daniels JS, Southall N, Jadhav A, et al. Inhibitors of the menin–mixed lineage leukemia (MLL) interaction. Journal of Medicinal Chemistry 2012;55(9):4020–5. Available from https://doi.org/10.1021/jm300028w.

Medina-Franco JL, Naveja JJ, López-López E, Martínez-Mayorga K. Cheminformatics applications in natural product drug discovery. Molecular Informatics 2020;39(1):e2000032. Available from https://doi.org/10.1002/minf.202000032.

Meghwal M, Goswami TK. Piper nigrum and piperine: an update. Phytotherapy Research 2013;27(8):1121–30. Available from https://doi.org/10.1002/ptr.4972.

Meng XY, Zhang HX, Mezei M, Cui M. Molecular docking: a powerful approach for structure-based drug discovery. Current Computer-Aided Drug Design 2011;7(2):146–57. Available from https://doi.org/10.2174/157340911795677602.

Moshawih S, Goh HP, Kifli N, Idris AC, Yassin H, Kotra V, et al. Synergy between machine learning and natural products cheminformatics: application to the lead discovery of anthraquinone derivatives. Chemical Biology and Drug Design 2022;100(2):185–217. Available from https://doi.org/10.1111/cbdd.14062.

Mullowney MW, Duncan KR, Elsayed SS, Garg N, van der Hooft JJJ, Martin NI, et al. Artificial intelligence for natural product drug discovery. Nature Reviews Drug Discovery 2023;22(11):895–916. Available from https://doi.org/10.1038/s41573-023-00774-7.

Najmi A, Javed SA, Al Bratty M, Alhazmi HA. Modern approaches in the discovery and development of plant-based natural products and their analogs as potential therapeutic agents. Molecules 2022;27(2). Available from https://doi.org/10.3390/molecules27020349.

Najmi A, Javed SA, Al Bratty M, Alhazmi HA, et al. Modern Approaches in the Discovery and Development of Plant-Based Natural Products and Their Analogues as Potential Therapeutic Agents. Molecules 2022;27(2):349. Available from https://doi.org/10.3390/molecules27020349.

Nandi S, Ahmed S, Saxena AK. Combinatorial design and virtual screening of potent antitubercular fluoroquinolone and isothiazoloquinolone compounds utilizing QSAR and pharmacophore modeling. SAR and QSAR in Environmental Research 2018;29(2):151–70. Available from https://doi.org/10.1080/1062936x.2017.1419375.

Nandi S, Bagchi MC. 3D-QSAR and molecular docking studies of 4-anilinoquinazoline derivatives: a rational approach to anticancer drug design. Molecular Diversity 2010;14(1):27–38. Available from https://doi.org/10.1007/s11030-009-9137-9.

Ng SSS, Lu Y. Evaluating the use of graph neural networks and transfer learning for oral bioavailability prediction. Journal of Chemical Information and Modeling 2023;63(16):5035–44. Available from https://doi.org/10.1021/acs.jcim.3c00554.

Oduah EI, Linhardt RJ, Sharfstein ST. Heparin: past, present, and future. Pharmaceuticals 2016;9(3). Available from https://doi.org/10.3390/ph9030038.

Romano JD, Tatonetti NP. Informatic approaches for identifying metabolic interactions and reactions. Frontiers in Genetics 2019;10:368. Available from https://doi.org/10.3389/fgene.2019.00368.

Romo-Hernández A, Cortazar-Moya S, González-Pérez JE, Jiménez-González O, López-Malo A, Morales-Camacho JI. In silico strategies for drug discovery: optimizing natural compounds from foods. Discover Chemistry 2025;2:133. Available from https://doi.org/10.1007/s44371-025-00201-3.

Sareen A, Shah S, Patil SM. A review on indian plant tulsi (Ocimum sanctum) and its medicinal uses. Systematic Reviews in Pharmacy 2024;15(5):176–82. Available from https://doi.org/10.31858/0975-8453.15.5.176-182.

Schrör K. History. In: Schrör K, editor. Acetylsalicylic Acid. Wiley-VCH; 2008. p. 5–24.

Simoben CV, Babiaka SB, Moumbock AFA, Namba-Nzanguim CT, Eni DB, Medina-Franco JL, et al. Challenges in natural product-based drug discovery assisted with in silico-based methods. RSC Advances 2023;13(45):31578–94. Available from https://doi.org/10.1039/d3ra06831e.

Sorokina M, Steinbeck C. Review on natural products databases: where to find data in 2020. Journal of Cheminformatics 2020;12(1). Available from https://doi.org/10.1186/s13321-020-00424-9.

Agu PC, Afiukwa CA, Orji OU, Ezeh EM, Ofoke IH, Ogbu CO, et al. Molecular docking as a tool for the discovery of molecular targets of nutraceuticals in diseases management. Scientific Reports 2023;13(1). Available from https://doi.org/10.1038/s41598-023-40160-2.

Sow P, Dey S, Dey R, Majumder A, Nandi S, Bera M, et al. Poly lactide-co-glycolide encapsulated nano-curcumin promoting antagonistic interactions between HSP 90 and XRCC1 proteins to prevent cypermethrin-induced toxicity: An in silico predicted in vitro and in vivo approach. Colloids and Surfaces B: Biointerfaces 2022;220:112905. Available from https://doi.org/10.1016/j.colsurfb.2022.112905.

Strawbridge R, Javed RR, Cave J, Jauhar S, Young AH. The effects of reserpine on depression: a systematic review. Journal of Psychopharmacology 2023;37(3):248–60. Available from https://doi.org/10.1177/02698811221115762.

Swanton EW. Economic and folk lore notes. Transactions of the British Mycological Society 1914;5:408–9. Available from https://doi.org/10.1016/s0007-1536(14)80040-5.

Szymański P, Markowicz M, Mikiciuk-Olasik E. Adaptation of high-throughput screening in drug discovery-toxicological screening tests. International Journal of Molecular Sciences 2012;13(1):427–52. Available from https://doi.org/10.3390/ijms13010427.

Thomas J, Kuruvilla KM. 10 - Cinnamon. In: Peter KV, editor. Handbook of Herbs and Spices: Volume 1. second ed.Woodhead Publishing; 2012. p. 182–96. Available from https://doi.org/10.1533/9780857095671.182.

Van Zanden JJ, Wortelboer HM, Bijlsma S, Punt A, Usta M, Bladeren PJV, et al. Quantitative structure activity relationship studies on the flavonoid mediated inhibition of multidrug resistance proteins 1 and 2. Biochemical Pharmacology 2005;69(4):699–708. Available from https://doi.org/10.1016/j.bcp.2004.11.002.

Waksman SA, Reilly HC, Johnstone DB, et al. Isolation of Streptomycin-producing Strains of *Streptomyces griseus*. Journal of Bacteriology 1946;52(3):393–7. Available from https://doi.org/10.1128/jb.52.3.393-397.1946.

Wang F, Feng K-R, Zhao J-Y, Zhang J-W, Shi X-W, Zhou J, et al. Identification of novel STAT3 inhibitors bearing 2-acetyl-7-phenylamino benzofuran scaffold for antitumour study. Bioorganic & Medicinal Chemistry 2020;28(24):115822. Available from https://doi.org/10.1016/j.bmc.2020.115822.

Williams JA, Day M, Heavner JE. Ziconotide: an update and review. Expert Opinion on Pharmacotherapy 2008;9(9):1575–83. Available from https://doi.org/10.1517/14656566.9.9.1575.

Wink M. Modes of action of herbal medicines and plant secondary metabolites. Medicines 2015;2(3):251–86. Available from https://doi.org/10.3390/medicines2030251.

Mullowney MW, Duncan KR, Elsayed SS, Garg N, van der Hooft JJJ, Martin NI, et al. Artificial intelligence for natural product drug discovery. Nature Reviews Drug Discovery 2023;22(11):895–916. Available from https://doi.org/10.1038/s41573-023-00774-7.

Zeng T, Li J, Wu R. Natural product databases for drug discovery: features and applications. Pharmaceutical Science Advances 2024;2:100050. Available from https://doi.org/10.1016/j.pscia.2024.100050.

Zhang M, Aguilar A, Xu S, Huang L, Chinnaswamy K, Sleger T, et al. Discovery of M-1121 as an orally active covalent inhibitor of menin-MLL interaction capable of achieving complete and long-lasting tumor regression. Journal of Medicinal Chemistry 2021;64(14):10333–49. Available from https://doi.org/10.1021/acs.jmedchem.1c00789.

Zhang S, Liu K, Liu Y, Hu X, Gu X. The role and application of bioinformatics techniques and tools in drug discovery. Frontiers in Pharmacology 2025;16. Available from https://doi.org/10.3389/fphar.2025.1547131.

Zibara V, Costanian C, Al Haddad N, Kilani H, Tohme F, Aoun Bahous S. Epidemiology and management of hypertension among refugees in the middle east: a review of the literature. Journal of Human Hypertension 2021;35(8):657–66. Available from https://doi.org/10.1038/s41371-021-00508-5.

Ziemert N, Alanjary M, Weber T. The evolution of genome mining in microbes-a review. Natural Product Reports 2016;33(8):988–1005. Available from https://doi.org/10.1039/c6np00025h.

Zjawiony JK. Biologically active compounds from aphyllophorales (polypore) fungi. Journal of Natural Products 2004;67(2):300–10. Available from https://doi.org/10.1021/np030372w.

Zoste P, et al. Advances in molecular docking in natural product drug discovery. Medical Informatics and Decision Making 2023;4(2):842. Available from https://doi.org/10.47852/bonviewMEDIN42023842.

CHAPTER 9

From integrated control to next-generation interventions against major hemoprotozoan parasites

Andreas Meryk[1], Omnia Hamed[2], Abdulsalam Alkhudhayri[3], and Mohamed Dkhil[2]
[1]Department of Pediatrics, Medical University of Innsbruck, Innsbruck, Austria,
[2]Department of Zoology and Entomology, Faculty of Science, Capital University, Cairo, Egypt,
[3]Department of Biology, College of Science, University of Hafr Albatin, Saudi Arabia

9.1 Introduction

Hemoprotozoan diseases constitute a diverse group of parasitic infections that remain among the most persistent threats to global health, food security, and socioeconomic stability. Affecting both humans and animals, these infections are caused by protozoa inhabiting the bloodstream and reticuloendothelial system and are widely distributed across tropical and subtropical regions, where ecological, climatic, and socioeconomic conditions favor their transmission (Kabli, 2025; Salim et al., 2025). Despite decades of research and control efforts, diseases such as malaria, trypanosomiasis, babesiosis, theileriosis, toxoplasmosis, and anaplasmosis continue to impose a substantial burden through high morbidity and mortality, reduced livestock productivity, and escalating health care costs (Maharana et al., 2016a; Capela et al., 2019). Their impact is particularly pronounced in low- and middle-income countries, where fragile health systems, limited diagnostic capacity, and environmental change intensify transmission dynamics (Kabli, 2025).

Beyond their direct health consequences, hemoprotozoan diseases exert profound economic effects, especially in the veterinary sector. Livestock losses due to reduced growth rates, decreased milk production, infertility, and mortality undermine rural livelihoods and national economies dependent on agriculture (Salim et al., 2025; Maharana et al., 2016a). In parallel, the increasing circulation of vector-borne pathogens in companion animals highlights the growing interface between animal and human health, reinforcing the importance of zoonotic considerations in disease management (Kongtawee et al., 2026). The convergence of globalization, climate change, urbanization, and land-use transformation has further reshaped epidemiological patterns, enabling vectors and reservoirs to expand into new geographic areas and exposing previously unaffected populations to infection risks (Elwakil et al., 2023; Ryan et al., 2019).

Innovative Strategies Against Blood Parasites
DOI: https://doi.org/10.1016/B978-0-443-48509-1.00008-2

Traditional control strategies are primarily reliant on chemotherapy, vector control, and mass drug administration. These strategies have achieved notable successes but are increasingly constrained by emerging drug resistance, insecticide resistance, and the absence of effective vaccines for many parasites (Capela et al., 2019; Maharana et al., 2016b). These limitations underscore the need for more holistic and sustainable solutions. Consequently, the global health community has shifted toward integrated control frameworks that combine biomedical innovations with ecological and social interventions, particularly under the One Health paradigm (Kabli, 2025).

Recent advances in molecular diagnostics, genomics, and bioinformatics have enhanced our understanding of parasite biology, transmission networks, and host–pathogen interactions, opening new avenues for targeted interventions (Chiuya, 2020; Kipanga et al., 2014b). Simultaneously, innovations such as drug repurposing, host-directed therapies, and artificial intelligence-driven surveillance are redefining how hemoprotozoan diseases are detected, monitored, and treated (Kourbeli et al., 2021a; Zhao et al., 2025). However, translating these scientific breakthroughs into practical solutions remains challenging because of regulatory barriers, infrastructure gaps, and resource constraints in endemic regions (Prasad et al., 2024a).

This chapter provides a comprehensive overview of the global burden and evolving epidemiology of major hemoprotozoan diseases, highlighting the rationale for integrated control approaches and examining current strategies across clinical, veterinary, and public health domains. It also explores cross-cutting challenges including resistance, diagnostic limitations, and socioeconomic disparities while outlining emerging innovations and future research priorities. By synthesizing evidence across disciplines, the chapter aims to present a strategic framework for the sustainable control and eventual reduction of hemoprotozoan diseases, emphasizing that long-term success will depend on coordinated global efforts, strengthened health systems, and continued investment in research and innovation (Shripat et al., 2025).

9.2 Comparative epidemiology in endemic regions

9.2.1 Geographic distribution and disease burden

The epidemiology of hemoprotozoan diseases demonstrates marked geographic heterogeneity, with the highest burden concentrated in tropical and subtropical regions, where climatic and ecological conditions favor vector survival and parasite transmission (WHO, 2023; GBD 2021 Collaborators, 2022). Global burden of diseases study 2021 results (The Lancet., no date). Sub-Saharan Africa remains the epicenter of several major blood parasitic diseases, including malaria, human African trypanosomiasis, and bovine theileriosis, accounting for a disproportionate share of global morbidity and mortality (WHO, 2023; Franco et al., 2020). This uneven distribution reflects the convergence of environmental suitability, socioeconomic vulnerability, and limitations in health care infrastructure (Albareedy and Ramadan, 2023a).

Climate variability plays a critical role in shaping disease landscapes. Rising temperatures and altered rainfall patterns have expanded the altitudinal and latitudinal ranges of vectors such as *Anopheles* mosquitoes and *Glossina* spp., leading to the emergence of transmission in previously nonendemic highland regions (Ryan et al., 2019; Rocklöv and Dubrow, 2020). In parallel, rapid urbanization in Africa and Asia has created peri-urban ecosystems that facilitate vector breeding while increasing human exposure (Tatem et al., 2013). These dynamics are further compounded by population displacement, conflict, and inadequate vector control programs, which collectively sustain persistent transmission cycles (WHO, 2023).

In Asia, countries such as India and Southeast Asian nations continue to report high burdens of malaria and zoonotic babesiosis (Yadav and Upadhyay, 2021), while the Middle East and North Africa are experiencing reemergence linked to climate change and migration (Al-Shehri et al., 2020). In livestock, endemic hemoprotozoan infections including babesiosis and anaplasmosis remain major constraints to agricultural productivity, particularly in regions reliant on pastoral systems, where animal movement promotes pathogen spread (Jongejan and Uilenberg, 2004).

9.2.2 Transmission pathways

The transmission ecology of blood parasites like in Fig. 9.1 is complex, involving multiple interconnected pathways shaped by environmental, biological, and social determinants (CDC, 2022; WHO, 2023).

9.2.2.1 Vector-borne transmission

Vector-borne spread is the dominant route for most hemoprotozoan diseases. Mosquitoes (*Anopheles* spp.) transmit *Plasmodium*, tsetse flies transmit *Trypanosoma*, and ticks such as *Rhipicephalus* and *Hyalomma* transmit *Babesia* and *Theileria* (Jongejan and Uilenberg, 2004; CDC, 2022). Vector competence, abundance, and biting behavior are strongly influenced by climatic variables, including temperature, humidity, and wind speed, which regulate vector lifespan and parasite development (Elwakil et al., 2023;

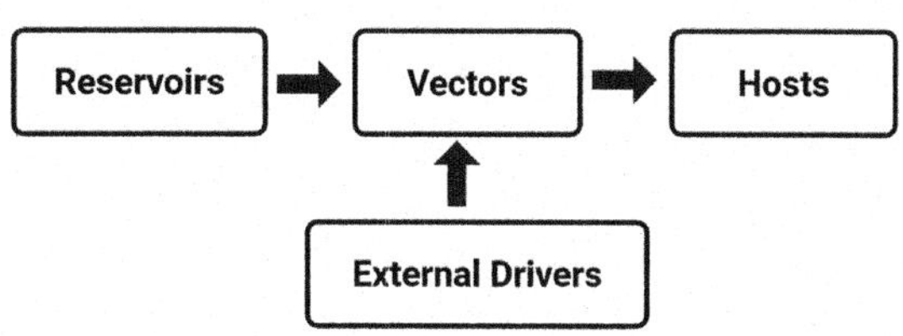

Figure 9.1 shows how the parasites (plasmodium, babesia, etc.) move through the environment. Parasite movement through the environment.

Rocklöv and Dubrow, 2020). Seasonal fluctuations therefore drive periodic peaks in disease incidence (WHO, 2023).

9.2.2.2 Zoonotic and bridging transmission

Many blood parasites circulate within animal reservoirs before infecting humans, exemplifying the One Health nature of hemoprotozoan epidemiology (Destoumieux-Garzón et al., 2018). Wildlife hosts maintain parasite populations during interepidemic periods, while domestic animals act as amplifying hosts (Veronesi et al., 2023b). Climate-induced habitat shifts are increasing interspecies contact, facilitating spillover events and the emergence of new transmission foci (Elwakil et al., 2023).

9.2.2.3 Food-borne and iatrogenic pathways

Although less common, transfusion-transmitted malaria and babesiosis represent important clinical concerns, particularly in nonendemic regions where screening may be limited (Kitchen and Chiodini, 2006; CDC, 2022). Additionally, foodborne exposure to protozoan stages contributes to the epidemiology of certain infections, highlighting the importance of integrated surveillance (Jofre et al., 2010).

9.2.2.4 Behavioral and cultural determinants

Human behavior significantly modifies transmission risk. Occupational exposure among farmers, herders, and forest workers increases contact with vectors, while traditional practices and limited access to protective measures further elevate vulnerability (Watson-Jones and Macpherson, 1988a; Tatem et al., 2013). These social determinants often explain localized differences in disease prevalence, even within the same ecological zone (WHO, 2023).

9.2.3 Reservoir hosts and ecological determinants

Reservoir hosts are central to the persistence and spatial distribution of hemoprotozoan diseases (Destoumieux-Garzón et al., 2018). A wide range of domestic and wild mammals—including cattle, dogs, rodents, and wildlife ungulates—harbor parasites without severe clinical manifestations, enabling silent transmission cycles (Veronesi et al., 2023b). For example, cattle act as reservoirs for *Babesia bovis* and *Theileria annulata*, while dogs maintain zoonotic *Babesia* species and other vector-borne pathogens (Jongejan and Uilenberg, 2004).

Ecological disturbances such as deforestation, agricultural expansion, and urban encroachment alter host–vector interactions by disrupting natural habitats and increasing contact between wildlife and humans (Atkinson et al., 2013). Fragmented landscapes often support higher vector densities because of the creation of breeding sites and reduced biodiversity, which might otherwise regulate pathogen transmission (Patz et al., 2004).

Aquatic ecosystems also influence disease ecology, particularly for parasites with vector stages dependent on water availability. Changes in water management, irrigation schemes, and dam construction can create new habitats for vectors, thereby reshaping local epidemiological patterns (Popoola et al., 2021).

9.2.4 Impact of climate change and environmental actors

Climate change is increasingly recognized as a dominant force reshaping the epidemiology of blood parasitic diseases (Ryan et al., 2019; Rocklöv and Dubrow, 2020). Rising global temperatures accelerate parasite development within vectors, shortening the extrinsic incubation period and increasing transmission efficiency (Mordecai et al., 2019). Even modest temperature increases can significantly enhance vectorial capacity, particularly in marginal transmission zones (Mordecai et al., 2019).

Extreme weather events, including floods and droughts, further influence disease dynamics. Flooding creates breeding habitats for mosquitoes and can trigger outbreaks, while drought conditions may drive human and animal populations toward shared water sources, intensifying exposure risk (Elwakil et al., 2023; WHO, 2023).

Another major consequence of climate change is the geographic expansion of vectors into temperate regions. Predictive models suggest the continued northward spread of several mosquito and tick species, potentially exposing immunologically naive populations to new infections (Ryan et al., 2019). This shift underscores the need for proactive surveillance and adaptive control strategies (Rocklöv and Dubrow, 2020).

Environmental factors such as land-use change, agricultural intensification, and biodiversity loss interact synergistically with climate drivers, producing complex and often unpredictable epidemiological outcomes (Patz et al., 2004; Atkinson et al., 2013). Consequently, integrated approaches that incorporate ecological monitoring, climate modeling, and public health surveillance are essential to anticipate future disease risks and design targeted interventions (Destoumieux-Garzón et al., 2018).

9.3 Current integrated control strategies

9.3.1 Chemotherapy and clinical management

9.3.1.1 Antimalarial therapies

Antimalarial management focuses on drugs that target different stages of the *Plasmodium* parasite's life cycle. Artemisinin derivatives, such as artesunate, artemether, and dihydroartemisinin, are the fastest-acting drugs available for clearing the blood stages of all *Plasmodium* species (Srinivasamurthy and Bairy, 2021). To mitigate the development of resistance, artemisinin combination therapy (ACT) is utilized, where short-acting artemisinin derivatives are paired with long-acting partner drugs such as lumefantrine, amodiaquine, or mefloquine (Srinivasamurthy and Bairy, 2021). Other specialized treatments include pyronaridine, which targets the parasite's food vacuole to inhibit hemozoin formation, and the combination of atovaquone-proguanil, which disrupts two separate pathways in pyrimidine biosynthesis (Srinivasamurthy and Bairy, 2021). For the prevention of *P. vivax* relapses, tafenoquine acts as a long-acting analoge of primaquine that targets both hepatic and blood stages (Srinivasamurthy and Bairy, 2021).

9.3.1.2 Antitrypanosomal treatments

The clinical management of trypanosomiasis, such as surra caused by *Trypanosoma evansi*, requires specific chemotherapeutic agents to eliminate the parasites from the host's system. In livestock such as buffalo and equines, the most common agents used are diminazene aceturate and quinapyramine salts (Shirale et al., 2024; Ullah et al., 2025). Furthermore, experimental efficacy studies conducted in Pakistan have evaluated various therapeutic agents to determine the most effective treatment for blood protozoa in exotic cattle (Khan et al., 2024).

9.3.1.3 Antibabesial drugs

The treatment of babesiosis varies depending on the host species and the specific variant of the parasite involved. Imidocarb dipropionate serves as a primary treatment for babesiosis in a wide range of animals, including cattle and horses (Azhar et al., 2023; Ullah et al., 2025). Diminazene aceturate is another frequently employed drug for livestock infections (Azhar et al., 2023). For pet animals such as dogs and cats, clinicians often use a combination of atovaquone and azithromycin, although there is an increasing emergence of drug-resistant *Babesia* variants (Azhar et al., 2023). In cases where *Theileria* coinfections are present, buparvaquone is typically incorporated into the treatment regimen (Azhar et al., 2023).

9.3.1.4 Management of toxoplasmosis

The management of *Toxoplasma gondii* involves both traditional antibiotics and newer therapeutic models. Clindamycin is a key antibiotic active against the parasite and is standard in clinical management (Srinivasamurthy and Bairy, 2021). Atovaquone has also demonstrated effectiveness, particularly in murine models of the disease (Azhar et al., 2023). For immunocompetent hosts, it is critical for clinicians to remain aware of atypical strains that can lead to severe clinical presentations requiring intensive management (Sobanski et al., 2025).

9.3.2 Vector and transmission control

9.3.2.1 Mosquito control strategies

Effective mosquito control is vital for reducing the global burden of malaria transmission. Beyond environmental management, transmission reduction is supported by using gametocidal drugs such as primaquine in infected patients; this reduces the reservoir of parasites available for mosquitoes to ingest and subsequently transmit to others (Srinivasamurthy and Bairy, 2021).

9.3.2.2 Tsetse fly management

While specific management techniques are less detailed in the current literature compared to the diseases they carry, controlling tsetse flies remains essential for managing trypanosomiasis in livestock and equines (Ullah et al., 2025).

9.3.2.3 Tick control programs

Tick control serves as the cornerstone for preventing the spread of babesiosis and theileriosis in animals. These programs specifically target vector species such as *Rhipicephalus* spp. and *Hyalomma* spp., which are the primary transmission agents for *Babesia* in cattle and horses (Azhar et al., 2023; Ullah et al.,et al., 2025). Standard practices in livestock-heavy regions involve the regular application of acaricides combined with environmental management to limit tick populations (Azhar et al., 2023).

9.3.2.4 Prevention of congenital and foodborne transmission

Preventing the spread of toxoplasmosis involves behavioral interventions such as avoiding the consumption of undercooked or raw meat and maintaining high standards of hygiene to prevent the accidental ingestion of oocysts (Sobanski et al., 2025). Additionally, livestock screening is essential; the importation of dairy animals or the transportation of pets requires rigorous diagnostic testing to prevent the introduction of blood protozoa into new geographical areas (Azhar et al., 2023).

9.3.3 Preventive and host-targeted measures

Vaccination represents a primary strategy for ensuring the biological safety of both humans and livestock by blocking the transmission of tick-borne pathogens (Yadav and Upadhyay, 2021). Research has highlighted the use of aquaporin antigens as effective active ingredients in cattle vaccines, specifically to manage infestations of *Rhipicephalus microplus* (Yadav and Upadhyay, 2021). Furthermore, protective components such as VirB2, VirB7, and VirB11 proteins have been tested to provide serological responses against pathogens such as *Anaplasma marginale* (Yadav and Upadhyay, 2021). Despite these advancements, many zoonotic diseases still lack widely available vaccines, which often necessitates a shift in focus toward controlling the vectors themselves or managing the surrounding ecology (Chiuya, 2020).

Chemoprophylaxis Preventive chemotherapy is a cornerstone of the World Health Organization's integrated approach to controlling neglected tropical diseases (NTDs) (Nsakashalo, 2019). This strategy often involves mass drug administration (MDA) using specific medications such as ivermectin (IVM) or diethylcarbamazine (DEC), combined with albendazole (ALB), to combat lymphatic filariasis (Nsakashalo, 2019). Additionally, praziquantel (PZQ) is utilized for the treatment of schistosomiasis, while soil-transmitted helminthiasis is managed through the administration of albendazole or mebendazole (MBD) (Nsakashalo, 2019). In some ecological settings, antibiotic-laden baits are also deployed to target pathogens within rodent populations that serve as disease reservoirs (Yadav and Upadhyay, 2021).

Livestock and Reservoir Management The management of livestock and wild reservoirs is essential because these animals act as the primary hosts and amplifiers for various zoonotic diseases (Chiuya, 2020). Implementing control measures at strategic points, such as livestock markets and slaughterhouses, can effectively reduce tick populations on cattle through the application of acaricides (Chiuya, 2020). Beyond chemical treatments, strict quarantine protocols are necessary to prevent the international movement of ticks via goods and materials (Yadav and Upadhyay, 2021). Alternative methods, including the use of natural oils, bioinsecticides such as Bt toxins, and biological control agents, offer nonchemical ways to suppress tick populations on livestock (Yadav and Upadhyay, 2021; Chiuya, 2020).

9.3.4 Surveillance and public health interventions

Diagnostic Tools and Screening The development and application of molecular diagnostics are vital for the early detection of pathogens in both vectors and hosts. High-resolution melting (HRM) analysis and PCR-based screening have been instrumental in identifying low-level *Plasmodium* spp. infections in patients who otherwise appeared negative under traditional microscopy (Chiuya, 2020; Kipanga et al., 2014b). Effective surveillance programs allow researchers to measure outbreak risks, identify novel pathogens, and better understand the complex interactions between pathogens and their vectors (Chiuya, 2020). Furthermore, the use of IgM serology alongside RT-PCR provides a more sensitive means of detecting fragile viruses in various field samples (Chiuya, 2020).

Community Engagement and Health Education Successful disease elimination programs rely heavily on community-directed delivery of treatments and public health education (Nsakashalo, 2019). Research indicates that female household heads and spouses often act as primary caregivers and are central to disseminating knowledge about mosquito control to their families (Chiuya, 2020; UNDP, 2015). Moreover, improving health literacy among patients and the general public is a significant factor in managing the transmission of diseases within a community (Yadav and Upadhyay, 2021; Belman et al., 2013).

Integrated Vector Management (IVM) Programs Integrated Vector Management (IVM) utilizes a combination of strategies to reduce vector-human contact and suppress vector populations. This includes the use of physical barriers such as insecticide-treated nets (ITNs), window screens, and the application of repellents (Chiuya, 2020; Steketee, 2003). Modern IVM also explores transmission-blocking technologies, such as the use of *Wolbachia* to create "superinfection exclusion" in mosquito populations (Chiuya, 2020). In regions such as Zambia, the synergy between mass drug administration and widespread vector control has been credited with the successful movement toward eliminating lymphatic filariasis (Nsakashalo, 2019). Environmental management to eliminate breeding sites remains a sustainable way to reduce vector biting rates (Chiuya, 2020).

9.4 Cross-cutting challenges

Drug Resistance Mechanisms Protozoan parasites have developed diverse and innovative mechanisms to evade the effects of existing medications like in Fig. 9.2, significantly reducing the effectiveness of current therapies (Capela et al., 2019). Resistance is frequently driven by specific genetic mutations in the parasite, such as the *K76T* mutation in the *Pfcrt* gene, which serves as a primary marker for chloroquine resistance in *Plasmodium falciparum* (Capela et al., 2019). Furthermore, parasites often utilize transmembrane proteins, particularly from the ABC transporter superfamily such as *PfMDR1* and *Pfmrp1*, to act as efflux pumps that actively remove drugs from cellular compartments (Capela et al., 2019). Resistance also arises through target alteration, such as mutations in the *Pfdhfr* and *Pfdhps* genes which confer resistance to antifolate drugs, as well as adaptive metabolic changes and increased production of neutralizing enzymes (Capela et al., 2019; Singh Cheema and Singh, 2022).

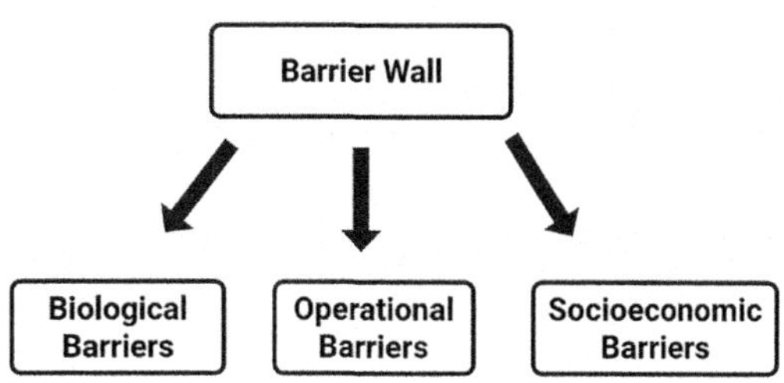

Figure 9.2 Obstacles to disease elimination.

Diagnostic Limitations and Access Effective disease management is heavily hindered by significant barriers in identifying and monitoring infections across affected regions. A critical pillar for malaria elimination is universal access to timely and accurate diagnosis, yet surveillance gaps remain a major threat to effective control (Capela et al., 2019). Monitoring drug resistance itself is a complex task that requires specialized methodologies, including *in vivo* efficacy studies, *in vitro* susceptibility testing, and advanced molecular assays to detect gene mutations (Capela et al., 2019). Additionally, current diagnostic strategies often fail to eliminate or even detect asymptomatic reservoirs and hepatic (liver-stage) forms of parasites, which allow the disease to persist and spread within populations (Capela et al., 2019).

Coinfection and Comorbidity Interactions The interplay between different infections and the host's underlying health status creates complex obstacles for successful treatment outcomes. A host's immune system may be strong enough to control, but not fully eliminate, a parasitic infection, leading to a "carrier" status that provides a constant source of reinfection for the community (Capela et al., 2019). Treatment is further complicated by host genetic factors, most notably G6PD deficiency, which can lead to severe and life-threatening side effects such as hemolysis when certain antimalarials, such as dapsone or primaquine, are administered (Capela et al., 2019).

Socioeconomic and Health System Constraints Economic and structural factors significantly limit the reach and success of global disease eradication programs. The lack of safe, effective, and affordable drugs remains a primary barrier, particularly in tropical and subtropical regions, where the disease burden is most concentrated (Capela et al., 2019). Many countries struggle to maintain early successes in disease eradication because of operational and socioeconomic challenges, which frequently lead to the resurgence of diseases such as malaria (Singh Cheema and Singh, 2022). In rural areas, these challenges are compounded by zoonotic factors, where the incorrect use of chemically similar drugs for both human and animal health accelerates the development of drug resistance (Capela et al., 2019).

Policy and Implementation Barriers High-level management and regulatory hurdles often prevent the effective deployment of medical advances where they are needed most. There is currently a critical lack of new drug leads with novel mechanisms of action, which reduces the long-term viability of current treatment protocols (Capela et al., 2019). This issue is exacerbated by the continued absence of effective vaccines for many protozoal diseases, forcing heavy and often unsustainable reliance on chemotherapy alone (Capela et al., 2019; Singh Cheema and Singh, 2022). As resistance to first-line treatments such as artemisinin combination therapy (ACT) spreads, the need for constant policy updates and the development of alternative strategies becomes urgent, yet these resources are not always immediately available (Singh Cheema and Singh, 2022; Capela et al., 2019).

9.5 Emerging and innovative strategies

9.5.1 Novel therapeutics

9.5.1.1 Natural products and bioactive compounds

Plants serve as a significant source of natural products with therapeutic properties against various diseases (Nasim, 2022). Several phytochemicals have shown potential in host-directed therapy (HDT) for TB by modulating host immune responses rather than targeting the bacteria directly (Raqib and Sarker, 2024).

Curcumin: Isolated from turmeric, curcumin enhances the fusion of phagosomes with lysosomes and induces apoptosis and autophagy in human monocytes and alveolar macrophages to clear *Mycobacterium tuberculosis* (Mtb) (Muvva, 2021). It also attenuates inflammatory responses by inhibiting the p38 MAPK pathway (Guimarães et al., 2013).

Epigallocatechin gallate (EGCG): This green tea polyphenol downregulates the TACO gene, which Mtb uses to arrest phagosome maturation, and promotes lysosome acidification to inhibit mycobacterial survival (Anand et al., 2006).

Piperine: Derived from black pepper, piperine acts as a bioenhancer that increases the bioavailability of anti-TB drugs such as rifampicin (Raqib and Sarker, 2024). A novel formulation called Risorine, which combines piperine with rifampicin and isoniazid, has demonstrated higher sputum conversion rates and a better safety profile in a phase III clinical trial (Patel et al., 2017).

Other Bioactive Compounds: Silymarin, 6-gingerol, and allicin have been shown in animal models to induce protective Th1 cytokine responses (IFN-γ, IL-12, and TNF-α), which help reduce bacterial load and lung inflammation (Guzman-Beltran, 2017; Raqib and Sarker, 2024).

9.5.1.2 Drug repurposing

Repurposing existing FDA-approved drugs for TB treatment offers a faster and more cost-effective alternative to developing new antimicrobials (Raqib and Sarker, 2024).

Metformin: Originally a diabetes drug, metformin is being investigated as an adjunctive HDT because it enhances mitochondrial reactive oxygen species (ROS) production, promotes phagocytosis, and reduces chronic lung pathology (Singhal et al., 2014; Padmapriyadarsini et al., 2022).

Statins: Typically used for high cholesterol, statins such as atorvastatin and pravastatin inhibit cholesterol synthesis, which is exploited by Mtb, and promote autophagy and phagosome maturation in infected cells (Parihar et al., 2019; Wolmarans, 2022).

Imatinib: Approved for leukemia, imatinib promotes phagosomal acidification by inhibiting Abelson tyrosine kinase, thereby improving the killing of Mtb within macrophages (Steiger et al., 2016).

Anti-inflammatory Drugs: Aspirin and ibuprofen are being studied for their ability to shorten treatment duration and improve outcomes by inhibiting cyclooxygenase (COX) enzymes and reducing excessive inflammation (Arias et al., 2023).

9.5.1.3 Host-directed therapies (HDT)

Host-directed therapies represent a shift from traditional antibiotics by targeting host defense processes to enhance antimicrobial capacity and minimize tissue damage (Jeong et al., 2022).

Mechanism of Action: HDTs work by modulating immune cells, regulating cytokine signaling, inducing autophagy, or repairing host defense processes that have been manipulated by Mtb (Tiberi et al., 2018; Raqib and Sarker, 2024).

Prevention of Resistance: Because HDTs target conserved host factors rather than the microbe, they are less likely to lead to the development of drug resistance in Mtb strains (Raqib and Sarker, 2024).

Adjunctive Benefits: When used alongside standard anti-TB chemotherapy, HDTs can amplify treatment effectiveness, potentially reducing the required dose of antibiotics and the overall length of treatment (Raqib and Sarker, 2024).

Clinical Potential: HDT is particularly promising for treating multidrug-resistant (MDR) and extensively drug-resistant (XDR) TB, as well as latent TB, where bacilli may be insensitive to conventional antibiotics (Raqib and Sarker, 2024).

9.5.2 Artificial intelligence and digital epidemiology in blood parasite control

The integration of Artificial intelligence (AI) into parasitology has ushered in a transformative era for the surveillance, diagnosis, and control of hemoprotozoan infections. Blood parasites such as *Plasmodium*, *Trypanosoma*, *Babesia*, and *Theileria* present complex epidemiological patterns driven by vector ecology, host immunity, and environmental variability, making them ideal candidates for AI-assisted modeling and precision public health strategies (Zhao et al., 2025; Kourbeli et al., 2021a). By processing vast and heterogeneous datasets, AI enables real-time insights into transmission dynamics and supports evidence-based decision-making for targeted interventions.

9.5.2.1 AI-driven predictive modeling and early warning systems

One of the most impactful contributions of AI in hemoprotozoan epidemiology is predictive modeling. Machine learning algorithms, including random forests, support vector machines, and deep neural networks, can integrate climate variables, vector distribution data, and human mobility patterns to predict outbreaks of malaria and other blood parasitic diseases with high accuracy (Zhao et al., 2025).

Natural language processing (NLP) tools further enhance early detection by mining digital data streams—such as online health reports, veterinary records, and social media—to identify unusual disease signals before official case notifications occur. These digital surveillance approaches have demonstrated particular value in malaria-endemic regions, where underreporting is common and traditional surveillance systems may lag behind real transmission trends (Zhao et al., 2025).

Graph-based models, including Graph convolutional networks (GCNs), are increasingly used to map connectivity between geographic regions and simulate how vector-borne pathogens spread across ecological corridors. Such models are especially useful for predicting the expansion of tick-borne hemoprotozoa such as babesiosis under changing climatic conditions (Ryan et al., 2019; Zhao et al., 2025).

9.5.2.2 Machine learning in drug discovery and parasite biology

Beyond epidemiological forecasting, AI has become a powerful tool in therapeutic discovery for blood parasites. Machine learning pipelines can analyze genomic, proteomic, and metabolomic datasets to identify essential parasite pathways and prioritize drug targets (Kourbeli et al., 2021a). For example, computational screening platforms have been used to predict inhibitors of *Trypanosoma* enzymes involved in energy metabolism, accelerating the early stages of drug development and reducing associated costs (Kourbeli et al., 2021a).

AI-assisted structure-based drug design also enables the rapid evaluation of compound libraries against parasite proteins, improving hit-to-lead optimization. Such approaches are particularly valuable for neglected hemoprotozoan diseases, where traditional pharmaceutical investment is limited (Kourbeli et al., 2021a).

9.5.2.3 Digital pathology and automated diagnosis

Artificial intelligence-based digital pathology (AI-DP) has significantly improved the diagnostic accuracy of blood parasite detection. Deep learning models trained on thousands of microscopic images can automatically identify infected erythrocytes, quantify parasitemia, and differentiate species with performance comparable to expert microscopists (Cure-Bolt et al., 2024b).

In malaria diagnosis, convolutional neural networks (CNNs) have demonstrated sensitivities exceeding 95%, reducing observer bias and enabling high-throughput screening in endemic settings (Cure-Bolt et al., 2024b). Similar systems are being adapted for veterinary diagnostics to detect *Babesia* and *Theileria* species infections in livestock, supporting rapid clinical decision-making and improving herd health management.

9.5.2.4 Digital epidemiology and precision surveillance

AI-driven digital epidemiology integrates multiple data streams to generate real-time risk maps for hemoprotozoan transmission. Clustering algorithms, such as Gaussian mixture models, identify spatial hotspots where interventions such as vector control or targeted treatment campaigns—can be prioritized (Zhao et al., 2025).

In addition, anomaly detection systems can monitor physiological or clinical data to identify unusual trends that may signal emerging outbreaks. For instance, automated analysis of electronic health records can detect increases in febrile illness patterns consistent with malaria transmission surges (Zhao et al., 2025).

Digital microfluidic (DMF) platforms further complement these approaches by enabling portable, point-of-care testing capable of detecting parasitic DNA or antibodies in field conditions. These lab-on-chip technologies are particularly valuable in remote or resource-limited regions, where access to conventional laboratories is limited (Sklavounos, 2022).

9.5.2.5 Remote monitoring and decision support systems

AI-enabled remote monitoring platforms and mobile health applications provide continuous surveillance and facilitate communication between health care providers, veterinarians, and public health authorities. Chatbots and decision-support tools can assist in triaging suspected malaria cases, guiding treatment protocols, and improving adherence to control programs (Zhao et al., 2025).

Collectively, these innovations support a shift from reactive to proactive disease management, where interventions are guided by predictive analytics rather than retrospective data. This paradigm is particularly important for hemoprotozoan diseases, whose transmission is highly sensitive to environmental fluctuations and vector behavior.

9.5.2.6 Challenges and future directions

Despite their promise, AI applications in blood parasite control face several challenges, including data scarcity in endemic regions, a lack of standardized datasets, and ethical considerations related to data privacy. Moreover, integrating AI tools into existing health systems requires capacity building, infrastructure development, and interdisciplinary collaboration between parasitologists, data scientists, and public health professionals (Zhao et al., 2025).

Future research should focus on developing explainable AI models to improve transparency, integrating genomic surveillance for real-time tracking of drug resistance, and expanding digital tools for veterinary surveillance to strengthen the One Health approach. As these technologies mature, AI-driven digital epidemiology is expected to become a cornerstone of global strategies aimed at reducing the burden of hemoprotozoan diseases.

9.6 Translational challenges: rom discovery to implementation

The transition of advanced medical technologies from laboratory discovery to field implementation involves a complex interplay of logistical, regulatory, biological, and economic hurdles. A primary barrier to deployment, particularly in developing regions, is the lack of robust infrastructure needed to maintain the cold chain for vaccine stability during transport and storage (Tessema et al., 2021; Prasad et al., 2024a). Many vaccines and biologics for blood parasites, including malaria, trypanosomiasis, and babesiosis, are thermolabile and lose efficacy if exposed to temperature fluctuations. In addition, shortages of trained personnel for handling, administering, and monitoring these interventions reduce their overall effectiveness, even when technological solutions exist.

This challenge is further compounded by a historical disparity in research funding, with livestock and veterinary diseases receiving significantly less attention than human medicine, despite the role of animals as critical reservoirs for zoonotic pathogens (Lew-Tabor, Rodriguez Valle, 2016b; Prasad et al., 2024a). Hemoprotozoan parasites such as *Babesia bovis*, *Theileria annulata*, and *Trypanosoma evansi* threaten livestock productivity and occasionally serve as sources of human infection, emphasizing the interconnectedness of human and animal health. The lack of investment slows innovation, limits field trials, and perpetuates dependence on outdated interventions.

Biological realities also impose constraints on intervention strategies. For example, the Asian longhorned tick (*Haemaphysalis longicornis*) can survive unfed for up to 12 months, making strategies such as pasture rotation or destocking economically unfeasible for many farmers (Jongejan and Uilenberg, 2004; Bickerton, 2024). Similarly, hemoprotozoan parasites exhibit complex life cycles involving multiple hosts and vector species, complicating the timing and design of vaccines or chemotherapeutics. From a material science perspective, nanomaterials must be engineered to navigate host immunological barriers while remaining stable and bioavailable under diverse environmental conditions, ensuring targeted delivery to parasites (Zhang et al., 2022; Prasad et al., 2024b).

Navigating the regulatory and ethical landscape adds further layers of complexity. The integration of nanotechnology into veterinary science requires rigorous safety and toxicity evaluations to prevent harm to living organisms and the environment (Lew-Tabor, Rodriguez Valle, 2016b; Prasad et al., 2024b). Regulatory bodies often face difficulties in establishing standardized definitions, measurement protocols, and approval pathways for nanomaterials, slowing translation into field use. To protect the human food supply, antiprotozoal and antifungal treatments must be strictly administered under veterinary guidance to ensure precise dosing, adherence to withdrawal periods, and minimal drug residues in animal products (WHO, 2023; Prasad et al., 2024b). These requirements demand close collaboration between researchers, regulatory agencies, and practitioners to implement safe, operationally feasible strategies.

Ultimately, the success of these technologies depends on their cost-effectiveness and scalability within industries threatened by high-mortality diseases such as trypanosomiasis, babesiosis, and bovine theileriosis (Lew-Tabora and Rodriguez Valle, 2016b; Prasad et al., 2024c). Traditional interventions, including area-wide acaricide spraying or repeated chemoprophylaxis, are often uneconomical, labor-intensive, and environmentally damaging (Jongejan and Uilenberg, 2004; Bickerton, 2024). In contrast, nanotechnology offers innovative solutions. "Multiplexing" platforms enable a single device or formulation to target multiple pathogens, reducing operational costs. Sustained-release nanovaccines provide long-term immunity with a single dose, eliminating repeated boosters and reducing labor demands. Targeted nanocarrier systems allow lower drug concentrations to achieve therapeutic efficacy while minimizing systemic toxicity and environmental impact (Zhang et al., 2022; Prasad et al., 2024c).

Collectively, these translational challenges highlight the need for integrated strategies that combine technological innovation with infrastructure development, regulatory alignment, and community engagement. Only by addressing logistical, biological, and economic constraints in parallel can laboratory discoveries meaningfully reduce the global burden of blood parasitic diseases (WHO, 2023; Prasad et al., 2024c).

9.7 Future research priorities

9.7.1 Identification of conserved therapeutic targets

The development of novel antibiotics targeting DNA double-strand break (DSB) repair pathways is a top priority in drug discovery, as unrepaired DSBs are lethal to parasites (Amarh & Arthur, 2019). Research has shown that inhibiting the *Plasmodium falciparum* protein kinase G (*PfPKG*) demonstrates excellent *in vivo* efficacy and is being explored as a target for drug repositioning against other protozoa such as *Cryptosporidium* spp. (Arnold et al., 2019). Regarding energy metabolism, studies indicate that the simultaneous inhibition of glycerol kinase and alternative oxidase results in parasite death by cutting off ATP production (Balogun et al., 2019). Additionally, Lysyl-tRNA synthetase is being investigated as a promising drug target across various apicomplexan parasites (Baragana et al., 2019). Furthermore, restoring mitochondrial structural and functional integrity using molecules such as M1 is being explored as a host-directed therapy to enhance pathogen clearance (Banerjee et al., 2019). Finally, research focuses on identifying structural differences between parasitic proteases, such as falcipains, and human homologs to design selective drugs with minimal host toxicity (Stephen et al., 2019).

9.7.2 Integrated one health research frameworks

Future research must investigate the transmission roles of waterways and sanitation in the spread of zoonotic parasites such as Echinococcus granulosus (Christofi, 2022). Collaboration between the veterinary and human medical sectors is essential for the effective delivery of prevention programs for neglected zoonoses (Christofi, 2022). It is also recommended to combine prevention methods and manage multiple canine diseases simultaneously within a unified One Health framework to ensure comprehensive control (Christofi, 2022).

9.7.3 Capacity building in endemic regions

The efficacy of health programs can be monitored by training local community members, including workers in human and veterinary clinics, to conduct simple data collection and recognize clinical signs of infection (Christofi, 2022). There is a critical need to improve medical and veterinary training and resource sharing in endemic regions (Christofi, 2022). Moreover, research emphasizes the importance of establishing sustainable guidelines regarding the frequency of administering vaccines and preventive treatments such as Praziquantel (Christofi, 2022).

9.7.4 Multidisciplinary and international collaborations

International consortia, such as the structure-guided drug discovery coalition (SDDC), facilitate hit-to-lead projects by bringing together diverse global research centers (Baragana et al., 2019). Effective disease control requires formal representation of both internal stakeholders, such as government health sectors, and external stakeholders, including abattoir workers and international organizations such as the WHO (Christofi, 2022). Additionally, organizations such as PATH bridge the gap between bench research and clinical application by connecting public institutions, businesses, and investors (Stephen et al., 2019).

9.8 Strategic roadmap toward sustainable control of blood parasites

9.8.1 Short-term priorities: improved tools and surveillance

The immediate focus of global control strategies for blood parasites is strengthening surveillance systems to detect outbreaks early and respond rapidly (Shripat et al., 2025; WHO, 2023). Timely identification of infections is critical for diseases such as malaria and human African trypanosomiasis, where delayed diagnosis can lead to severe morbidity and continued transmission.

Enhanced diagnostics form the cornerstone of short-term control. Rapid diagnostic tests (RDTs) for malaria, molecular assays for *Babesia* spp., and antigen-based detection for *Trypanosoma* spp. enable health workers to initiate prompt treatment, thereby reducing parasite reservoirs in human and animal populations (Mohan et al., 2022; Kourbeli et al., 2021a). For livestock, point-of-care tests such as lateral flow assays for bovine babesiosis and anaplasmosis are increasingly employed to reduce losses in endemic pastoral regions (Lew-Tabor and Rodriguez Valle, 2016b).

Digital surveillance tools enhance the speed and accuracy of reporting. Mobile phone-based reporting systems, electronic health registries, and cloud-based dashboards allow near-real-time mapping of cases and vector abundance (Shripat et al., 2025; Salathé et al., 2012). These platforms reduce errors associated with paper-based reporting, improve data coverage in remote or underserved areas, and facilitate early outbreak warnings. Integration with geographic information systems (GIS) and environmental data further enables the identification of hotspots and targeted vector control interventions (Rocklöv and Dubrow, 2020).

Additionally, community-based surveillance is critical. Training local volunteers to recognize clinical signs of hemoprotozoan infections or vector proliferation provides a decentralized layer of detection, particularly in rural and high-risk settings (WHO, 2023; Franco et al., 2020).

9.8.2 Medium-term goals: integrated interventions

In the medium term, the focus expands beyond reactive surveillance toward building resilient health systems capable of sustaining disease control programs (Shripat et al., 2025). Rather than disease-specific silos, integrated primary health care systems are emphasized, which combine services for hemoprotozoan infections, other infectious diseases, and noncommunicable diseases. This approach addresses overlapping determinants such as nutrition, sanitation, and occupational exposure (Tatem et al., 2013; Atkinson et al., 2013).

Multisectoral collaboration is essential. Health authorities must coordinate with the education, urban planning, and agricultural sectors to mitigate vector breeding and reduce human–animal contact that facilitates spillover of zoonotic blood parasites (Destoumieux-Garzón et al., 2018; Veronesi et al., 2023b). For example, urban drainage management and peri-urban livestock control can minimize mosquito and tick habitats while promoting safe livestock practices in pastoral communities.

Capacity building is also a core component of the medium-term strategy. Training health care providers, veterinarians, and community health workers ensures effective case management, surveillance, and vector control. Community engagement programs increase trust and compliance with interventions, particularly for interventions requiring behavioral changes such as bed net usage or livestock vaccination (Watson-Jones and Macpherson, 1988a; Lew-Tabor and Rodriguez Valle, 2016b).

Moreover, integrated vector management (IVM) is promoted, combining chemical, biological, and environmental methods to sustainably reduce vector populations while minimizing ecological disruption (WHO, 2017). For livestock, this includes acaricide rotation, pasture management, and tick-resistant breeds, which help control bovine babesiosis and theileriosis (Jongejan and Uilenberg, 2004).

9.8.3 Long-term vision: reduction and elimination

The long-term vision centers on the sustainable reduction and elimination of blood parasites through sustained investments, community participation, and global cooperation (Shripat et al., 2025; WHO, 2023).

A critical priority is universal health coverage (UHC), ensuring equitable access to prevention, diagnosis, and treatment for all populations, including remote and marginalized communities. For human malaria, this includes the continuous distribution of insecticide-treated nets (ITNs), indoor residual spraying, and prophylactic interventions in high-risk regions (WHO, 2023). In livestock, veterinary extension services provide routine vaccination, treatment, and education to prevent hemoprotozoan infections that impact livelihoods (Lew-Tabor and Rodriguez Valle, 2016b).

Planetary health integration recognizes the interconnections between climate change, environmental modification, and disease transmission. Strategies include predictive modeling of vector range shifts because of warming climates, adaptive vector control measures, and ecosystem-based interventions to maintain biodiversity that naturally regulates vector populations (Ryan et al., 2019; Popoola et al., 2021).

Finally, community empowerment and global equity are central to long-term success. Programs designed to involve local populations in surveillance, health education, and decision-making foster sustainable engagement. International collaboration ensures that resources and technology reach regions with the greatest burden, supporting elimination targets for diseases such as malaria, human African trypanosomiasis, and bovine babesiosis in endemic regions (Franco et al., 2020; WHO, 2023).

References

Al-Shehri H, et al. Re-emergence of vector-borne diseases in the middle east. Parasites & Vectors 2020;13:460.

Albareedy A, Ramadan HK. Infectious diseases and change of disease pattern in Africa. In: Saad-Hussein A, Elwakil R, Khomsi K, editors. Impact of Climate Change on Health in Africa: A Focus on Liver and Gastrointestinal Tract. Springer Nature Switzerland AG; 2023. p. 79–96.

Amarh V, Arthur PK. DNA double-strand break formation and repair as targets for novel antibiotic combination chemotherapy. Future Science OA 2019;5(8). Available from https://doi.org/10.2144/fsoa-2019-0034.

Arnold SJ, et al. Potent inhibitors of malarial P. falciparum protein kinase G: Improving the cell activity of a series of imidazopyridines. Bioorganic & Medicinal Chemistry Letters 2019;29(3):509–14.

Anand PK, Kaul D, Sharma M. Green tea polyphenol inhibits Mycobacterium tuberculosis survival within human macrophages. International Journal of Biochemistry and Cell Biology 2006;38(4):600–9. Available from https://doi.org/10.1016/j.biocel.2005.10.021.

Arias L, Otwombe K, Waja Z, et al. SMA-TB: study protocol for the phase 2b randomized double-blind, placebo-controlled trial to estimate the potential efficacy and safety of two repurposed drugs, acetylsalicylic acid and ibuprofen, for use as adjunct therapy added to, and compared with, the standard WHO recommended TB regimen. Trials 2023;24:435. https://doi.org/10.1186/s13063-023-07448-0.

Atkinson PM, et al. Environmental drivers of vector-borne disease dynamics. Philosophical Transactions of the Royal Society B 2013;368:20120276.

Azhar M, Gadahi JA, Bhutto B, Tunio S, Vistro WA, Tunio H, et al. Babesiosis: current status and future perspectives in Pakistan and chemotherapy used in livestock and pet animals. Heliyon 2023;9(6). Available from https://doi.org/10.1016/j.heliyon.2023.e17172.

Balogun EO, Inaoka DK, Shiba T, Tsuge C, May B, Sato T, et al. Discovery of trypanocidal coumarins with dual inhibition of both the glycerol kinase and alternative oxidase of Trypanosoma brucei brucei. The FASEB Journal 2019;33:13002–13. Available from https://doi.org/10.1096/fj.201901342R.

Baragaña B, Forte B, Choi R, Hewitt SN, Bueren-Calabuig JA, Pisco JP, et al. Lysyl-tRNA synthetase as a drug target in malaria and cryptosporidiosis. Proceedings of the National Academy of Sciences of the United States of America 2019;116(14):7015–20. Available from https://doi.org/10.1073/pnas.1814685116.

Belman S, et al. Public health literacy and its role in disease management and patient compliance in hospital settings. Journal of Health Communication 2013.

Bickerton M. Advances in nanotechnology for veterinary parasitology: efficiency and sustainability. Veterinary Science Today 2024;12(3):45–62.

Bose D, Banerjee S, Chatterjee N, Das S, Saha M, Saha KD. Inhibition of TGF-β induced lipid droplets switches M2 macrophages to M1 phenotype. Toxicology in Vitro 2019;58:207–14.

CDC. (2022). Parasites and vector-borne diseases overview.

Capela R, Moreira R, Lopes F. An overview of drug resistance in protozoal diseases. International Journal of Molecular Sciences 2019;20(22):5748. Available from https://doi.org/10.3390/ijms20225748.

Chiuya T. Integrated control strategies and surveillance systems for vector-borne diseases. Parasites & Vectors, 13, 412.," no date). One Health approach to vector biology and epidemiology of arboviruses, Rickettsia, and protozoa in smallholder livestock systems in western Kenya (Doctoral dissertation). University of Pretoria; 2022.

Christofi. (2022). Journal of Zoological Systematics and Evolutionary Research. [File: Cystic Echinococcosis An Impact.pdf].

Cure-Bolt N, et al. Artificial intelligence in digital pathology for parasitic disease diagnosis. Nature Medicine 2024;30:112–20.

Destoumieux-Garzón D, Mavingui P, Boetsch G, Boissier J, Darriet F, Duboz P, et al. The One Health Concept: 10 years old and a long road ahead. Frontiers in Veterinary Science 2018;5. Available from https://doi.org/10.3389/fvets.2018.00014.

Elwakil H, et al. Climate-driven changes in vector-borne disease transmission dynamics. Environmental Research 2023;216:114489.

Franco JR, et al. Monitoring the elimination of human African trypanosomiasis. Lancet Infectious Diseases 2020;20:e241–8.

GBD 2021 Collaborators. Global burden of diseases study 2021 results. The Lancet; 2022.

Guimarães MR, Leite FRM, Spolidorio LC, Kirkwood KL, Rossa C Jr. Curcumin abrogates LPS-induced pro-inflammatory cytokines in RAW 264.7 macrophages: Evidence for novel mechanisms involving SOCS-1, -3 and p38 MAPK. Archives of Oral Biology. 2013;58(10):1309–1317. https://doi.org/10.1016/j.archoralbio.2013.07.005.

Guzmán-Beltrán S, Torres M, Arellano M, Juárez E. Human macrophages chronically exposed to LPS can be reactivated by stimulation with MDP to acquire an antimicrobial phenotype. Cellular Immunology 2017;315:45–55.

Jeong I, et al. Regarding the shift toward targeting host defense processes 2022.

Jofre J, Lucena F, Blanch AR, Muniesa M. Health-related water bacteriology in the 21st century: Are we facing a new paradigm? Water Research 2010;44(20):6003–22.

Jongejan F, Uilenberg G. The global importance of ticks. Parasitology 2004;129(S1):S3. Available from https://doi.org/10.1017/s0031182004005967.

Kabli A. Global burden and integrated management of protozoan parasitic diseases. Infectious Disease Reports 2025;17:102–18.

Khan AY, Shaukat A, Muneeb M, Shah MK, Shaukat I, Aleem MT, et al. Prevalence of Blood Protozoa and Impact of Chemotherapy in Exotic Cattle, With Special Reference to Haematological Parameters. Egyptian Journal of Veterinary Sciences 2024:1–8.

Kipanga PN, et al. High-resolution melting analysis for detection of low-density malaria infections. Malaria Journal 2014;13:24.

Kitchen AD, Chiodini PL. Malaria and blood transfusion. Vox Sanguinis 2006;90(2):77–84. Available from https://doi.org/10.1111/j.1423-0410.2006.00733.x.

Kourbeli V, et al. An overview of drug development for parasitic diseases using computational approaches. Drug Discovery Today 2021;26:1327–36. no date). Machine learning approaches in drug discovery for parasitic diseases. Computational and Structural Biotechnology Journal, 19, 425–436.

kongtawee R, Junsiri W, Narapakdeesakul D, Thiptara A, Beugnet F, Taweethavonsawat P. High burden and spatial clustering of canine hemoparasitic infections in southern Thailand: a molecular survey of free-roaming dogs. One Health 2026;22:101365. Available from https://doi.org/10.1016/j.onehlt.2026.101365.

Lew-Tabor AE, Rodriguez Valle M. Tick-borne protozoan diseases of livestock. Veterinary Parasitology 2016;167:30–45.

Maharana BR, Kumar B, Prasad A, Patbandha TK. Prevalence and assessment of economic impact of hemoprotozoan diseases in livestock. Veterinary World 2016a;9:148–52.

Maharana BR, Tewari AK, Saravanan BC, Sudhakar NR. Important hemoprotozoan diseases of livestock: challenges in current diagnostics and therapeutics: an update. Veterinary World 2016b;9(5):487–95. Available from https://doi.org/10.14202/vetworld.2016.487-495.

Mohan K, et al. Rapid diagnostics for malaria and other hemoprotozoan infections. Frontiers in Microbiology 2022;13:833971.

Mordecai EA, Caldwell JM, Grossman MK, Lippi CA, Johnson LR, Neira M, et al. Thermal biology of mosquito-borne disease. Ecology Letters 2019;22(10):1690–708. Available from https://doi.org/10.1111/ele.13335.

Muvva JR, Ahmed S, Rekha RS, Kalsum S, Groenheit R, Schön T, et al. Immunomodulatory agents combat multidrug-resistant tuberculosis by improving antimicrobial immunity. The Journal of Infectious Diseases 2021;224(2):332–44.

Nasim N, Sandeep IS, Mohanty S. Plant-derived natural products for drug discovery: Current approaches and prospects. Nucleus 2022;65:399–411. Available from https://doi.org/10.1007/s13237-022-00405-3.

Nsakashalo, M. (2019). Developing an integrated implementation plan for control and elimination of NTDs: Nationwide mapping surveys for lymphatic filariasis, schistosomiasis and soil-transmitted helminthiasis in Zambia (Doctoral dissertation). University of Liverpool.

Padmapriyadarsini, C., et al. (2022). Phase 2 trial of Metformin for reducing lung tissue damage.

Parihar, S.P., et al. (2019). StAT-TB trial regarding Pravastatin and phagolysosome maturation.

Patel N, Jagannath K, Vora A, Patel M, Patel A. A randomized, controlled, phase III clinical trial to evaluate the efficacy and tolerability of Risorine with conventional rifampicin in the treatment of newly diagnosed pulmonary tuberculosis patients. Journal of the Association of Physicians of India 2017;65(9):48–54. PMID: 29313577.

Patz JA, et al. Unhealthy landscapes: policy recommendations. Environmental Health Perspectives 2004;112:1092–8.

Popoola, S., Fazio, F., Noreen, S., et al. (2021). Impacts of Climate Change on the Epidemiology of Parasitic Diseases in Marine and Freshwater Fish Species.

Prasad M, Kumar R, Ghosh M, Syed SM, Chakravarti S. Nanotechnology Theranostics in Livestock Diseases and Management Livestock Diseases and Management. Singapore: Springer Nature; 2024. Available from http://doi.org/10.1007/978-981-16-1610-5.

Prasad R, Sharma V, Singh A. Translating nanovaccines and nanotherapeutics from laboratory to livestock: challenges and opportunities. Frontiers in Veterinary Science 2024;11:1023–45.

Prasad R, Singh K, Tiwari S. Translational challenges in implementing novel technologies for parasitic disease control. Frontiers in Veterinary Science 2024;11:1287456.

Raqib R, Sarker P. Repurposed drugs and plant-derived natural products as potential host-directed therapeutic candidates for tuberculosis. Biomolecules 2024;14(12):1497. Available from https://doi.org/10.3390/biom14121497.

Rocklöv J, Dubrow R. Climate change and vector-borne diseases. Nature Immunology 2020;21:479–83.

Ryan SJ, et al. Global expansion of vector-borne disease risk. PLoS Neglected Tropical Diseases 2019;13:e0007213.

Salathé M, Bengtsson L, Bodnar TJ, Brewer DD, Brownstein JS, Buckee C, et al. Digital Epidemiology. PLoS Computational Biology 2012;8(7):e1002616. Available from https://doi.org/10.1371/journal.pcbi.1002616.

Salim B, Alasmari S, Bakheit MA. Genetic resistance to vector-borne hemoprotozoa in livestock: molecular markers, host-parasite interactions, and implications for breeding and control. Journal of Veterinary Science 2025;26(5). Available from https://doi.org/10.4142/jvs.25125.

Salim B, Taha KM, Hassan SM. Epidemiology and economic impact of major livestock hemoprotozoan infections. Tropical Animal Health and Production 2025;57:45.

Shirale SY, Palampalle HY, Meshram PV, Pawankar KN, Vaidya MM, Dhenge SA. Therapeutic management of trypanosomiasis in buffaloes: a clinical study. International Journal of Advanced Biochemistry Research 2024;8(3):203–7.

Shripat C, Prakash P, Kumar Y, Prajapati J, Vihan S. Global Health and Preventive Strategies. 1st ed. New Delhi: AkiNik Publications; 2025.

Singh Cheema H, Singh MP. Drug resistance in plasmodium, future malaria management strategies and importance of medicinal plants. Journal of Ayurvedic and Herbal Medicine 2022;8(2):107–12. Available from https://doi.org/10.31254/jahm.2022.8209.

Singhal A, Jie L, Kumar P, Hong GS, Leow MK, Paleja B, et al. Metformin as adjunct antituberculosis therapy. Science Translational Medicine 2014;6(263):263ra159. Available from https://doi.org/10.1126/scitranslmed.3009885.

Sklavounos, A. (2022). Preparing for Resource-Limited and High-Stakes Settings: a Digital Microfluidic Approach (Doctoral dissertation). University of Toronto.

Sobanski V, et al. (2025). Referenced regarding severe toxoplasmosis management and atypical strains; cited within internal documentation.

Srinivasamurthy R, Bairy LK. Chemotherapy of malaria and other protozoal infections. Paul A, editor. Introduction to Basics of Pharmacology and Toxicology, Volume 2. Singapore: Springer Nature; 2021. p. 1025–45.

Steiger C, et al. (2016). Regarding Imatinib and phagosomal acidification.

Steketee RW. Pregnancy, nutrition and parasitic diseases. The Journal of Nutrition 2003;133(5):1661S. Available from https://doi.org/10.1093/jn/133.5.1661S.

Stephen AO, Omokehinde EA, Kato K. Keystone Symposia-Poster Abstracts: 21st-Century Drug Discovery and Development for Global Health (S3) 2019.

Tatem AJ, et al. Urbanization and global malaria risk. Malaria Journal 2013;12:133.

Tessema B, Haile D, Alemayehu G. Cold chain challenges for vaccine delivery in Sub-Saharan Africa. Vaccine 2021;39(45):6541–50.

Tiberi S, et al. (2018). Regarding mechanisms for modulating immune cells and cytokine signaling.

Ullah A, Geng M, Chen W, Zhu Q, Shi L, Zhang X, et al. Effect of parasitic infections on hematological profile, reproductive and productive performance in equines. Animals 2025;15(22). Available from https://doi.org/10.3390/ani15223294.

UNDP. Gender and Malaria: Combined efforts for Disease Control. United Nations Development Programme Report; 2015.

Veronesi F, et al. Wildlife reservoirs and zoonotic parasite transmission. International Journal for Parasitology 2023;53:215–28.

Watson-Jones C, Macpherson C. Cultural and socio-economic factors in the epidemiology of hydatid disease. Annals of Tropical Medicine & Parasitology 1988;82(2):173–9.

Wolmarans K. Regarding Atorvastatin and autophagy in Mtb-infected cells 2022.

WHO. (2017). Integrated vector management: strategic framework. Geneva: World Health Organization.

WHO. (2023). World malaria report 2023. Geneva: World Health Organization., no date). World Health Organization guidelines on veterinary therapeutics and food safety. Geneva: World Health Organization.

Yadav N, Upadhyay RK. Tick-borne diseases, transmission, host immune responses, diagnosis and control. Journal of Human Physiology 2021;3(2). Available from https://doi.org/10.30564/jhp.v3i2.3788.

Zhang X, Li Y, Wang J. Nano-carrier systems for targeted delivery in parasitic infections. Journal of Nanobiotechnology 2022;20:190.

Zhao J, Jin Y, Shen X, Ruan X, Kucherenko M. AI applications in public health: a review of epidemic monitoring, epidemiological analysis, and health management. Artificial Intelligence and Medicine 2025;1(1).

Index

Note: Page numbers followed by "*f*" and "*t*" refer to figures and tables, respectively.

O

P

Printed and bound by CPI Group (UK) Ltd, Croydon, CR0 4YY
14/09/2026
02216409-0008